INDEXING BOOKS

Chicago Guides
to *Writing*, Editing,
and Publishing

On Writing, Editing, and Publishing
    Jacques Barzun

Getting into Print
    Walter W. Powell

Writing for Social Scientists
    Howard S. Becker

*Chicago Guide for Preparing
Electronic Manuscripts*
    Prepared by the Staff of the
    University of Chicago Press

*A Manual for Writers of Term
Papers, Theses, and Dissertations*
    Kate Turabian
        Sixth edition revised by
        John Grossman and Alice Bennett

A Handbook of Biological Illustration
    Frances W. Zweifel

The Craft of Translation
    John Biguenet and Rainer Schulte,
    editors

Style
    Joseph M. Williams

Mapping It Out
    Mark Monmonier

Writing Ethnographic Fieldnotes
    Robert M. Emerson, Rachel I.
    Fretz, and Linda L. Shaw

Tales of the Field
On Writing Ethnography
    John Van Maanen

Glossary of Typesetting Terms
    Richard Eckersley, Richard
    Angstadt, Charles M. Ellerston,
    Richard Hendel, Naomi B.
    Pascal, and Anita Walker Scott

The Craft of Research
    Wayne C. Booth, Gregory G.
    Colomb, and Joseph M. Williams

A Poet's Guide to Poetry
    Mary Kinzie

INDEXING BOOKS

Nancy C. Mulvany

The
University of Chicago
Press

Chicago and London

Nancy C. Mulvany
is a professional indexer and past president
of the American Society of Indexers. She has written articles on indexing for
a variety of publications and teaches basic indexing at the University of
California Extension in Berkeley.

The University of Chicago Press, Chicago 60637
The University of Chicago Press, Ltd., London
© 1994 by Nancy Claire Mulvany
All rights reserved. Published 1994
Printed in the United States of America

09 08 07 06 05 04 03   4 5 6 7

ISBN: 0-226-55014-1 (cloth)

Library of Congress Cataloging-in-Publication Data

Mulvany, Nancy C.
Indexing books / by Nancy C. Mulvany
p.   cm.—(Chicago guides to writing, editing, and publishing)
Includes bibliographical references and index.
1. Indexing.   I. Title.   II. Series
Z695.9.M8   1994
025.3—dc20   94-22934
                                        CIP

Contents

Preface   vii
Acknowledgments   xi

1   INTRODUCTION TO BOOK INDEXING   1

2   THE AUTHOR AND THE INDEX   16

3   GETTING STARTED   35

4   STRUCTURE OF ENTRIES   68

5   ARRANGEMENT OF ENTRIES   109

6   SPECIAL CONCERNS IN INDEXING   128

7   NAMES, NAMES, NAMES   152

8   FORMAT AND LAYOUT OF THE INDEX   183

9   EDITING THE INDEX   214

10   TOOLS FOR INDEXING   239

Appendixes
A   Index Specifications Worksheet   281
B   ASCII Table   284

C   Summary of Generic Codes Most Often Needed in
    Electronic Index Manuscripts   285
D   Summary of Generic Codes for Roman Characters for
    Latin-based Languages   286
E   Summary of Generic Codes for Greek Characters,
    Monetary Symbols, Punctuation for Latin-based
    Languages, and Some Mathematical Symbols   287
F   Resources for Indexers   289
                    References   295
                    Index   301

Preface

MANY TIMES DURING THE writing of this book I asked myself why I had taken on the task. My first motivation was quite pedestrian: I needed a text for my classes. After teaching book indexing for several years, I grew tired of piecing together course materials. I exposed my students to a bit from here and a bit from there, often contradictory material that had to be put into perspective through lectures or with my own additional written material. While G. Norman Knight's book *Indexing, the Art of,* or Margaret Wheeler's article "Indexing: Principles, Rules and Examples," would have been fine primary texts, both are out of print. Also, I recognized that not every aspiring indexer could take my class or one of the few others offered in this country that are devoted to book indexing. Those who wish to know about book indexing methods have few places to turn for reference.

Like my classes, this book attempts to address the real-world aspects of book indexing. But I must include here the caveats I present to my students during our first class session.

Book indexing is something you will either enjoy or detest; there is little middle ground. You will have a knack for it or you won't. I do not believe that indexing can be taught. Rules, and the reasons for following or not following them, can be presented. Various index formats can be discussed. However, the ability to objectively and accurately analyze text and to produce a conceptual map that directs readers to specific portions of the text involves a way of thinking that can only be guided and encouraged, not taught. I compare my book indexing class to a studio painting class. I can tell you various methods for preparing a canvas and for mixing pigments. We can discuss types of paints and brushes. We can look at the work of other painters to see how they handled color or perspective. But I cannot turn you into a painter.

So, too, in indexing, although many rules can indeed be taught and learned, a very important aspect of this work comes down to the individual indexer's judgment and communicative abilities. Indexing cannot be reduced to a set of steps that can be followed. It is not a mechanical process. Indexing books is a form of writing. Like other types of writing, it is a mixture of art and craft, judgment and selection. With practice and experience, indexers develop their own style—as do other writers. The best we can do as teachers of indexing is to present the rules and offer guidance.

So much for my first and most immediate reason for writing this book. While satisfying my desire to present the many diverse practices in indexing, the book attempts to come to terms with the seemingly elusive aspects of our craft. After grading hundreds of indexes of the same material, I have learned from my students that good indexes come in a variety of forms. Just when I think I have seen all the possible permutations of the one standard index assigned in all of my classes, someone comes up with a new and quite brilliant way of handling the material. Perhaps I shouldn't be surprised at this. After all, an index by its very nature is interpretive. Therein lies the challenge and creativity in indexing. In this book I have attempted to explain what it is we indexers *really* do. But I feel my efforts are preliminary in this regard. My discussions with other indexers clearly reveal that in the midst of following rules and creating entries in an accurate and complete fashion, a synergy is at work that is difficult to describe.

This is not a "how-to" book in the sense that its rules, if followed, will result in a perfect index. I do hope, however, that readers seeking information about how to handle a particular aspect of an index will find direction here. Nor is this book intended to be an encyclopedic or historical treatment of indexing like Hans Wellisch's fascinating book *Indexing from A to Z*. My book primarily addresses authored indexes such as those found in books. Unlike Gerard Salton's *Automatic Text Processing* or F. W. Lancaster's *Indexing and Abstracting in Theory and Practice,* my book does not provide detailed treatment of index methods used for online information retrieval. Yet I believe that many principles presented apply equally to the development of both online and print media information access structures.

This book pulls together various approaches to book indexing. It is about practice, not theory. It is my hope that novice indexers will find within these pages the guidance they seek and that my colleagues, experienced book indexers, will find that I have described our methods and our profession well.

When I first considered writing about book indexing, I wondered who might publish such a book. I decided quite early that I wanted the University of Chicago Press to publish my book. In my mind, it would be a perfect match. I am honored and extremely pleased that this book is being published by the University of Chicago Press. However, I caution readers to keep in mind that much of the material presented in these pages does not reflect the recommendations of the University of Chicago Press. Because of the widespread acceptance by the North American publishing community of the indexing guidelines in *The Chicago Manual of Style*, UCP's preferences for index presentation are of course discussed. But the opinions expressed in this book are mine and are not necessarily endorsed by UCP. If you are preparing an index for the University of Chicago Press, do review the guidelines presented in the 14th edition of *The Chicago Manual of Style* before proceeding.

Acknowledgments

THIS BOOK IS THE RESULT of both the knowing and the unknowing collaboration of many people in the indexing and publishing community. I am indebted to those who so willingly shared their thoughts with me and gave of their time.

To begin, I would like to thank my Dad's cousin Barbara Porter for encouraging me to take Dr. BevAnne Ross's indexing course at the University of California Berkeley Extension. I thank BevAnne for her generous guidance, support, and encouragement over the years.

The hundreds of students who have taken my courses, particularly the USDA Correspondence Study Course (C-EDIT 360) and the UC Berkeley Extension course (X400), have contributed greatly to my abilities as a teacher. There is one three-letter word that all good students have on the tip of their tongue—"why." I thank all the students who wouldn't let me get away with answers like "It's the rule" or "That's the way we've always done it."

In early 1990 when I first seriously considered writing this book, I knew that I wanted it to be published by the University of Chicago Press. I want to thank Jennie Lightner, a manuscript editor at UCP, for encouraging me to present my book proposal to her press. Additional thanks are due to Penny Kaiserlian, associate director of the Press, who with a firm and gracious hand guided this project from a two-page outline to the bound book that it is today. Later when I learned that Jennie Lightner would be my editor, I was delighted. Jennie is an expert editor. She has made my book much more readable, for which I am extremely grateful.

The wry wit and wise counsel of Georg Feuerstein, whose advice spanned such topics as contract negotiations and the writing and editing of the book, were always much appreciated.

In order to update my collection of indexing style guides I wrote to many publishers asking for their current versions. I would like to thank the many editors at American and Canadian publishing houses and those in computer documentation departments for providing me with their indexing instructions.

Thanks are due to those who read the entire second draft of this manuscript: Victoria Agee, Linda Fetters, Jane Maddocks, Carolyn McGovern, Mark Monmonier, Rosemary Simpson, Diane Ullius, and Cecelia Wittmann. I extend a special thanks to Dr. Mark Monmonier, who for a very long time was known to me only as "Reader 1." Dr. Monmonier was involved in the review process early on as one of the readers of my initial book outline. His suggestions regarding indexing by authors were invaluable.

Sections of this manuscript were reviewed by others, whom I wish to thank: Trisha Feuerstein, Elinor Lindheimer, Hugh Maddocks, Shirley Manley, AnnMarie Mitchell, and Janet Shuter. Then there are those individuals who generously offered advice about very specific topics: James D. Anderson, John Grossman, Jessica Milstead, Kathy Pitcoff, Barbara Roos, Linda Toy, and Hans Wellisch.

Carolyn McGovern, whom I call my First and Last Reader, deserves a special mention. Carolyn brings to this project an extensive background in both editing and indexing. She was the First Reader of this manuscript. Her insights and comments as both an editor and an indexer on the first draft of the book were extremely helpful. I am so very pleased that Carolyn agreed to write the index for this book. In the role of the indexer, she will be the Last Reader of the book before it is printed. As Last Reader/Indexer she comes full circle with this manuscript; indeed, this is an exciting collaborative effort.

Writing a book while also running a full-time business can have its maddening moments. I would like to thank Ty Koontz and Gale Rhoades for giving me the gift of time. They relieved me of my office duties at crucial periods during the writing of this book.

Last, I would like to thank my parents, Audrey and Hy Mulvany, for giving me the greatest gift of all—belief in myself. They brought me up to believe that I could do anything I set my mind to. This belief enabled me to persevere with this project.

Appendixes B, C, D, and E are reprinted, with permission, from Hugh C. Maddocks, *Generic Markup of Electronic Index Manuscripts*, tables 1–4 (Port Aransas, Tex.: American Society of Indexers, 1988).

The material in chapter 10 concerning what to look for in dedicated indexing software is taken, with permission, from Linda K. Fetters, "Explanation of Program Features," *A Guide to Indexing Software*, 4th ed. (Port Aransas, Tex.: American Society of Indexers, 1992). Figure 3.1 is reprinted from *The Chicago Manual of Style*, 14th edition, © 1969, 1982, 1993 by The University of Chicago.

1

INTRODUCTION TO BOOK INDEXING

SEVERAL YEARS AGO I sat at a conference listening to various people talk about hypermedia applications.[1] There were demonstrations of hypertext systems and interactive video. Talk was of the global electronic village where we would all be linked together via computers and telephone lines. At the tap of a key or a click of a mouse we could access an amount of information previously unimaginable. I became fascinated with the dazzling technology and enchanted with the notion that hypermedia would be as important as the development of the printing press in the history of information dissemination.

The discussion became heady. Then, one of the speakers brought us back to earth when she predicted that "a very respected profession ten years from now will be that of an indexer." I was astonished. I had thought that only indexers knew this! I looked around the room for nods of agreement. But nothing had changed. The speaker had moved on to a discussion of problems with unstructured linking in hypertext systems.

Now, as I reflect back on that conference, I realize that the speaker's words, which still ring in my ears, were not *really* heard by most of the others in the audience. I am sure that all would agree that a massive amount of information is of little value if there is no access to the content of that information. What is not so well understood is that an index is a device for providing access to information—and that is what this book is about.

We see the word *index* in many contexts—index of leading eco-

1. Hypertext is a method used to link related information in an electronic document. Readers can choose to review linked topics in a nonlinear way. For example, an electronic encyclopedia that discusses Abraham Lincoln may refer to the Gettysburg Address. The phrase "Gettysburg Address" may be highlighted in some way to convey to readers that it is a linked topic. If they wish, readers can select the Gettysburg Address and be shown its complete text. A hypermedia system is a hypertext system that may combine text, graphic, video, and audio material.

nomic indicators, consumer price index, indexed database files, the
Roman Catholic church's *Index Librorum Prohibitorum,* index of re-
fraction, index finger. Even within the indexing and information science communities, indexing processes cover a wide spectrum of applications. The *Proceedings* of the American Society of Indexers'
25th Anniversary Conference (Mulvany 1993) provide evidence of
the diversity of topics related to indexing. We are concerned here
with the preparation of what is often called a back-of-the-book index. The framework for this discussion is the indexing of books. The
methods presented, however, have far-reaching application beyond
printed media, into the dimension of the electronic environment. It
is worth recalling what Jessica Milstead wrote: "Whenever a collection of information, by reason of its size, its location, or the medium
on which it is stored, cannot conveniently be scanned in its entirety
by any would-be user, the quality of the index determines its value
perhaps more than any other factor" (Milstead 1984: 192).

Today, not only are we confronted with a voluminous amount of
printed information; we also must make our way through tangles of
electronic information. Very diverse material is stored electronically.
Full-text databases cater to a wide variety of professional interests.
In many offices, paper versions of forms and documents are optically
scanned and placed online—this is called document-image processing (DIP). CD-ROMs hold the contents of an encyclopedia or
several large collections of books. The desktop Rolodex is fast becoming the only information collection that can be conveniently scanned
by any user.

In an article about the retrieval of documents stored in online
document-image processing systems, Christopher Locke (1991) also
noted the value of indexing. "The dark side of document-image processing is the question of retrieval. Indexing documents properly and
consistently for later retrieval isn't a low-order clerical task but a
complex exercise requiring knowledge engineering skills. DIP tends
to underestimate, or underemphasize, the complexity of this task."
An interesting discussion of information access in electronic image
collections can be found in *Indexing Electronic Images and Text* (Bellardo et al. 1993).

PC Computing magazine surveyed its readers in December 1991
on the importance of various components of computer documenta-

tion. The published results of the survey (Grech 1992) overwhelmingly indicated that the index is considered by users the most important feature in both software and hardware manuals. The article concluded, "The plain truth is that many users are left to their own devices, and a responsible and competent manufacturer/publisher should see to it that documentation is complete, accurate, and thoroughly indexed."

Dependable, efficient information management has become a priority. Information that cannot be located might as well not exist. The index is one of the oldest information retrieval devices. When the earliest scribe produced a document that could not be easily browsed, the need for an index emerged. Hans Wellisch (1992: 70) writes,

> Indexing of books did not begin, as is commonly thought, after the invention of printing. It started with the rise of the universities in the 13th century. Although no two manuscripts of the same work were exactly alike and folio or page numbers were seldom used, indexes to theological treatises, lives of the saints, medical and legal compendia and, most of all, to collections of sermons were compiled, using chapter and section numbers instead of pagination.

Although the exact date of the first index is a matter of debate, we can safely say that indexes have been around for several hundred years. Nonetheless, the answer to the question What is an index? is not self-evident.

What Is an Index?

In the United States, the American National Standards Institute (ANSI) has adopted a standard for indexes, the *American National Standard for Library and Information Sciences and Related Publishing Practices—Basic Criteria for Indexes*. In ANSI Z39.4-1984 an index is described as "a systematic guide to items contained in or concepts derived from a collection. These items or concepts are represented by entries arranged in a searchable order, such as alphabetical, chronological, or numerical. This order is normally different from that of the items in or concepts in the collection itself."

The British Standards Institution has provided a more succinct definition (BS 3700:1988): "a systematic arrangement of entries designed to enable users to locate information in a document." Note that both standards stress the importance of *systematic* arrangement.

The *Oxford English Dictionary* (*OED*) takes us back to the Latin root *index* (n), the forefinger; *index* (v), to point out. The *OED* devotes many column inches to the various meanings of the word *index*, both as a noun and as a verb. For more on the history and meaning of *index*, see the fascinating discussion provided by Hans Wellisch in his *Indexing from A to Z* (1991: 159–70).

In his classic *Indexing, The Art of* (1979), G. Norman Knight turns to the British standard of 1976, the standard current at the time he wrote his book, for a full, cogent definition: BS 3700:1976 states that an index is "a systematic guide to the location of words, concepts or other items in books, periodicals or other publications. An index consists of a series of entries appearing, not in the order in which they appear in the publication, but in some other order (e.g. alphabetical) chosen to enable the user to find them quickly, together with references to show where each item is located."

I myself find the following definition useful: An index is a structured sequence—resulting from a thorough and complete analysis of text—of synthesized access points to all the information contained in the text. The structured arrangement of the index enables users to locate information efficiently.

What an Index Is Not

An index is *not* a concordance, a list of all the words that appear in a document. A concordance lacks analysis and synthesis. It is simply a list of words. A concordance, even in alphabetic order, is not a "systematic guide to items contained in or concepts derived from a collection."

An index is *not* a mere appendage to a book. It is a separate and distinct written document. Indexes are written, not generated. As creative, authored works, indexes are granted copyright registration. Like other types of writing, indexes are communicative by nature. The writing of an index differs from other types of writing in that an index employs only the very basic writing tools needed for ultimate clarity. Index writers strive for directness, succinctness, and clarity without the use of prefatory remarks or complete sentence structures. Communication goals are achieved with a minimum amount of communication tools.

An index is *not* a more elaborate version of the table of contents. Neither is the index simply an outline of the book. The term *index*, as it will be used in this book, is not an umbrella under which any alphabetic list can huddle. An index serves only one purpose: it enables readers to locate information efficiently.

The Index as a Knowledge Structure

The value of an index lies in how it is organized. While a poor index may contain references to all the important information in the text, if it is not systematically organized for easy access, such an index has limited value to the user.

A proper index is an intricate network of interrelationships. The very nature of the hierarchical arrangement implies a graded series of relationships and results in an obvious structure for access to the information. Ideally this structure is transparent to readers. Readers turn to an index with a very specific purpose, to locate information about a topic. When that topic is easily located, the readers' needs are satisfied; they can leave the index and return quickly to the text. However, when readers are unable to locate their topic, they must stop and more closely examine the structure of the index. At this point the index has failed to provide quick and easy access to information. In order to better understand the components of the index network we must go beyond definitions and examine the purpose of an index.

THE PURPOSE OF AN INDEX

One of the most cogent discussions of the purpose of an index can be found in the British standard (BS 3700:1988) (numbering added):

FUNCTION OF AN INDEX

1. Identify and locate relevant information within the material being indexed.
2. Discriminate between information on a subject and passing mention of a subject.
3. Exclude passing mention of subjects that offers nothing significant to the potential user.

4. Analyse concepts treated in the document so as to produce a series of headings based on its terminology.
5. Indicate relationships between concepts.
6. Group together information on subjects that is scattered by the arrangement of the document.
7. Synthesize headings and subheadings into entries.
8. Direct the user seeking information under terms not chosen for the index headings to the headings that have been chosen, by means of cross-references.
9. Arrange entries into a systematic and helpful order.

The first three items above require that the indexer judge the difference between relevant and irrelevant information. That indexers should actually pass judgment on the relevancy of information in a text makes some observers uncomfortable. Often indexers are instructed to index every name in the text regardless of relevancy. We have all looked up entries in an index only to find nothing of value in the text at the point referenced. It is indeed the job of indexers to distinguish between substantive information and passing mention of a topic. If we do not make these distinctions, we waste the readers' time.

Item 4 addresses two important functions of an index. First, concepts are to be identified and analyzed. Concepts in a book are not always stated verbatim. For example, in a book about raising dogs, several paragraphs may be devoted to various types of dog food. Never is the word *nutrition* mentioned; however, the concept *nutrition* should be in the index. The indexer reads between the lines, analyzes text, and identifies relevant concepts whether they are mentioned or not.

Second, item 4 directs us to use the terminology of the document. The author's language should always take precedence over alternative terms. Later in this book I will discuss various ways to handle synonyms. In regard to indexes in general, the language of the text dictates to a great degree the language that should be used in the index. An indexer should not impose an external taxonomy that is not reflected in the document itself. If the author uses the term *autos* in the text, then the information about autos should be posted at *autos*, not at *cars*. Strict adherence to this guideline does become difficult when working with multiauthored works, which will be discussed in more detail in chapter 6.

Items 5 and 6 relate to building the network of interrelationships in the index. The basic hierarchy of an index entry—that is, main heading with subentries—indicates a relationship between concepts. The *See also* cross-reference is another tool used in the index to indicate relationships. However, item 6, "Group together information on subjects that is scattered by the arrangement of the document," refers to a much more subtle aspect of the index network. When readers look up a particular term in an index, they should find references for all relevant information about that term. Using the earlier example about dog food and nutrition, we might find an index entry like the following:

> nutrition
> and bone development in puppies, 67–70
> food and, 30–35
> skin problems and diet, 120–125
> vitamin supplements, 89

As we can see from the page references in the example above, information about nutrition was presented in various parts of the book. The indexer has assembled for the reader the relevant information about nutrition. Identifying related information and gathering it together in an appropriate place is one of the more difficult aspects of indexing. All too often inexperienced indexers focus on the minutiae of the text and neglect the big picture.

When readers discover that information in an index is scattered, their confidence in the index suffers, and rightly so. Users of an index should be able to look up a term and feel confident that all the relevant information has been gathered there. They should not have to second guess the indexer and try to figure out if more information might be found at some other place, or, worse, at many other places in the index.

Item 7 instructs the indexer to "synthesize headings and subheadings into entries." The indexer's ability to put together distinct topical and conceptual elements so as to form a whole, synthesized entry contributes greatly to the integrity of the index network. At times this effort is as simple as resolving differences between synonymous terms. At other times the synthesis process is more complex, as when, say, objective realism is discussed in a passage in which the phrase is not stated verbatim.

While item 7 refers to the design of individual index entries, item 9 discusses the arrangement of index entries. The most common arrangement order for index entries is alphabetic. However, as we shall see in chapter 4, there is more than one way to alphabetize.

Item 8 addresses the crucial element of cross-references in an index—in particular, the *See* cross-reference. Cross-references are an integral part of the index network. *See* cross-references control the scattering of information in an index. They anticipate the language of index users and reconcile the language of the document with the users' language.

In the "autos" example used earlier, although the information about automobiles should be listed at this term, there should also be a cross-reference for "cars. *See* autos" in the index. Judicious use of cross-references can greatly enhance the usability of an index. Without cross-references, readers have no guidance; they must spend time discovering the various ways a topic has been cited. When appropriate cross-references are lacking, the cadence of their search for information is disrupted; the usability of the index has been compromised.

In order to provide appropriate cross-references the indexer must be intimately familiar with the language of the book and the audience for the book. Again, the primary purpose of an index is to enable readers to locate information efficiently. Indexers must always ask themselves, Who are these readers?

THE AUDIENCE: WHO USES INDEXES?

We can begin by dividing the audience into two general categories: those who have read the book and those who have not. There are books that are read from cover to cover. Readers of these books inevitably become familiar with the author's language. They are the readers who are likely to look up terms that were used by the author. This is one reason it is so important for the indexer to retain the author's terminology. An index that is thorough and complete will meet the needs of this portion of the audience.

Meeting the needs of those who have *not* read the book is far more difficult. People who have not read the book are not familiar with the author's language. The burden is on the indexer to anticipate the language of readers that may differ from that of the author, and to anticipate the expectations of different readers. We can assume that most index users will not have read a book in its entirety. This is particularly true of reference books. By their very nature reference books are designed to be referred to, not to be read straight through.

Reference books deserve further comment. Included in this category are a wide range of books: computer software manuals, cookbooks, employee benefits handbooks, style manuals, corporate policy and procedures manuals, and many gardening books. However, the audiences for reference books can be quite different. We need to ask, Will the readers have specialized subject knowledge? How will they use the index?

Specialized Subject Knowledge

Some books clearly require of their readers specialized subject knowledge. A general trade book about growing roses will have an audience very different from a book about chemical pest management in citrus groves. In the book on growing roses an entry for "aphids" may be sufficient, whereas in the pest management book we may need an entry for "aphidoidea" as well as for the various genera and species using their Latin names.

Generally speaking, the more specialized knowledge that is required of readers, the easier it is to identify their language needs. For example, in a book that assumes a background in information science an entry named "search techniques" will be adequate; the index does not need to provide access for those readers who might look up "find" or "locate."

In a mass market book that assumes little or no specialized knowledge the indexer must anticipate that some items may be looked up by readers in a variety of ways. A reference manual for a word processing program may have an entry "searching for text." This time the indexer cannot assume that most readers will know that information about finding or locating text will be posted at "searching for text." The indexer anticipates that readers may look up "finding text" or "loca :ng text" and provides cross-references to direct readers to the "searching for text" entry.

There are books whose audience is composed of readers with and without specialized subject knowledge. Cookbooks are a good example of this type of book. One cook may look up "sauces," while another cook may be more focused and look up "Madeira sauce." A thorough cookbook index will anticipate the needs of both types of readers.

How Are Indexes Used?

Depending on the type of book, we can make some general assumptions about the way indexes are used. Although there are exceptions—some people actually do "read" indexes—for the most part, readers turn to the index because they want information about a specific topic. We should distinguish between casual indexer users and desperate index users.

Casual index users have time and patience. Suppose I want to use leftover chicken for dinner. I turn to my cookbook index and look up "kung pao chicken" in the K's. Not finding it there, I would then look under "chicken" and, if unsuccessful there, I would look under "poultry." Although I might experience some irritation on the third try, I would continue my search.

At the other end of the spectrum are desperate index users, who have no time or patience. The readers of computer manuals often fall into this category. Most likely the only portion of the manual they ever read was the "Getting Started" section. Now there is a problem, and as a last resort they turn to their manual. Let's suppose an office manager is printing a report that he must deliver in twenty minutes to his boss. The paper has jammed in the laser printer. He doesn't know how to open the printer to dislodge the paper. He grabs his printer manual. It turns out that paper jams are discussed in the "Troubleshooting" section along with a myriad of other problems. He is lucky that the indexer thoroughly indexed this three-page section. He finds an entry for "jammed paper." The topic was also indexed as "paper, jamming of" and "troubleshooting."

Imagine a more serious situation. A mother frantically turns to a home medical guide to find out how to stop her child's arm from bleeding. This index user has no time to examine the internal structure of the index or to think about whether she should look up general terms or specific terms. If she is fortunate, the indexer will have provided several access points for the information she needs.

The indexes for the printer manual and the home medical guide should address the needs of both casual and desperate index users. For the latter category of users, the index should be "action" oriented. These index users should be able to locate terms like "jammed paper" and "stopping bleeding" in the indexes.

To provide reasonable access points for information, indexers must have a thorough understanding of a book's audience. As a communicative network, the index does not exist independent of its audience. Users of an index that anticipates their needs find the internal structure of the index transparent. They need not think about the index structure or spend a lot of time searching the index itself. They turn to the index, find the information they seek, and immediately return to the text.

The Ideal Index

As we shall see in the chapters that follow, many factors contribute to the writing of the "ideal" index. A stellar index that meets the needs of a majority of users does not emerge without careful thought and design choices by the indexer. There are times to follow rules; there are times to break rules. The bottom line is always to provide efficient access to information.

It can certainly be argued that there is no such thing as a perfect index. Every index can be examined and found wanting in some respects. However, the indexer's goal is to write the best index possible given the circumstances. There are indeed circumstances that by their very nature compromise the quality of the index. Some of these will be discussed in chapter 2.

The American Society of Indexers (ASI) has formulated criteria for judging an annual book indexing competition. Two sections of the criteria—"Content of the Index" and "Structure and Accuracy of the Index Entries"—clearly list many of the components of the "ideal" index.

3. CONTENT OF THE INDEX

3.1 The index must bring together references to similar concepts that are scattered in the text, or that are expressed in varying terminology. This can be done through the establishment of a single heading and a set of subheadings, through the use of cross-references, or through other appropriate devices.

3.2 All significant items in the text must appear in the index. However, if there is a category of material that is not indexed, this should be stated in the introduction.

3.3 Items and concepts in the text must be represented in the index by appropriate, precise, accurate, unambiguous headings.

3.4 The index entry headings should be consistent in form and in usage. Inclusion of synonymous headings and spelling variations, if used, should be intentional to facilitate access.

3.5 The index should represent the text and not be a vehicle for expressing the indexer's own views and interests.

4. STRUCTURE AND ACCURACY OF THE INDEX ENTRIES

4.1 The index entries should be arranged in a recognizable, or stated searchable order, such as alphabetical, classified, chronological, or numerical order.

4.2 The locators given in the index should tally with the text.

4.3 Strings of undifferentiated locators should generally be avoided by use of appropriate subheadings or other appropriate devices. If the number of locators in a given entry is so large that aspects of the heading are not adequately differentiated, additional headings, subheadings, or modifiers should be introduced. Headings should be as specific as the nature of the collection permits, and the purposes of the users require.

4.4 There must be a sufficient number of cross-references in the index so that related items are connected, and obsolete or idiosyncratic terms in the text are related to terms in current use.

4.5 Abbreviations, acronyms, or other abridgment of a word or phrase should be explained in an appropriate manner.

Careful readers will notice many similarities between the ASI judging criteria and the British standard's "Function of an Index." If we ever lose sight of what the purpose of an index is, re-reading of these excerpts should refresh our minds.

TERMINOLOGY

Would that the indexing profession could agree on terms
so that the members of the profession could understand
each other.

Dorothy Thomas (1989: 18)

In May of 1988, Dorothy Thomas, an indexer and a past president
of the American Society of Indexers, spoke at the annual ASI conference about a variety of topics including the lack of standard terminology within the indexing profession. Unfortunately the language
situation has not improved since 1988.

There are five terms that will be used throughout this book that
require identification: *main heading, subentry, reference locator,
cross-reference,* and *the entry.* Figure 1.1 labels these five items.

1. Main Heading

This is the top line in the index entry hierarchy. As Thomas points
out, it has been referred to by at least six terms: access point, entry,
index entry, heading, main heading, and subject heading.

2. Subentry

The lines of indented text that immediately follow the main heading
(and are not cross-references) will be referred to here as subentries.
Other writers refer to them as subheadings.

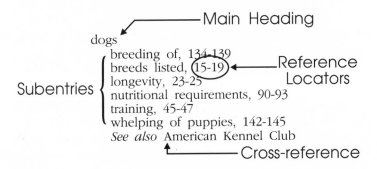

FIG. 1.1. THE INDEX ENTRY.

3. Reference Locator

Usually in a book index the reference locators are page numbers. However, in some books the reference locator is not a page number. For example, many legal books are indexed to section numbers. In this book both terms, reference locator and page number, will be used.

4. Cross-reference

Cross-reference will refer to internal index navigation guides. These guides generally take the form of *See* or *See also.*

5. Entry

A main heading along with the entire block of information that follows it will be referred to as an entry. In figure 1.1, "dogs," its reference locators, subentries, and the cross-reference together constitute the entry. The term will be used in a general sense, such as "index entries are alphabetized." The term, when qualified, such as in "the 'dogs' entry," will refer to the main heading and everything that follows it.

REFERENCES

Several texts will be referred to frequently throughout this book. While only portions of these references will be discussed here, all are deserving of a complete reading and all would make a valuable addition to an indexer's library.

British Standard Recommendation for Preparing Indexes to Books, Periodicals and Other Documents (BS 3700:1988). As this book is being written, two other important standards are being revised, namely, the American standard (ANSI Z39.4, *Basic Criteria for Indexes*) and the international standard (ISO 999, *Guidelines for Preparing Indexes to Books, Periodicals and Other Documents*). The British standard has been used in this book primarily because of its lucid discussion of germane topics. Much of BS 3700 has been incorporated into the draft version of the emerging ISO 999 standard. Information about BS 3700 can be obtained from either the British Standards Institution or the Society of Indexers in England. In the United States, information about standards can be obtained from the National Information Standards Organization (NISO). Addresses for these organizations are provided in appendix F, "Resources for Indexers."

The American standard, Z39.4, is being extensively revised. The references in this text to the NISO committee's revision of Z39.4-199x are drawn from draft 3 (1993). As a member of this NISO committee, I have attempted to cite portions of the draft that I suspect will appear in the final version of the standard. However, readers interested in the guidelines of the revised American standard are advised to refer to either future drafts or the final version of Z39.4-199x when it becomes available.

The Chicago Manual of Style, both the 13th edition, because of its widespread use, and the 14th edition, because of changes in style, will be discussed. The primary discussion of the *Manual of Style* will focus on the chapters about indexes. In the 13th edition, citations will be to chapter 18 of the *Manual*; in the 14th edition, to chapter 17. References to other sections of the *Manual of Style* will, as the occasion requires, be to the 13th or the 14th edition, or to both.

Knight, G. Norman, *Indexing, The Art of*. Unfortunately this delightful book is out of print. However, it can be located at major university libraries in the United States.

2

THE AUTHOR AND THE INDEX

WHETHER AUTHORS DECIDE to prepare indexes for their own books or instead engage a professional indexer, a few preliminary matters should be addressed. A little planning early in the writing process will reap rewards later during the indexing.

THE BOOK CONTRACT AND THE INDEX

A standard clause in most American nonfiction book contracts states that the author will provide an index. Should the author fail to provide an index or fail to provide a satisfactory index, the contract often states that the publisher may supply an index and charge the cost of the index against the author's royalty account. Either way, the author pays for the index in time or money.

The clause in the contract regarding the index is often given little scrutiny by authors. In the whirlwind of activities that surround the signing of a book contract, neither party, publisher or author, is likely to be thinking of the index. Yet the index for some books can have a direct impact on sales. It is in the interest of both parties that the best possible index be written for the book.

Later in this chapter the pros and cons of author-prepared indexes will be discussed. Here I shall focus solely on the contractual provisions regarding the index. Even those authors who are committed to writing their own index should consider revising the index clause in their book contract. The contract should state that the cost of the index shall be shared jointly between the publisher and author, and that the author's portion shall be charged against future royalties. This type of provision provides the author with more financial flexibility should a professional indexer be required. In 1988 the British journal *The Indexer* reported in the article "Contracted Indexes" that the Society of Authors and the Writers' Guild of Great Britain had reached agreements with several British publishers regarding a fifty-fifty division of the cost of indexing as a standard clause in a book contract.

When the author is completely responsible for provision of an index, an unfortunate chain of events is often set into motion. Although many authors realize that by the time the book pages are paginated they will be quite tired of dealing with the book, they often think that the indexing will not take much time. It is certainly something they can whip out in a couple of days or a week, they think. Their editor has sent them a copy of the press's indexing style guide or has referred them to *The Chicago Manual of Style*. But they have rarely read any of this material prior to receiving the first set of galleys; they've been too busy writing the book.

Perhaps the author has tagged index terms in the word processor files. Or perhaps the author has highlighted some index terms in the galleys while proofreading the book. Some authors do both, thinking that, without too much trouble, they can repaginate the word processor files to match the typeset pages by marking final page breaks on galley pages so that the final page numbers can be assigned to index entries.

Finally, the author gets around to reading the index style specifications. Let's say the index is to be provided in run-in (or run-on) format with letter-by-letter alphabetizing. Leading prepositions, articles, and conjunctions in subentries are not to be alphabetized. Page ranges are to be elided in a specific way. The *See* cross-references are to run off from the main entry while the *See also* cross-references are to be placed as the last subentry. And all of this has to be done within two weeks of receiving the final page proofs, which arrived yesterday.

The clock is ticking, the author is exhausted, and the editor is waiting for the index. The author calls the editor and asks about finding someone to do the index. Since editors know that most experienced indexers are booked weeks if not months in advance, locating an indexer who will be able to provide an index quickly enough to maintain the printing schedule will not be an easy task. Sometimes the editor is lucky—an indexer is free because the schedule for another book has slipped. More often than not, the editor is not lucky. Phone calls produce only referrals to other indexers. The search goes on across the country for any indexer who happens to be free.

Authors who are new to publishing often do not know that contractual indexing services can be expensive. Presuming a good indexer can be located at all, the cost of indexing often shocks the author who must pay for it. A typical three-hundred-page book can easily cost close to a thousand dollars to index, especially if it is a rush job. How many books will have to be sold to pay for that? Some editors, appearing as advocates for the author, quite blatantly ask indexers to lower their fee "because the author has to pay for this." Of course, the author has to pay for it because the publisher wrote that clause into the contract and the author did not object.

The scenario above is not farfetched. It happens far too frequently. The moral of the story is simple: arrangements for the index should be planned; the author should have the financial flexibility to contract for indexing.

The Writing Process and the Index

Indexers know that a well-written, well-edited, structured book is far easier to index than a poorly written book. While writing, the author can maintain some simple lists that will help to resolve mundane indexing problems later.

Names of People

If a book refers to people, these names are often included in the index. Superficially, indexing names of people may seem quite easy. However, the task is often more complicated because of the variations in references to names. When citing an individual in the index, the indexer must cite the most complete name used in the text. The individual's complete name is usually provided when the person is first mentioned in the text. Later an abbreviated name or even a nickname may be used. It would be helpful if the author maintained a list of important names in full, with entries such as "Butler, James Francis—AKA—Frank Butler." A simple list of personal names can save indexing time. For example, James Francis Butler may be introduced on page 78 and not appear again until page 310, when he is referred to as Frank Butler. If a list of names is available, the indexer

THE AUTHOR AND THE INDEX

can quickly locate the formal name and check the text to be sure these two names in fact refer to the same individual.

Names of Organizations

Like names of people, names of organizations should be cited in full in the index. It is to be hoped that, when an organization is first mentioned in the text, the complete name will have been provided along with any acronyms or abbreviations associated with it. A simple list of organization names, acronyms, and abbreviations can help the indexer maintain consistency in the index. Such a list can also help proofreaders spot name errors, which easily creep into the text. For example, on page 35 we find a reference to the "Society of Indexers" while on page 210 we find the "Society for Indexers." Which is correct? An author's list of organization names would quickly resolve such discrepancies, avoiding last-minute queries from the indexer to the editor.

Names of Places

Some geographic names pose the same problems as names of people and organizations. Let's take a book called *A Climber's Guide to Mountains of the Western States and Alaska*. While many geographic names are straightforward, such as the Rocky Mountains or Half Dome in Yosemite, others are troublesome. Many readers of this book will not know that in 1980 Mount McKinley was renamed Denali, so the index will need an entry for "McKinley, Mount. *See* Denali." If the author maintains a list of such idiosyncrasies, checking the index for term consistency will be much easier.

Controlled Vocabulary

As a book is being written, terms that have synonyms will be introduced. The author should decide upon a term of choice and use it consistently throughout the book. The index will cross-reference from synonymous terms to the term of choice. In a book called *Getting the Most Out of Your Computer in Ten Easy Steps* we find the following statement: "Throughout this book we will not distinguish between the MS-DOS and PC-DOS operating systems. Instead, we will refer only to DOS."

These two sentences cleanly resolve a potential vocabulary problem. The indexer will provide two cross-references:

MS-DOS. *See* DOS
. . .
PC-DOS. *See* DOS

Authors should be encouraged to offer synonymous terms in the text. In some cases it might help to keep a list of such terms. The list can be used by both the editor and the indexer to ensure term consistency throughout the book and the index.

Deciding Ahead of Time What Gets Indexed

Several years ago I indexed a book that contained a lot of footnotes. Before I turned the index over to the editor, I sent a copy to the author for review. She called me and was quite pleased with the index except for one thing: she had expected to see several more names in the index. I was alarmed to learn that I had missed so many names! When we went through her list, name by name, I discovered that each was mentioned only in a footnote citation. Often the mention took the form of

19. For a useful discussion of this concept, see Joseph Tussman, *Government and the Mind* (Oxford: Oxford University Press, 1977), p. 149.

In the example above, "Joseph Tussman" would not ordinarily be indexed. The general rule is not to index the footnote if it merely serves as a bibliographic reference. Footnotes are indexed when they add substantive information not otherwise included in the text. Authors should put indexable names in the body of the text rather than burying these names in footnotes if they want them to appear in the index. Or the author can request that a separate index of "Authors and Works Cited" be prepared. If such an index is desired, the request should be made early so that additional index pages can be allowed for in the production phase.

Another portion of a book that is often not indexed is the appendixes. Some editors routinely tell indexers not to index the appendixes. In many books a wealth of information is contained in the appendixes that should be indexed. If authors want the appendixes indexed, they may need to express this desire to the book editor.

Who Should Prepare the Index?

Much debate has been devoted over the years to the virtues of author-prepared indexes compared with indexes written by professional indexers. Although the 13th edition of *The Chicago Manual of Style* declared that "the author most nearly approaches the ideal as indexer" (18.20), that opinion was considerably modified in the 14th edition (17.21):

> It might be supposed . . . that authors are their own ideal indexers, and sometimes this is indeed the case. The best scholarly indexes are probably made by authors who have the ability to be objective about their work, who understand what a good index is, and who, having mastered the craft, know how such an index is achieved. . . . Not all authors have mastered the skills or acquired the experience necessary to make a good index. In such a case, the surest way to attain a suitable index is to enlist the aid of a professional indexer.

According to John A. Vickers, an author and a winner of the esteemed Wheatley Medal (for indexing), "It may well be true in general that the author should be the last person to index his own book, being too close to the text." Hans Wellisch echoes Vickers's thoughts when he writes (1992: 73),

> Many publishers claim (and some even say so in their instructions to authors) that the author is the person best qualified to be his or her own indexer. Who else knows all the details and important points of the book better than the author? There may be some kernel of truth in this idea, but in most instances authors have never had any training in indexing; certainly, "underlining every important word or name and alphabetizing the resultant entries after some editing" (another frequent instruction to authors) is inadequate advice for the would-be author-indexer. Authors are also often much too close to their

works and are therefore unable to envisage how prospective users will search for information.

While this debate will certainly not be resolved here, we can say that it is very difficult to generalize about author-prepared indexes. Some authors take to the task of indexing well and prepare useful indexes for their books. Others will flounder and develop an intense dislike for the entire process. A common pitfall is deciding to index one's book without knowing what is actually involved. Aside from a familiarity with the mechanics of indexing, which will fill the remaining chapters of this book, there are some practical issues that should be considered before anyone decides to index a book.

Authors as Indexers: Strengths and Weaknesses

The primary strength authors bring to the indexing process is familiarity with the text and general subject matter. Authors, better than anyone else, know what is covered in their books and are in a good position to anticipate the needs of the audience for which they have written the book. Many authors, particularly textbook authors, realizing that the index will play a crucial role in many buying decisions, have a vested interest in the publication of a good index. A good index will help the sales of the book. With this synergy of crucial elements in place, what could possibly go wrong?

Two factors that can greatly hinder authors who prepare their own indexes are (1) a lack of knowledge of the indexing process and (2) general fatigue and too much self-involvement with the book when it is ready for indexing. The extent to which these factors apply to an author's situation should help authors decide whether or not to index their own book.

Virtually all who encourage authors to prepare their own indexes insist that authors learn the mechanics of indexing. Some publishers send authors attractive pamphlets that outline the indexing process in quite simple terms. Other publishers refer their authors without additional comment to the discussion of indexing in *The Chicago Manual of Style.* If indexing were such a straightforward and simple task, there would be no need for a book such as this; we could issue a training leaflet instead.

It is not my intention to inflate the index-writing process. On the contrary, I wish to provide information about the substance and nuances of the process to improve the performance of those who undertake the writing of an index. However, after teaching book-indexing techniques to hundreds of students over the years, I've discovered that the art and craft of indexing is mastered by few. Even after thirty hours of classroom instruction, matched by at least thirty hours of outside preparation time, some students learn the rules but still cannot write a proper index. Other students do an excellent conceptual job with term selection but muddle up the rules so badly that their indexes suffer. Hans Wellisch (1991: xv) sums up the situation as follows:

> Indexing does not come naturally, like breathing. It is rather more like playing the fiddle: some learn to do it reasonably well, a few will become virtuosi, but most people will never know how to do it at all. This simple truth seems to be lost on publishers and editors, who almost always assume that someone who can write a book will also be able to index it. But this assumption, enshrined in most authors' contracts, is tantamount to the belief that an author can also design and cut the type from which the book will be printed.

To suggest that writing an index can be done by anyone with a minimum amount of preparation is a disservice to author-indexers. At the same time, to suggest that indexing is best tackled by a professional indexer is not fair either. Some authors naturally want to index their own books; the index is a crucial component of their book. Authors who wish to index their own books should be encouraged to do so, provided they are made aware of the demands of the task. Index writing is indeed a form of writing, but one very different from expository writing. Book writers will have to switch creative gears when they become index writers. There will be rules to follow, deadlines to be met. Indexing one's own book is certainly not an impossible task, but it is a demanding task when done well.

In addition to learning how to index, author-indexers must also face the problem of exhaustion and overinvolvement with the book by the time it is ready for indexing. As I contemplate the indexing of this book, I am quite concerned about my own ability to index it well. I will have written and rewritten, edited and rewritten the book many times. I will have proofread pages at least once, if not twice. I suspect that by the time this book is ready for indexing I will be quite tired of it!

The element of fatigue should not be overlooked. Many authors turn the indexing task over to someone else simply because they are too tired of the book to write the index themselves. This is as good a reason as any to hire a professional indexer.

We can generally gauge the amount of fatigue we are feeling; it can be more difficult, however, to ascertain the degree of self-involvement we have with our book. Author-indexers must be true not only to themselves but also to the readers of the index. In order to anticipate the needs of their readers, they must become somewhat detached from the book. While authors know their own language quite well, this language may not be helpful to people who use the index. Even though the author has deliberately chosen particular terms for use in the book, the author-indexer must methodically consider various ways to provide the reader access to the terms and concepts in the book. Intense involvement with one's book can make it very difficult to anticipate the index user's needs accurately.

Those authors who will be writing indexes for their own books can rest assured that they will not need to know every tidbit of information that follows in the remaining chapters. They may wish to jump ahead to the next chapter, "Getting Started," paying particular attention to the section on deciphering indexing style guides.

Professional Indexers: Strengths and Weaknesses

The primary strength a professional indexer brings to the task can be summed up in one word: experience. Professionals know how to index. They know how to budget their time so that the publisher receives the index on schedule in the desired format. Also of extreme importance, professionals can be objective about the book. The professional can read the book with fresh eyes. Even those indexers who specialize in a particular field realize that each book is unique; each index is a special blending of the language of the text with the language of the audience.

Professional indexers are familiar with publishing practices. They frequently work with authors, manuscript editors, production editors, and typesetters. Instructions full of publishing jargon that may sound like gibberish to the uninitiated make complete sense to the professional.

Many indexers specialize in subject areas. Some may have advanced degrees, while others may have years of hands-on experience. Often indexers who do specialize join appropriate professional organizations and keep current with the language of the field by regularly reading the professional literature.

Indexers must be able to empathize with both the author and the readers. Indexers must possess an array of inductive and deductive thinking skills. Additionally, the professional must work in a detailed, careful, and accurate manner. Indexers must also possess the rare commodity of common sense. When the rules do not apply and there is nowhere to turn for guidance, common sense and sound judgment will provide an answer.

The most obvious handicap that a professional indexer may have is lack of familiarity with the subject matter. With many mass market books, this is not an issue. Any book written for a literate, general audience can be indexed by a well-read, intelligent indexer. Books that contain specialized and complex subject matter will often require the indexing skills of an individual with a substantial background knowledge of the subject. For example, any good indexer could index a mass market book about reducing cholesterol with a vegetarian diet. The indexer would not need an advanced degree in nutritional science. However, a medical school text about renal disease can be an indexing challenge. While the indexer of such a book need not have a medical degree, knowledge of medical terminology will be important. Ideally, the indexer of the book about renal disease will be an experienced medical indexer familiar with the nuances of medical indexing and the standard vocabulary of the discipline. Readers interested in legal indexing will find Elizabeth Moys's article "Legal Vocabulary and the Indexer" quite informative.

Without a doubt some books contain such specialized subject matter that locating a professional indexer with the appropriate background may be difficult. Some argue that a good indexer can index anything; I submit that indexers often need subject-area expertise to index well.

At the other end of the spectrum are authors and editors who assume that the material is so complex that the indexer will need help with term selection. Often this "help" takes the form of lists of terms to be included in the index, or manuscripts in which the author has highlighted indexable terms. I have often found that the material to be indexed is not complex but quite straightforward to anyone with a rudimentary background in the field. It is important to maintain a clear picture of the nature of the material to be indexed and to locate an indexer with an appropriate background.

RELATIONSHIP BETWEEN AUTHOR AND INDEXER

When authors decide not to index their own books, they must locate someone who will do the indexing. By now it should be clear that indexing is not a task to carelessly hand over to a graduate student or somehow persuade a brother-in-law to do. The index will reflect upon both the author and the publisher. A poorly written index will be a source of embarrassment to both parties. Authors are advised to spend time and locate an appropriate indexer.

Locating an Indexer

An indexer should be selected well in advance of the date that final, paginated pages are expected. Given the typical turnaround time for an index, the indexer will need to plan for a book. Usually six weeks to a month is enough notice for an indexer to block out the time needed.

Indexers are often located by referral. Most editors have a list of indexers with whom they have worked. Your colleagues can be another source of information. If you liked the index in a particular book, try to locate the indexer who wrote it.

Another source of information is the *Register of Indexers* published annually by the American Society of Indexers. The *Register* lists ASI members who offer freelance indexing services. Indexers are listed by subject-area specialty, by geographic location, and by type of indexing services. Indexers are also listed in the *Literary Market Place* (*LMP*), the source book for the American publishing industry. Outside the United States, the Australian Society of Indexers (AusSI) publishes *Indexers Available*, the Indexing and Abstracting Society of Canada (IASC) publishes *Register of Indexers*

Available, and the Society of Indexers (SI) in Great Britain publishes *Indexers Available.*

When time allows, it is often a good idea to interview and accept bids from several indexers. You need to find an indexer with whom you can work. The author and the indexer must be able to communicate very clearly. Ask if the indexer has worked on books similar to yours. The indexer will surely ask you to describe your book and its audience. If you do not feel comfortable with the conversation, then most likely you are not talking to the person who should index your book.

If the interview does go well, you will undoubtedly be asked questions you may not be able to answer. You might be asked if the index is to be in indented or run-in style, or if the index is to be delivered on disk with typesetting codes embedded. Authors should feel free to refer all questions regarding index specifications to their editor (see the section below, "What the Indexer Needs").

Many authors turn the entire matter of indexing over to their editors. However, a complete lack of author involvement in the indexing process is far from ideal. In response to a very negative review of an index that placed blame on the indexer and the publisher, British author Bernard Levin addressed the matter of the author's responsibility:

> This authorial willingness to be left out of the picture is widespread; I cannot count the number of fellow-authors who have complained in my hearing about, say, a rotten jacket for their books. When I ask why they did not demand to see the jacket in all its stages, from the first sketch, it almost invariably transpires that it never occurred to them to ask, whereupon I have a struggle to refrain from telling them that they have no one to blame but themselves. When I wrote my first book, some seventeen years ago, I announced that I was going to interfere in every stage of the publication, right down to the typeface it was set in, and I have done so ever since. And surely if a book includes an index, a self-respecting author should be as jealous of its quality as of his own.

Authors are advised to make clear to their editors very early in the book production schedule the degree of involvement they wish to have with the index. If an author wants to review an index before it goes to press, time will need to be allocated for that review. When an author demands to see actual page proof of the index, planning for this time is even more crucial. Time for thorough author review of the index needs to be budgeted from the very beginning of the production cycle.

Contractual Matters

When an index is paid for either by the author alone out of royalties or jointly by the publisher and author—again, the author's portion out of royalties—typically the publisher formally contracts with the indexer. Authors who will pay the indexer directly will need their own contract with the indexer.

Most problems between indexers and publishers or authors arise from a lack of communication about aesthetic and practical expectations regarding the index. Many indexers have their own contracts. Publishers have their own contracts. Often these indexing contracts are woefully lacking in clarity and professionalism.

At the very least, an indexing contract should cover the following items:

the work to be indexed; expected length of the work
time schedule for indexing
provisions regarding late delivery of material to the indexer; provisions regarding late delivery of the index to the author/publisher
complete specifications regarding index format and submission format for the index
rate of pay for the index; the payment schedule
assignment of rights for the index

Written contracts. Like any other contract, the indexing contract must be signed by both parties. A surprising number of publishers and indexers work without written contracts; they rely solely on oral agreements. This arrangement appears to work well until there is a problem. When a problem does arise, the lack of a written contract does not reflect well on the professionalism of either the indexer or the publisher.

A very detailed example of an indexing contract can be obtained from the American Society of Indexers. Request a copy of the "ASI Recommended Indexing Agreement."

Assignment of rights. Many people within the publishing community mistakenly assume that an index is automatically considered a "work made for hire." The U.S. Copyright Act of 1976 (sec. 101) very clearly states that a work is a work made for hire "if the parties expressly agree in a written instrument signed by them that the work shall be considered a work made for hire." Without a written agreement signed by both parties an index cannot be considered a work made for hire. If both parties sign an agreement stating that the index will be a work made for hire, then the commissioning agent, usually the publisher, will be the copyright owner (see sec. 201). For more information about copyright and indexes, see the article "Copyright for Indexes, Revisited" (Mulvany 1991).

How much will it cost? Generalizing about the cost of an index is very difficult. Indexing rates vary greatly depending upon the type of material to be indexed.

One of four basic formats are used by indexers when preparing bids. Many indexers charge by the hour; others charge by the page or by the entry. Some indexers will present a flat fee bid.

When an indexer charges by the hour, the indexer must stipulate, in writing, an expected range, with the maximum number of hours clearly understood by both parties. An experienced indexer is able to judge accurately how much time an assignment will take. Hourly rates in 1993 started at $20 to $25 per hour and went up from there.

Many indexers bid jobs on a per-page rate. This way both parties know exactly how much an index will cost. When calculating a per-page rate, the indexer will be taking into account the density of text per page. Clearly, if a book is three columns of eight-point type, the per-page rate will be higher than for a book of less densely printed material. Another item considered in this type of bid format is the amount of illustrative material. Are there tables or photographs or line drawings? Is the illustrative material to be indexed? If not, does it take up space on the pages, reducing the amount of indexable material? Are footnotes to be indexed? Another important consideration is the nature of the material. For example, a multiauthored graduate-level text about economics will very likely cost more to index than an introductory, single-authored text about economics. In 1993, per-page rates generally started at $3–$4 per page, depending on geographic area, publisher, and type of book; many medical texts, for instance, are indexed at a rate of $5–$6 per page.

Some indexers submit per-entry bids. This format requires a very clear understanding of what constitutes an entry. For example, is the entry "dogs, 34–37, 55, 103–4" one entry? Is it three entries? Or is it seven entries? In my opinion, it is three entries—the indexer had to type the entry "dogs" three times because "dogs" appeared in three separate locations in the text. Others would consider the example as one entry. In this case, the per-entry rate is really a per-line rate. Another concern with this type of bidding is the possibility that an index will become "padded" with entries. Given the disparity in the interpretations of what constitutes an entry, it is difficult to arrive at a general rate for this type of bidding. Usually, the rate is less than $1.00 per entry or per line.

Indexers who provide a flat fee bid have undoubtedly taken into account the various bidding formats used. In any type of contract work, all parties like to know what it will cost. This is not always possible, but it is always desirable.

One last remark about fees. Occasionally an editor will call and say, "We need a really short index, only about 900 lines," implying that it takes less time to design a short index than to design a longer index for the same material. Therefore, the price should be less. This reasoning is flawed. First, regardless of the size of an index, the indexer must still read the same number of words. Second, it is not only difficult but also time-consuming to produce a 900-line index instead of the 1,500 lines that may really be called for. Many indexers index a book the way it should be indexed, then edit it to meet space requirements. It is difficult to distill five entries to one entry and remain fair to the material. Short indexes do not necessarily imply reduced fees.

What the Indexer Needs

The indexer will need a complete set of final page proofs for the book. It is usually the publisher's responsibility to provide a set of these pages to the indexer. Often the typesetter is asked to send final pages by overnight delivery to the indexer at the same time that the pages are sent to the publisher.

The indexer's copy of the final pages must be clear and readable. Poor photocopies will slow down the indexing and very likely cause the indexer grief.

Given the proliferation of "desktop publishing," a few comments about *final* pages are warranted. Publishers who generate final pages in-house often succumb to the temptation to make last-minute adjustments that change the pagination of a book. Since the indexer is assigning page numbers to index entries, any changes in pagination will affect the index. It can be very time-consuming, and therefore costly, for the indexer to readjust reference locators in the index. Once pages have been sent out for indexing, every effort should be made to ensure that the pagination of the book does not change. If the pagination does change, the indexer should be notified immediately.

The indexer must be given specifications for the index or a comprehensive style guide. Index "specs" should cover such things as rules of alphabetization, format of the index (run-in or indented), format and placement of cross-references, and electronic manuscript requirements. The likely source for this information is the editor at the publishing house. More on index specifications will be presented in chapter 3.

If the author has maintained lists of personal names, geographic names, or names of organizations, these lists should be given to the indexer. A copy of the editor's style sheet can also be helpful to the indexer. Any general editorial guidelines regarding such matters as transliteration or density of indexing should be discussed prior to the beginning of indexing work.

Collaboration between Author and Indexer

A cooperative working relationship between the author and the indexer can be extremely beneficial. An author who is available for consultation during the indexing process can be a very valuable technical resource for the indexer.

In some books the indexer may have questions about the organization of certain terms. "Would it be better to list this as *xyz*, or would people tend to look it up first as *abc*?" Authors should respond to such questions with directness; there is no time to give the indexer a graduate-level education in the topic at hand. If the author and the indexer have established a good rapport, the indexer will feel free to call upon the author as need arises; a much better index will result. This is one reason authors should be involved in the selection of the indexer.

Alternatively, authors (and editors) can become overinvolved in the indexing process, much to the dismay of the indexer. Calls to the indexer to say "I just want to make sure you indexed *xyz* on page 52" are not helpful. A far more difficult situation arises when the indexer is provided with a long list of terms that the author wants to see in the index. Such lists are very distracting to the indexer. The cadence of indexing is disrupted when the indexer must doublecheck selected index terms against the author's list. Another problem with these lists is the assumption that the indexer needs help. It would be more productive for the author to hold on to such a list and use it later when the index is being reviewed. If there are terms on the author's list that do not appear in the index, the author can discuss these terms with the indexer and the two of them together can figure out how to integrate the missing terms into the index.

Author highlights. Equally unhelpful, in my experience, are "author highlights." An author highlight is a set of page proofs on which the author has highlighted the terms that should be indexed. The quality of highlights varies greatly. I have seen pages with practically nothing marked. Others have been so heavily marked up with various Day-Glo colors representing different levels of entries that the pages resembled a psychedelic smorgasbord. One editor went so far as to tell me that the only terms that should be in the index were those terms that were highlighted. The editor should have hired a data entry clerk, not an indexer, for this task.

There are several problems with author highlights. First, it is the indexer's job to know what should be indexed. If the editor's or author's confidence in the indexer is so low that they feel the indexer needs to be told what to index, then perhaps they have not found the right indexer for the job.

Second, working from pages that have been marked up by someone else is, again, distracting. The rhythm of indexing is interrupted as the indexer second-guesses every decision. It is difficult for the indexer to see the book on its own terms; the highlights interfere with the indexer's perception of the book. Given the short amount of time available for indexing, anything that slows the process should be eliminated.

Third, some author highlights are not only distracting but impossible to work with. I have seen pages with thirty or more terms marked per page. An indexer needs clear, legible copy. When an editor insists on providing an author highlight, I insist on a second set of unmarked pages. Usually I put the author highlight in a corner and never look at it. It takes a great deal of the author's time to highlight pages. This time could be better spent putting together lists of names or synonyms for the indexer.

Interim review of the index. Sometimes an author or editor asks to see the index while it is in progress. The value of an interim review of the index is that the author or editor can check to see that certain types of material are being handled as desired. The disadvantage of an interim review is that it places the indexer in an awkward position. Writing an index is not a linear process. As an index evolves, changes are made to various parts of the index. The structure of entries on Wednesday may bear little resemblance to the structure of entries on Friday.

Again, given the typical time allotted for indexing, there is little chance that an interim review of an index can be scheduled at a productive point. When an indexer works on the usual deadline, stopping midway and waiting for interim review comments are not possible. By the time review comments come back to the indexer, the index at hand will very likely be different from the index that was reviewed. It is also important to keep in mind that much of the editing of the index does not occur until the end of the indexing process.

There are some situations when an interim review might be desirable to all parties. An interim review can be helpful in a very large indexing project, particularly if multiple indexers are involved. Such review periods need to be specifically scheduled and time allowed to incorporate the reviewer's comments.

Final review of the index. Ideally the indexing schedule will allow time for author review of the index. Author review is separate from the editor's review. While the publishing house editor will be concerned primarily with index format and length, the author will be concerned with the content of the index. See chapter 9 for a detailed discussion of editing tasks.

Authors must be prepared to review the index very quickly, usually within a day or two of its receipt. Authors are intimately familiar with the content of the book. When reviewing the index, authors must evaluate the index's ability to provide access to the content of the book. One way to do this is to randomly choose a page of text to look at. Imagine how readers might look up information appearing on that page. Check to see if those terms are in the index.

The index should also be reviewed as a whole. Authors should read through the index. Check for cross-referencing of synonymous terms. Do not forget to truly read the entries. Do not scan them. Do the entries make sense? If an entry does not make sense, look it up. Perhaps you, as the author, can provide a better term.

Make notes and keep a list of questions. The next step is to talk with the indexer. The author and indexer should have prearranged a time to talk. At this point time is crucial. The editor is waiting for the index. Quite likely, the indexer will send the index to the publisher within twenty-four hours of conferring with the author.

Most indexers are pleased to work with authors who have carefully reviewed the index. Often authors' insights result in a better index. It is also important for authors to listen to the indexer, who may have very sound reasons for designing the conceptual structure of an index in one way and not another. At the same time, indexers must remember that authors know their books best. This is not the time to be overly defensive about one's work! It is the time to listen to the author and attempt to integrate the author's suggestions into the index.

Some authors have no desire to become involved in the indexing process. The editors of books by such authors will find themselves responsible for the entire review and editing cycle. Chapter 9, "Editing the Index," will present a detailed discussion of the index editing process.

3

GETTING STARTED

THIS CHAPTER WILL provide a general overview of the indexing process, beginning with a look at how indexers work. Since the primary focus throughout this text is the indexing of books, a brief description of the book production process will be provided. Next, I will discuss what is and is not indexable; suggestions will be offered about how to index the indexable material. Lastly, I will look at several publishers' index style specifications and a handy way to estimate the size of an index.

THE NATURE OF INDEXING WORK

Before diving into the intricacies of indexing, I shall describe the way many indexers work. Most professional book indexers do not begin work until final page proofs of the book are available. Final page proofs are typeset and paginated book pages. Indexers must have final proofs in hand in order to be able to assign page numbers to index entries.

Indexers should understand where indexing falls in the book production cycle. The general sequence of events in the book production cycle is as follows:

Copyediting
Author review of copyediting
Cleanup copyediting
Galley production
Author proofreading
Page proof production
Proofreading/Indexing (one or the other may come first; both may go on simultaneously)

Before production of final page proofs, galleys of the book are produced. Galleys are typeset book copy that has not yet been divided into numbered pages with illustrations in place. Some publishers bypass reviewing the book in galley form and instead ask the typesetter not to send proof until it has been made up into pages. While a book is in galley form, the production team or the typesetter breaks the galleys into pages, inserting illustrations where needed. The book is proofread at either the galley or the page proof stage.

Even in this age of electronic manuscript preparation, there is still a gap between the first run of typeset copy and the final page proof. Despite the use of sophisticated book design software, inevitably changes will be made to various pages of the book. Some page breaks will not be quite right. Sometimes an illustration that falls at the bottom of a page will need to be moved to the top of the next page. Any adjustments to book pages that affect the pagination should be completed before indexing begins.

Occasionally indexers are asked to index from galleys. The editor hopes that this will reduce the time needed for indexing after the final pages are complete. Rarely is this the case. It can be a very tedious matter, and quite time-consuming for the indexer, to write an index using temporary galley numbers and then to go through final pages of a book and assign correct final page numbers to index entries. At the very least, the indexer will have to go through the text copy *twice*.

Since so many books are now written on personal computers, it would at first glance seem to make sense to index the book using the indexing module in the word processing program. A lot of time could be saved this way, one would think. If the index entries were already embedded in the text files, one would not need to wait for final page proofs before beginning the index. The many problems with this approach to indexing will be discussed in chapter 10, "Tools for Indexing."

Once the indexer receives final book pages, time is of the essence, to put it mildly. The publisher has a firm date set with the printer and binder of the book. That date is rapidly approaching. Presumably the production editor or production controller has scheduled a reasonable amount of time for indexing, editing the index, typesetting the index, proofreading the index, and laying out and producing the final proofs of the index.

An informal survey of production editors revealed that once copy for an index is received by a publisher, usually a week or less remains before the index must be delivered to the printer. There is no time for slipped schedules at this point. Missing a date with the printer can have dire consequences. Publishers with a high printing volume may have some leeway insofar as rescheduling the printing date is concerned. However, a slipped print schedule can be very expensive when the book must be printed as a rush job in order to meet a binding and shipping date. Or a book could miss its shipping date altogether. It will be late going to distributors. Orders from bookstores will be placed on back order. The book cannot be presented at an important conference or will not be ready for the beginning of fall classes.

When the indexing work begins, often production schedules have already slipped—the copyeditor was late, the author was late getting corrections back, or the typesetter was delayed and the page proofs are late. There is often no cushion in the schedule by the time the indexer gets the pages. Indexers must be able to work within the bounds of rather tight schedules. Indexing is not a leisurely activity.

How Indexers Work

The way indexers work will vary from individual to individual and from project to project. Some indexers will receive the entire set of final pages at one time. Others will receive pages in batches, such as chapters 1 through 3, then 4 through 6, and so on. When pages are sent in batches, the indexer often has more time to devote to the index. Ideally, the batches are sent in order so that the indexer can work through the text in a linear manner.

Believe it or not, one question frequently asked of indexers is, "Do you really have to read the whole book?" Yes, we read the whole book, every word. Once in possession of book pages, some indexers skim through the book. Others thoroughly read the book, marking appropriate entries as they go. Still others sit down with the pages and jump right in on page 1 and create index entries.

Chapter 10, "Tools for Indexing," discusses the various methods used by indexers to collect the entries and turn them into a formatted index. Here I wish only to discuss the general nature of indexing work.

Reading a book as an indexer is very different from reading the book as an interested reader. The indexer must be able to read quickly and at the same time accurately synthesize the material being read. In well-written and well-edited books, the overall structure of the index emerges in tandem with the discussion of the text. Highly structured books are often the easiest books to index. For example, a programmer's reference guide for a C Language programming product will be much easier to index than Martin Heidegger's *Being and Time*. Reference books for programming languages are often very structured documents that discuss discrete elements one at a time. *Being and Time* is also highly structured, but the discussion deals with complex conceptual issues that build upon one another.

The indexer becomes immersed in the flow of the writing. It is inevitable that the indexer will internalize the voice and tone of the author. At the same time, though, the indexer must consider the reader's perspective, adding cross-references where needed and picking up on nuances that are not clearly stated. The indexing process is very intense. Chances are that no other reader will read the book in such a focused manner in such a short amount of time as does the indexer.

Many indexers hold the structure of the index in their mind as they work. It always amazes me that while indexing page 324 I can remember that the same topic was discussed earlier, although that earlier discussion may have been as far back as page 98. For the length of time an indexer works on a book, the indexer lives and breathes the language of the book. This is why some experienced indexers turn down work they are quite capable of doing; they do not want their consciousness flooded with the theme of the book!

Indexers must be able to recognize details. More important, the indexer must be able to see relationships between details and to organize them into meaningful order. While indexers must be detail oriented, they must also be able to synthesize information and communicate the synthesis to the readers. This ability requires sharp communication skills and the ability to empathize with the audience.

The indexer is constantly balancing the words of the author with the needs of the reader. The index is ultimately an interface between the author and the reader. It is the most heavily used portion of some books. The indexer's ability to meet the demands of the text and the reader's needs will determine the overall usability of the index, and of the book as well.

Indexing by its very nature is intense. The intensity is compounded by the pressure of the book's production schedule. A two-week period to index a three-hundred-page book is not uncommon. A three-week schedule is considered generous.

As G. Norman Knight so clearly pointed out in the title to his book, indexing is an art. We can isolate the methodological components of indexing, but there is another dimension to indexing that does not lend itself to such rigorous examination. Indexing skills can be nurtured and rules can be learned. But the indexer's ability to thoroughly digest the intentions of the author and anticipate the needs of the readers, thereby producing a knowledge structure that is sensible and usable, involves the application of abilities and skills that are inherent in some individuals and not in others.

After the indexer has edited the index, the work is prepared for submission. Frequently the indexer delivers the index both in manuscript form and on disk. (Chapter 8, "Format and Layout of the Index," provides information about final submission formats.) Because time is of the essence, most indexes are sent to the publisher by overnight courier. For many indexers, delivery of the index signals the end of their involvement with the index. But indexers should always be available to answer any questions the editor may have.

The Book Production Process

A general understanding of how a book is physically produced can be very helpful to the indexer. For example, decisions regarding the actual page size of a book and the typography and layout will affect the cost of indexing. Decisions regarding the printing and binding of a book directly affect the number of pages that will be allotted to the index. Thorough overviews of typography, layout, and printing methods can be found in publishing handbooks such as *The Chicago Manual of Style, Words into Type,* and *Pocket Pal.*

Typography and Layout

There are many reasons why indexers should have a familiarity with the principles of typography and book layout. First, indexers often work with production editors rather than manuscript editors. Indexers need to be able to interpret the language used by production editors. Second, when space for an index is at a premium, indexers can sometimes have some influence over the typography and layout of the index. Effective communication between indexers and production editors can mean the difference between cutting an index down to size and printing the index in its entirety. Third, indexers familiar with typography will understand the difference in text density per page when the type is "10 on 12" compared to type that is "9 on 10." Lastly, indexers are only one of several types of professionals who work in the publishing industry. A general knowledge of publishing is appropriately expected of indexers.

Books are printed using particular typefaces in specific sizes. Typefaces have names such as Times Roman or Helvetica. The size of a typeface is expressed in points. The larger the point size, the larger the characters. Many books are printed in 9- or 10-point type. The text you are reading right now is in 10-point type. The spacing between the lines of type is referred to as leading, which is also measured in points. The expression above, "10 on 12," refers to a book that is printed with 10-point type on a 12-point base that allows 2-point leading.

The layout of book pages affects the density of type on the page. The pages for many computer manuals have a lot of "white space"—wide margins with the body text in one column. On the other hand, the pages for a graduate-level college textbook may be quite dense, with two columns of text and footnotes at the bottom of the page. The density of text on a page impacts not only the density of indexing, that is, the average number of index entries per page, but also the time it takes the indexer to read and extract index entries from a page of text. Thus, the cost of indexing is related to the layout of the book pages.

Printing and Binding of a Book

Production editors and indexers may find themselves at odds regarding the space allocated for the index. Often the indexer feels that the index needs more pages than are available whereas the production editor insists that the index fit into the specified number of pages. Unfortunately, such disputes arise at a time in the production cycle when little can be done to accommodate an index that is too long.

When a book is printed, the pages are not printed one at a time. Instead, the printer uses large sheets of paper, often called *press sheets.* Such a sheet might be 49 inches by 37 inches, with 64 pages to a sheet, 32 pages on each side. A sheet of this sort will be cut and folded into groups of 16 pages. These groups are called *signatures.* When a book is laid out, the production editor will arrange the book so that it will come out in even signatures. A 320-page book that is printed on a sheet that produces 32 pages on each side, 64 pages total, will require five 64-page press sheets for one copy of the book (320 pages divided by 64). If 10,000 copies of the book are printed, 50,000 press sheets will be required.

When a book is prepared for binding, the press sheets are folded and gathered into signatures in numerical order. The signatures are then sewn together, individually and to each other. Various methods are used to physically bind the signatures into one unit.

Long before a book goes to press, paper is ordered for the book. The cost of the paper is of real concern to a publisher; it directly affects the unit cost of a book. When an editor tells an indexer that only a specific number of pages are available for the index, that number is not arrived at capriciously. Most likely, front matter pages have been counted and recounted. Perhaps a half-title page and the blank page behind it have been removed so that two more pages can be set aside for the index.

It is highly unlikely that an additional signature will be added to a book to accommodate an index. Remember, in the 320-page book example above, the press sheets hold 64 pages. The printing press is set up for this particular paper size. Adding another signature will involve ordering more 64-page press sheets. This can be not only costly but difficult to do at the last minute. The paper manufacturer may not have the paper in stock. Or the paper manufacturer may not be able to ship the paper to the printer in time for the printer to get the pages to the binder. Also, the bindery is expecting to bind a book of a particular size. Adding another signature may affect the binding.

With careful planning, the production editor will give thought to the number of pages required for the index. Later in this chapter, estimating index size will be discussed.

What Not to Index

Before we look at what parts of a book are indexed, let's discuss what portions are not. There are some gray areas within a book that are indexed in some situations but not in others. Most books can be divided into three major sections: front matter, text, and back matter.

Front Matter

Generally the front matter of a book is not indexed. Included as nonindexable front matter are the following: title page or pages, copyright and printing history page, dedication or epigraph, table of contents, lists of illustrations or tables, and acknowledgments.

Many books also include a foreword, a preface, and an introduction. The foreword and preface that describe how a book came to be written should not be indexed unless the actual substance of the book is discussed therein. Certainly an introduction to the subject matter of the book is indexable.

Lowercase Roman numerals are generally used to paginate front matter pages. These reference locators precede the Arabic page numbers regardless of their numeric value. Note the order of the reference locators in the following entry:

atoms, discovery of, xv, 5–8

Although the front matter appears first in a book, it is often the last set of pages the indexer will receive. Some of the front matter sections, such as the table of contents, cannot be composed until the entire book is in pages. As noted above, it is often necessary to juggle the pagination of the front matter so that the book will fit within the desired number of signatures. A book that is running one page too long, perhaps because of the index, can sometimes be shortened by removing a blank page in the front matter. But removing pages from the front matter is easier said than done. Often the front matter pages are typeset and paginated by the time the index is submitted.

If there will be indexable material in the front matter, providing the copy to the indexer early on can be very helpful. The material need not be in final pages at this point; galleys or manuscript will do. For example, if a true introduction to the book appears as front matter, the indexer could benefit from reading the introduction before beginning work. The indexer would then have a general perspective on the entire work. The foreword or preface can also inform the indexer of the book's intended audience.

Many editors do not routinely provide front matter material for indexing. It is up to the indexer to inquire about the substance of the foreword, preface, or introduction and to ask for a table of contents even if the final version is not yet available.

Text

For the purposes of this discussion, the text of a book shall be defined as the main body of the book, often divided into chapters or sections. Most of the text of a book is routinely considered indexable.

In some books each chapter or section begins with a detailed table of contents. These "minicontents," like the contents page at the beginning of the book, are not indexed. Similarly, some books are divided into parts, which begin with display pages that list the title of the part. Such display pages are not indexed.

Chapters in textbooks often end with a series of "Questions for Students." These pages are not usually indexed. But like many guidelines in indexing, *usually* does not mean *never*. A fine example of an exception to this guideline is McGraw-Hill's *Schaum's 3000 Solved Problems in Electric Circuits*, a book that is composed entirely of questions and answers for students. The current edition contains an extremely detailed index that captures the topics of the questions.

Footnotes or endnotes that serve only a bibliographic purpose are usually not indexed. In other words, if the function of the note is solely to provide a reference to discussion in the text, it is not usually indexed. The matter of indexing footnotes or endnotes is discussed in more detail later in this chapter.

Back Matter

The back matter of a book often comprises appendixes, notes, glossary, bibliography, and, of course, the index. As a general rule, the contents of the bibliography and glossary are not indexed. However, if the back matter is lengthy, it may be helpful to readers to cite in the index the presence of the glossary or bibliography:

glossary of terms, 535–66

Although many technical publications contain glossaries, indexers are not always provided with them. Some editors assume that the glossary will not be indexed, so they do not provide the indexer with a copy. Or it may be that the glossary is not yet set in pages when indexing begins. Whenever possible, the indexer should receive the glossary: it can be used as a quick reference during indexing and as a handy checklist during the editing of the index. While not every term that appears in the glossary necessarily appears in the index, a great majority of glossary terms do.

Since the indexing of notes is tied very closely to the indexing of the text, the notes portion of the back matter will be discussed in the next section, "What Is Indexable?"

Whether appendixes are indexed depends on their content. The general feeling among editors and indexers is that appendixes that reproduce material cited in the text should not be indexed. The only reason not to index material is if the material is not really pertinent. The contents of the appendixes need not always be indexed. The presence of the material, however, should be cited.

Let's suppose that a book about civil liberties has an appendix containing the text of the *Declaration of Independence*. While the substance of the *Declaration of Independence* itself is not indexed, the presence of the document is cited. Readers who want to locate the actual text of the *Declaration of Independence* should be provided with access to that text. The civil liberties book may contain the following entry:

> *Declaration of Independence*
> authors of, 38–39
> French Revolution and, 45–48
> text of, 430–35
> writing of, 39–44

In the above, the subentry "text of" clearly references the presence of the document in the appendix. This subentry provides direct access to the reproduced document in the appendix.

In technical documentation, particularly that of the computer industry, a great deal of important information is often included in the appendixes. This information is not always indexed as thoroughly as it might be. Contract indexers are often not even given the appendix pages. Because the appendixes are frequently the last portion of the book to be written, there may be little time for thorough indexing. Unfortunately, appendixes in computer documentation may contain crucial information, such as troubleshooting tips, configuration tables, and hardware switch settings. Access to information like this is important to the users of the product. It is definitely a mistake to assume that appendixes should not be indexed merely because they reproduce documents or material discussed in the text.

It is very important when deciding whether to index appendixes to distinguish between indexing the appendixes in detail or indexing them in a general manner, simply citing the presence of certain material in the appendixes. Given the cost and effort that goes into publishing a book, it is difficult to imagine material in appendixes being of such minor importance that no indexing of the appendixes is required. The indexer's duty is to index the entire book. If a decision has been made to restrict the indexing, a statement to this effect should appear in an introductory note to the index.

What Is Indexable?
The Text Itself

All information presented in the body of the text that is directly relevant to the subject matter, scope, and audience of the book is indexable. An indexer with a clear idea of the scope of the book itself and a general understanding of the subject matter and the audience will be in a position to distinguish between relevant and peripheral information.

Distinguishing between relevant and peripheral information involves judgment. Careful exercise of such judgment is what sets a true index apart from a computer generated list of words. A computer could easily scan the text of a book and produce a listing of every occurrence of the words "Yellowstone Park." An indexer, however, has the ability to distinguish between passing mention of "Yellowstone Park" and information of substance relating to "Yellowstone Park." Users of indexes seek access to specific, relevant information. They do not expect to be guided to peripheral material.

Relevant information in a book can be both explicit and implicit. Explicit information is that which is stated verbatim in the text. Simple examples of explicit information are the names of people or organizations discussed in the text. Implicit information is that which is implied but not stated word for word in the text. Quite often, general concepts are implicit information that must be identified by the indexer.

An example of implicit information is found in a discussion of the mineral and vitamin content of dog food in a book about raising dogs. Although many types of minerals and vitamins are discussed in relation to wheat-based and corn-based dog food, never is the word "nutrition" used. In a case like this, "nutrition" is an implicit concept that will be identified by the indexer and added to the index.

The amount of judgment and interpretation required of indexers can make some people uncomfortable. It is the reasonable and experienced application of judgment and interpretation by the indexer that greatly contributes to the overall quality and usefulness of an index. It takes a trained and experienced mind to realize that just because a term is mentioned does not necessarily mean that the mention is important.

Yes, the indexer must pass judgment. Sometimes the indexer must conclude that something is not important; it is not indexable. The indexer does take on a great deal of subjective responsibility for each element in the index as well as for the general character of the index. Later in this book we shall see that computers are capable of automatically manipulating the text of a book in a variety of ways. Yet the computer is incapable of exercising the type of judgment and interpretation applied by experienced indexers on a daily basis.

Unlike the computer, the indexer is constantly filtering information: separating the trivial from the substantive, making the implicit concepts explicit in the index. The complex network of decisions that lie behind the successful index are often transparent to the index users. The common element of every successful index is the critical application of judgment and interpretation by the indexer.

Footnotes, Endnotes

The general rule regarding footnotes and endnotes is to index their contents only when they present material not found in the text itself. Notes that provide only a bibliographic reference for material in the text are not generally indexed. Scholarly books that contain notes often have a bibliography that lists all the references cited in the text. A reader seeking a reference cited in the text can locate that reference in the bibliography. However, many books with notes do not also contain a bibliography. If a bibliography is not present, a strong argument can be made for the indexing of references in footnotes as this will be the only access to these references provided for readers. Also, because the bibliography does not include page references for the discussion in the text, it is often difficult, if not impossible, for readers to work backwards from an entry in the bibliography to its context in the text.

There are certainly times when the readers' needs will be better served if the reference material in notes is indexed. For example, most of the text in *Labor Management Laws in California Agriculture* was written in "plain English" rather than in legalese. Very few case law citations found their way into the body of the text. Instead, the book made heavy use of footnotes to list the many pertinent case law citations. In the interest of attorneys who might use the book, all footnotes containing case law citations were indexed.

As with any general rule in indexing, it is always important to apply the rule judiciously within the context at hand. In some books, the reference material found in footnotes is of great importance. We have all wanted to locate a reference that appeared in a footnote only to discover that this material was not indexed. Keep in mind that properly indexing all reference material in footnotes can greatly add to the length of the index. In a heavily referenced book, the decision to index all reference material should be evaluated carefully in light of the space available for the index. (See chap. 4 for a discussion of the reference locator format for footnote and endnote entries.)

Illustrations, Tables, Charts, and Other Display Material

Before indexing begins, a decision should be made regarding the indexing of display material in the text. In the context of this discussion, display material refers to line drawings, photographs, tables, charts, screen displays, block diagrams, flowcharts—any special element that is not text.

If the display material appears on the same page as textual discussion of the material, it is usually not necessary to index the display individually. If a photograph of a kung pao chicken dish appears on the same page of a cookbook as the recipe, one entry is sufficient. But if the photograph is ten pages away from the page containing the recipe, two entries will be needed: one for the recipe, another for the photograph.

A distinction should be made between indexing the presence of a display and indexing the contents of a display. Let's take the example of a computer printer manual. Frequently a manual will begin with an illustration of the printer, with various parts of the printer labeled. In this illustration there may be an arrow indicating where the bank of DIP switches is located. The discussion of how to set the DIP switches may be separated from this illustration by twenty or thirty pages. It may help the reader to cite in the index the illustration that shows where the DIP switches are located. In a case like this, indexing the contents of display material contributes to the usability of the text.

When display material is indexed, the reference locator format often differs from that used to indicate textual entries. In chapter 4 various ways of citing display material will be discussed.

How to Index the Indexable Material

While most of the remainder of this book is about "how to index," some general comments are warranted here.

Depth of Indexing

> The *depth* of indexing is "the degree to which a topic is represented in detail in an index" (International Organization for Standardization 1981). It is not, as often thought, just the equivalent of exhaustivity but is always a *combination of exhaustivity and specificity* which, when both are at a high level (a large number of terms each of which is also highly specific), results in the greatest possible indexing depth. (Wellisch 1991: 122)

As Wellisch notes above, depth of indexing is often discussed in relation to exhaustivity and specificity. Gerard Salton, in his book *Automatic Text Processing,* makes the following point:

> The effectiveness of any content analysis or indexing system is controlled by two main parameters, indexing exhaustivity and term specificity. Indexing exhaustivity re-

flects the degree to which all aspects of the subject matter of a text item are actually recognized in the indexing product. When indexing is exhaustive, a large number of terms are often assigned, and even minor aspects of the subject area are reflected by corresponding term assignments. The reverse obtains for nonexhaustive indexing, in which only main aspects of subject content are recognized. Term specificity refers to the degree of breadth or narrowness of terms. (Salton 1988: 277)

Book indexes tend to be exhaustive and specific. When a book is cataloged for inclusion in a library, the cataloger is often restricted to the assignment of three to five terms that describe the content of the book. In contrast, the index in the book itself may well have over two thousand terms that reflect the subject matter of the book. The exhaustivity of a book index is greatly influenced by the indexer's analysis and synthesis of the text. Wellisch writes that "exhaustivity refers to the extent to which concepts and topics are made retrievable by means of index terms" (1991: 121). The book index that provides complete access to all the information in a document is exhaustive and satisfies the goal outlined in BS 3700 to "identify and locate relevant information within the material being indexed."

Salton defines term specificity as "the degree of breadth or narrowness of terms" (Salton 1988: 277). As Wellisch points out in his discussion of specificity (1991: 355–58), the terminology used in the text will influence the specificity of the index. I would add that the anticipated language and needs of the readers will also help the indexer determine the degree of breadth or narrowness of terms in the index. The index in a highly specialized text that will be read by readers fluent in the technical language of the text will very likely be composed of a large percentage of specific and precise terms, whereas a book written for a larger group of readers some of whom are not specialists will have a greater mixture of broad and specific terms in the index.

I am not convinced that exhaustivity and specificity provide a useful framework for the discussion of depth of indexing in regard to book indexes. The book indexer must work with restrictions imposed by the time available for indexing and the space allotted for the index. The depth of indexing, or the amount of detail to index, will be influenced by the nature of the text itself and any restrictions placed upon the indexer.

In the early portion of the indexing process, it is better to overindex than to underindex. Include every topic you think may be important. It is irritating to discover, midway through a book, detailed treatment of a topic that was discussed earlier but not indexed. Returning to the earlier chapters and searching for the initial discussion of the term can be quite tedious. It is much easier to codify or eliminate superfluous material than it is to locate information that was not indexed and later proves to be significant.

Term Selection

When selecting terms for the index, always attempt to structure the terms in a way that readers can locate them. Consider how the term will appear in the index. In an alphabetic index it is crucial that the first word be a word that readers are likely to look up. An example of improper term structure can be found in the 2d edition of Van Wolverton's book *Running MS-DOS* (Microsoft Press, 1985). In the *T* section of the index we find "The Find Filter Command" alphabetized under *The* rather than under *F* for *Find*. It is important to bring the significant term forward within each entry.

Term selection plays a significant role in determining the overall structure of the index. The wording of main headings in particular is of crucial importance since main headings are the primary access points in the index. Readers conduct their search for information at the main heading level. However, the ultimate structure of an index is often not fully intact until the indexer has gone through the entire document. For this reason much of the manipulation of terms is performed as an editing task. See the discussion "Substantive Editing Tasks" in chapter 9 for more detailed treatment of this topic.

Succinct and Clear Entries

Entries should be as succinct as possible while remaining clear. Avoid verbose, long entries whenever possible. When indexes are printed, they are often printed in multiple columns per page in a type size smaller than that of the text. Succinct entries help to reduce the density of the printed index pages. Dense index pages compromise the ability of readers to quickly scan the index and locate information. When the index entries are kept to the minimum number of words needed for clarity, the usability of the index is enhanced.

Terms from the Title; Subject Matter of the Book

Be wary of creating entries for the whole topic of a book or from terms in the title. Generally, such entries will be far too broad to serve a useful purpose in the index. A book called *A Guide to Michigan* will most likely not need an entry in the index for "Michigan." The entire book is about Michigan, so the entire index would be in the *M's*! It will be assumed that the entries appearing in the index are related to Michigan, and they will be found in different sections of the index.

Some indexers add an introductory note that explains the way particular terms have been handled in the index. In F. W. Lancaster's 1991 book *Indexing and Abstracting in Theory and Practice,* we find the following introductory note for the index: "Because the entire volume is about indexing and abstracting, the use of these terms as entry points has been minimized in this index."

Marking the Page Proofs

In chapter 10, "Tools for Indexing," the details of the mechanics of indexing, ranging from index cards to software for indexing, will be presented. Here the focus will be on the steps taken before entries are transcribed onto cards or entered into the computer.

The first step for many indexers is to mark up page proofs. For some, a great deal of the actual indexing process is done right on the page proofs. Others find that heavily marking up page proofs is an additional step that takes additional time without providing comparable benefits.

Inexperienced indexers are urged to mark up the page proofs to some degree. One advantage of marked pages is that they make it very easy to locate the context of an entry later during the editing process. Also, if entries are in page number order, marked pages can be used to help check that the correct page number has been assigned to index entries.

One primary goal of marking pages for indexing is to indicate the possible index entries on each page of text. Indexers use their own shorthand notations for page markup.

In figure 3.1 main headings are underlined. Subentries are preceded by a colon. At this stage include all the subentries that appear reasonable. During the editing process unnecessary subentries can be removed.

An unedited extraction of the marked entries would yield the following list. The list will move from left to right across and then down the page.

> copyediting: list of illustrations
> manuscript editor: and list of illustrations
> list of illustrations: preparing
> list of illustrations: when to include
> capitalization: in list of illustrations
> sentence style: in list of illustrations
> headline style: in list of illustrations
> plates: in list of illustrations
> figures: in list of illustrations
> maps: in list of illustrations
> folios: in list of illustrations
> numbers, page: in list of illustrations
> captions, picture: editing, for list of illustrations
> legends, picture: in list of illustrations

After the indexer has marked up the pages, the next step is to extract the entries from the pages. Whether writing on index cards or typing entries into the computer, the indexer will end up with citations like those above with reference locators attached to the end of the entries.

Some indexers are not concerned with actual term selection when marking pages. Instead they highlight particular types of terms that will be indexed. For example, if a book contains a great many personal names, it may be helpful to use a highlighting pen to mark the names. This way there is less chance that a name will be missed. Skimming through the book in this way gives the indexer an opportunity to get an overview of the material. When the writing of the index begins, the indexer has a good perspective on the overall structure of the book.

copyediting: list of illustrations
manuscript editor: and list of illustrations

LIST OF ILLUSTRATIONS : *preparing*

11.44 A task that often falls to the manuscript editor (but is more properly done by the author) is preparing the list of illustrations. Not every illustrated book requires such a list. The criterion is, Are the illustrations of interest apart from the text they illustrate? For a scientific monograph on interstellar particles, illustrated largely by graphs, the answer is obviously no. For a book on Roman architecture, illustrated by photographs of ancient buildings, the answer is obviously yes. For some other illustrated books, the answer may not be so easy to give, and the author and editor must decide whether the list of illustrations is worth the space it will take. *: When to include*

Preparing the List

11.45 The list of illustrations follows the table of contents, normally on a new recto page, and is headed simply Illustrations. The titles of the illustrations listed are capitalized in sentence style or headline style in agreement with the style used in the list of tables and so forth. If illustrations are of more than one type, they are listed by category—plates, figures, maps, and so forth—and by number if numbers are used in the text (see 11.28, also fig. 11.4). For figures and maps that print with the text (and hence have folios assigned to them, whether or not the folios are expressed on the page), page numbers are given (*000* or ■■■ in the copy as first prepared). For plates and for maps printed separately, another type of location is given. If plates are to be inserted in groups of four or more pages at one location, each group is listed under the tag *Following page 000* when copy is prepared. If they are to be inserted in the text two pages at a time (each page of plates accordingly lying opposite a text page), the location is given as *facing page 000*. The editor changes the zeros to real numbers once page proofs are out and page numbers are known. *-ation* *: in list of illustrations*

Editing Captions *; picture: editing; for list of illustrations*

11.46 It should be remembered that the list of illustrations is a *list*, not a reprinting of the captions and legends. If the captions are short and adequately identify the subjects of the pictures, they may do double duty in the list of illustrations. Long captions, however, should be shortened, and discursive legends should never be used here. *; picture: in list of illustrations*

Fig. 3.1. A sample page proof marked for indexing. From *The Chicago Manual of Style*, 14th edition, © 1969, 1982, 1993 by The University of Chicago.

Interpreting the Publisher's Instructions

Before any indexing begins, the indexer must understand what the publisher expects. Aside from the desire for the most brilliant and thorough index possible, the expectations of most publishers can be reduced to two: the index should conform to the house style, and the index should be of the desired length.

Deciphering Indexing Style Guides

Some publishers provide the indexer, be it the author or a professional indexer, with a booklet outlining the house index style. Other publishers provide a less polished, often much-photocopied list that describes the style required. A surprising number of publishers simply tell the indexer to "follow Chicago." What this means is that the indexer is to follow the guidelines outlined in the *The Chicago Manual of Style*, published by the University of Chicago Press. Because the indexing section of *The Chicago Manual of Style* has been published separately and is widely used within the publishing community, I will devote some discussion to the basic style requirements of the University of Chicago Press. It is interesting to note that a survey of 104 publishers by Liddy, Bishop, and Settel (1991: 68) revealed that the majority of the respondents (84 percent) viewed *The Chicago Manual of Style* as the preferred style guide for indexing. At the end of this section you will find a table that summarizes basic styles of various book publishers.

Most publishers specialize in particular types of books. Their index style guide has emerged from years of experience with a particular type of book. At the very least, the style guide is an attempt to distill general indexing guidelines as they apply to a particular type of book. Many publishers know that not every book will fit into this general mold. So it is important to know that not every facet of a publisher's style guide is cast in stone. When there is good reason to change a specification, many editors will accommodate the indexer. But such changes should not be made lightly. The indexer will have to present a strong and very persuasive argument regarding any changes to the house style. Unfortunately, the indexer will very likely be dealing with an editor who knows little about indexing and nothing about the raison d'être of the house index style.

It is crucial that the indexer correctly interpret house style and understand the implications of specifications on the usability of the index before suggesting any change in the specifications. Five elements will be covered in any indexing style guide. Here these five elements are discussed in a very general way. Later in this book I will discuss these elements in far more detail. In appendix A you will find an "Index Specifications Worksheet" which will provide an easy way to outline the index specifications of your publisher.

The five basic elements of index style are presented below. Keep in mind that there are many other elements that are commonly dealt with in an indexing style guide.

Alphabetizing of main entries
Arrangement of subentries
Format of entries
Format of reference locators
Format and placement of cross-references

Alphabetizing of main entries. Most publishers want main headings in an index alphabetized in one of two orders: either letter-by-letter order or word-by-word order. (For further discussion of this topic, see chap. 5.)

Arrangement of subentries. The prevalent choice for the order of subentries is alphabetic. The particular type of alphabetic order is the same as that used for sorting the main headings. However, some publishers want subentries sorted not in alphabetic order but chronologically. Frequently the chronological order is obtained by sorting the subentries in ascending page number (or reference locator) order. (For further discussion of this topic, see chap. 5.)

Format of entries. The format of entries refers to the way the entries will appear in print. The format is usually either indented style or run-in style. Within these two styles are many variations. (For further discussion of this topic, see chap. 8.)

Format of reference locators. The variations in specifications for reference locators often focus on different ways to cite inclusive discussion of a topic. In the case of a reference locator that is a page number, an indexing style guide will cover the way that page ranges are expressed. Often page ranges are not expressed in full but, rather, are compressed (or elided) by dropping some of the repeated digits. For example, a page range such as "232–239" has two repeated digits, the "2" and the "3." There are different rules for handling the compression of such numbers. If the inclusive page numbers are not to be expressed in full, the indexing style guide will outline the publisher's "page number compression" rules. (For further discussion of this topic, see chap. 4.)

Format and placement of cross-references. There are many, many variations in the format and placement of cross-references, particularly the *See also* cross-references. Some publishers will want the *S* in the *See* capitalized; others will want it lowercased. Many will want the *See* and *See also* in italics. Sometimes the *See also* cross-reference will be placed at the beginning of an entry right after the main heading and its page numbers. Other times the *See also* will be placed at the end of the entry after the subentries. (For further discussion of this topic, see chap. 4.)

Sample Index Styles

Four common index styles are illustrated below. All use the same set of entries, including some strange entries to demonstrate differences. The first two examples illustrate the style presented in *The Chicago Manual of Style* (14th ed.). The other two styles are not attributable to any particular publisher, but they are used by many publishers.

Sample 1

Alphabetizing of entries: letter-by-letter
Arrangement of subentries: letter-by-letter
Format of entries: run-in
Format of reference locators: compressed
Format and placement of cross-references:
    See is run off from the main entry, and *See also* is the last subentry; a period and space precede both

dog food, 125–29
dogs, 10–18; clumber spaniels,
75–83; collies, 1122–29; dalmatians, 243–49; English setters,
35–42; Gordon setters, 282–89;
Great Danes, 1541–49; Irish setters,
700–712; rottweilers, 342–56. *See
also* American Kennel Club
Dog Tooth Mountain, 56
hounds. *See* dogs

Sample 2

Alphabetizing of entries: letter-by-letter
Arrangement of subentries: letter-by-letter
Format of entries: indented
Format of reference locators: compressed
Format and placement of cross-references:
   See is run off from the main entry preceded by a period and a space, and *See also* is the last subentry

dog food, 125–29
dogs, 10–18
   clumber spaniels, 75–83
   collies, 1122–29
   dalmatians, 243–49
   English setters, 35–42
   Gordon setters, 282–89
   Great Danes, 1541–49
   Irish setters, 700–712
   rottweilers, 342–56
   See also American Kennel Club
Dog Tooth Mountain, 56
hounds. *See* dogs

Sample 3

Alphabetizing of entries: word-by-word
Arrangement of subentries: word-by-word
Format of entries: indented
Format of reference locators: in full
Format and placement of cross-references:
   See and *See also* are run off from the main heading; a period and space precede both

dog food, 125–129
Dog Tooth Mountain, 56
dogs, 10–18. *See also* American Kennel Club
    clumber spaniels, 75–83
    collies, 1122–1129
    dalmatians, 243–249
    English setters, 35–42
    Gordon setters, 282–289
    Great Danes, 1541–1549
    Irish setters, 700–712
    rottweilers, 342–356
hounds. *See* dogs

Sample 4

Alphabetizing of entries: letter-by-letter
Arrangement of subentries: page-number order
Format of entries: run-in
Format of reference locators: compressed
Format and placement of cross-references:
    see is run off from the main heading, and *see also* is the last
subentry; both are enclosed in parentheses

dog food, 125–9
dogs, 10–8
    English setters, 35–42; clumber
    spaniels, 75–83; dalmatians, 243–9;
    Gordon setters, 282–9; rottweilers,
    342–56; Irish setters, 700–12; col-
    lies, 1122–9; Great Danes, 1541–9
    (*see also* American Kennel Club)
Dog Tooth Mountain, 56
hounds (*see* dogs)

Most index style guides will include far more instructions than those outlined above. Some will indicate whether main headings should always be capitalized, whether there is a preferred citation format for notes and illustrations, or whether run-in subentries should start on the line below the main heading or run off from the main heading line. Later in the book these format topics as well as many others will be discussed.

Sample Styles from Various Publishers

Table 3.1 lists some of the style requirements of a selected group of publishers. The table demonstrates both conformity and variety regarding index style. The information was gathered for this table either from correspondence with the publishers or from style guides provided by the publishers. It is important to keep in mind that most publishers are willing to adapt style guidelines as necessary in order to present an index in the best possible manner. Table 3.1 lists only the *preferred* style, not necessarily every style allowed by the publishers. Indexers working in the future for any of the publishers listed in the table should confirm current style requirements, since requirements can change.

Indexing style information for British publishers has been compiled by Jean Simpkins in the article "How the Publishers Want It to Look" (Simpkins 1990). The publishers represented in this article are Blackwells, Butterworths, David and Charles, HMSO, Hutchinson, Oxford University Press, Routledge, Sage Publications, and Unwin Hyman. American indexers working for British publishers will find this article quite valuable. One of Simpkins's observations regarding British publishers is also generally applicable to the American publishing industry: "On many points remarkable unanimity is apparent on the part of publishers—as though they had all been studying the same handbook before compiling their lists of requirements."

Simpkins found that most publishers preferred the following: word-by-word alphabetizing; elision of page numbers; the alphabetization of subentries that begin with prepositions on the keyword following the preposition; avoidance of sub-subentries; and minimal use of capital initial letters in main headings. More specifically, Oxford University Press style appears quite similar to that of both the 13th and 14th editions of *The Chicago Manual of Style,* including preferring the letter-by-letter alphabetizing method noted above. HMSO will accept either alphabetical or page-number order for subentries. Butterworths will accept sub-sub-subentries for law books and requests that all page numbers be provided in full, not elided. It would seem that British publishers, like American and Canadian publishers, agree on some of the general style issues, as noted in table

TABLE 3.1: COMPARISON OF BASIC INDEX SPECIFICATIONS

	Main Heading Alphabetizing		Subentry Arrangement		Entry Format		Locator Format		Cross-References, Main Heading Capitalization
	Letter-by-Letter	Word-by-Word	Alphabetic	Page-number Order	Run-In	Indented	In Full	Compressed	Format and Placement
American Standard (ANSI/NISO Z39.4-199x, Draft 3)		X	X		NP	NP	X		term *see* xyz *see also* at the top of the entry, run off from the main heading
Apple Computer Inc.	X		X			X	X		term. *See* xyz *See also* at the top of the entry, run off from the main heading
British Standard (BS 3700: 1988)		X	X		NP	NP		X	term *see* xyz *see also* as the last subentry
Chicago: 13th	X		X		X			X	Term. *See* Xyz *See also* at the top or bottom of the entry in run-in format; at the

				top of the entry in indented format
Chicago: 14th X	X	NP	NP	X term. *See* xyz *(see also)* in run-in format or *See also* in indented format at the top of the entry; or, in both formats, *See also* as the last subentry
HarperSan Francisco X	X	X		X Term. *See* Xyz *See also* at end of entry
Harvard University Press X		X	X	Term. *See* Xyz *See also* at the end of an entry
Hoover Institution Press X		X	X	X Term, *see* Xyz *See also* at the top of the entry, run off from the main heading

(continues)

Table 3.1: Continued

	Main Heading Alphabetizing		Subentry Arrangement		Entry Format		Locator Format		Cross-References, Main Heading Capitalization
	Letter-by-Letter	Word-by-Word	Alphabetic	Page-number Order	Run-In	Indented	In Full	Compressed	Format and Placement
IBM Corp.		X	X			X	X		term (*see* xyz) (*see also*) as the first subentry
McGraw-Hill College Division		X	X			X	X		Term (*see* Xyz) (*See also*) as the last subentry
Oregon State University Press	X			X	X			X	Term. *See* Xyz *See also* at the end of the entry
Stanford University Press	X			X	X			X	Term, *see* Xyz *See also* at the end of the entry
WordStar International	X		X			X	X		term. *See* xyz *See also* as the last subentry

NP = No Preference.

3.1, but when we examine more specific aspects of style far more variety is found.

Estimating the Size of an Index

Before indexing begins, the indexer must know if there is a size limitation on the index. By the time a book is in final pages, ready for indexing, the production editor will have a fairly good notion of the number of pages available for the index.

Frequently an editor will tell an indexer that there are x number of pages available for the index. This is not enough information for the indexer to work with. The indexer needs to know how the index will be laid out. For example, will the index pages contain two columns or three columns of text? The type size and leading used also influence the number of index lines per page. Chapter 8, "Format and Layout of the Index," presents the details of page design and typography as they relate to the index. Here we shall concentrate on the number of pages available for the index, as this is often the only specification the indexer is given.

Correlating space available for the index with the density of indexing is very, very difficult. No foolproof formula exists. However, there are some general guidelines that the indexer can keep in mind while indexing. Before we examine these guidelines, let's consider why it is important that the index not exceed the length allotted for it.

Earlier in this chapter the point was made that a publisher will not be likely to add an additional signature of pages just to accommodate an index. If an index is too long, it is better that the indexer, rather than the in-house editor, reduce its size. Because the indexer knows the index intimately, she or he is in a far better position to edit the index to size than someone unfamiliar with the index. Chapter 9 will present techniques for reducing the size of an index. For the discussion at hand, suffice it to say that it is best to deliver an index that fits. When the indexer knows that space for the index is severely limited, he or she will make certain editorial decisions that will affect the density of indexing before indexing begins.

When an index must be short, the indexer, after consulting with the editor, may decide to restrict certain types of entries. For example, the indexer may post (enter) all book titles only as main headings rather than double-posting the title as a subentry under the author's name and as a main heading itself. Similarly, the indexer may decide against using sub-subentries; or perhaps material in the notes will be excluded.

The guidelines that follow are very, very general. The great number of variables that affect the length of an index make it extremely difficult to offer a set of rules that will apply to all circumstances. The entries in some indexes will be very short, and quite long in other indexes. An entry that is long most likely will not fit across the width of one column in the index. The line will "turn over" (or "run over") and continue onto the line below. Naturally, entries with run-over lines take up more space. An index formatted in run-in style will sometimes take up less space than an index in indented style. An index page with three columns will often hold more entries than a page with two columns.

Knowing the number of pages that have been reserved for the index can be quite helpful. With this information at hand the indexer can determine the proportion of the number of index pages to the number of indexable text pages of a book. Using simple arithmetic, the indexer can arrive at a percentage figure. Assume that a book with 200 indexable text pages has 10 extra pages reserved for the index. If we divide 10 by 200, we end up with 5 percent:

$$10 \div 200 = 0.05, \text{ or } 5\%.$$

We can refer to this as a 5 percent index. As a general rule of thumb, a 5 percent index is not an exceptionally dense index. To an indexer, this means that a moderate amount of indexing is expected, perhaps averaging five to six entries per indexable page. As the value of the percent figure increases, the density of indexing increases.

The ratio of indexable text pages to index pages varies for different types of book. The index for a style book such as *The McGraw-Hill Style Manual* can be expected to be somewhat dense and lengthy. Following are index page percentages for three style books:

The Chicago Manual of Style: 13th ed. 7%; 14th ed. 6%
The McGraw-Hill Style Manual: 8%
Webster's Standard American Style Manual: 8%

All three of these books are densely indexed, perhaps averaging eight to ten entries per indexable page. When an indexer is told that 6 percent (or more) of the indexable text pages have been reserved for the index, it is reasonable to assume that a fairly detailed index is desired. When the percentage drops below 5 percent, it is reasonable to assume that light indexing is desired.

In the case of technical manuals, a 10 percent index is not uncommon. Some complex manuals have 20 to 25 percent indexes. For example, the WordStar 6.0 *Reference* manual (1989, rev. a) included a 17 percent index. This manual averaged about 15 entries per indexable page. The significance of the variation in density becomes apparent when we realize that in a 200-page book the difference between an index with 5 entries per page and one with 15 entries per page is 2,000 entries.

An extreme example of a very dense index can be found in *The Oxford Dictionary of Quotations*. The index included in this book is a 54 percent index! At the other end of the spectrum, in general trade books, we often find 2 percent or 3 percent indexes. Theodore Roszak's book *The Cult of Information* has a 2 percent index, and John Muir's *Travels in Alaska* has a 2.3 percent index. A quantitative study of back-of-the-book indexes by Bishop, Liddy, and Settel (1991) found that the average ratio of index pages to book pages of all books reviewed (433 books) was 3.3 percent. Diodato and Gandt (1991), although working with a smaller sample of books (73 books), also found that the average ratio of index pages to book pages was 3 percent.

Occasionally there is little space available for an index not because of a conscious decision to reduce access to information in the text but, rather, because of poor planning. During the book design phase, ideally an appropriate number of pages will be reserved for the index. The designer can work with straightforward percentage numbers.

Table 3.2 gives the percentage of index pages allotted along with a rough estimate of index entries per page for various types of books.

The very general nature of the figures in the table is revealed when we examine two indexes. The index of the January 1967 edition of *The Joy of Cooking* occupied 60 pages of the book; the indexable text took up 787 pages. This is an 8% index. All who have used this index

TABLE 3.2: ESTIMATES OF INDEX LENGTH

Type of Book	Percent of Index Pages	Entries per Page
Mass market trade books	2–5%	3–5
Light text, not heavy on details		
General reference books	7–8%	6–8
Cookbooks		
Medical texts		
Scholarly texts		
Style manuals		
Technical documentation I	10%	8–10
General end-user manuals		
Introductory manuals		
Policy and procedures manuals		
Training manuals		
Technical documentation II	15%+	10+
Codes & regulations		
Service & repair manuals		
Specialized audience material		
Systems manuals		
Theory of operations		

know that it is dense. Terms are often double- and triple-posted. Cross-references abound.

On the other hand, *Greenhouses: Planning, Installing, and Using Greenhouses,* published by Ortho Books (1991), includes a 3% index. On the face of it, one might assume that the book is not thoroughly indexed or that the indexable text is not as dense as in *The Joy of Cooking.* On the contrary, this book is very densely indexed. The indexer reports that there is an average of 8.6 entries per page. The figures for entries per page in table 3.2 demonstrate that this index would fall into the Technical Documentation I category, which often has 10 percent indexes.

The critical difference between these two indexes is a matter of typography and layout. *The Joy of Cooking* index is set in 8-point type with 9-point leading at two columns per page, on a six and one-half inch by eight and three-quarters inch page. The *Greenhouses* index is set in 7-point type with 9-point leading at four columns per page, on an eight and one-half inch by eleven inch page. It is important to keep in mind that even when an adequate number of pages are not available for the index, it is still possible to provide a thorough index. The wizards in the production department have a variety of options available to fit a large number of index entries on a page.

The problem with setting up a table like table 3.2 is that some editors and indexers will consider the numbers immutable. Every book must be evaluated on its own terms—and according to its readers' needs. Some medical textbooks will need a 10 percent index, not a 7 percent index. If a 10 percent index is called for, then a 10 percent index should be created.

In *Book Indexing*, M. D. Anderson (1987: 7) offers another method for estimating index length. Anderson suggests that

> the number of lines from top to bottom of a page of index, multiplied by the number of pages in the index, and expressed as a percentage of the approximate number of lines in the rest of the book, gives a rough estimate of the relative length of the index. . . . Using this method of reckoning, it is found that short indexes run from 1% to 3% of the text, indexes for many "serious" books for the general reader from 4% to 7 or 8%, and those for specialized textbooks up to 15%.

If an indexer suspects that an index will need more space than has been assigned, it is the indexer's duty to bring this matter to the editor's attention as soon as possible so that the production department will have the lead time to consider changing the layout of the index pages. The indexer would do well to keep a running tally of entries per page as the work progresses.

To summarize, before indexing begins, the indexer must determine what major sections of the text will be indexed and which sections, if any, will not be indexed. The publisher's style requirements must be clearly understood. The indexer must have at least a general notion of the space that will be available for the index.

4

STRUCTURE OF ENTRIES

INDEXES ARE EVERYWHERE—we find them in reference books, in school books, in computer manuals, and in policy and procedures manuals. Although the presentation of an index may vary from book to book, we always seem to recognize one when we come across it.

One reason we recognize indexes so readily is that indexes are highly structured documents. The structure of an index is by design; it is not happenstance. Index writers who have a sound understanding of the interrelation of the parts of an index to its whole will be in a good position to write indexes that are cohesive, indexes that work. In this chapter we shall examine the external and internal structure of an index.

EXTERNAL STRUCTURE

The sequence of entries in an index follows a particular order. In the case of an alphabetic index, the entries follow the order of the alphabet, beginning with *A* and ending with *Z*. In a numeric index, the sequence followed is that of the value of numbers, beginning with lower values and progressing in ascending numeric order.

Superficially the order of main headings appears linear. *A*'s are followed by *B*'s, which are followed by *C*'s, and so on. There is indeed a linear progression from one main heading to another as determined by the ordering sequence. As noted earlier, though, an index can be viewed as a network. Although main headings are arranged as individual nodes in a particular order, these nodes are often related to one another through the use of cross-references. The cross-references form a web of interrelationships in the index network that help users to identify and to locate all relevant information about a topic.

The linear nature of an index is truly superficial and relates only to the external structure of the index. The ordered, linear sequence of main headings provides the index writer with a convenient way to refer to distant portions of the index using the ordered sequence itself as a guide.

Although printed book indexes are presented in a linear format, they are not used in a linear fashion. Indexes are not meant to be read in a linear order, from beginning to end. Index users jump around in an index seeking the location of the information they want. Internal *guideposts* in the index may send readers to another part of the index. Readers go directly to that other portion of the index; they do not read the material in between the two points.

The text of the index itself can be described as a hypertext. It is not truly a linear document. Many of the nodes are linked through cross-referencing. These links provide a path that leads users to related information in the index document. An index that is arranged in one of the formats described later in this chapter allows readers to browse the index network. One of the benefits of structured browsing is serendipity. While the primary focus here is on the presentation of indexes in a printed medium, many of the same principles are applicable to the presentation of indexes in an electronic medium.

INTERNAL STRUCTURE

Internally, the index structure is hierarchical. Within a complex index entry—that is, an entry composed of a main heading, subentries, and, possibly, sub-subentries—there is a hierarchical relationship between the various elements of the entry. The subentries present more specific aspects of the main heading; the sub-subentries present more specific aspects of the main heading and subentries.

An index entry has four structural elements: the main heading, subentries, reference locators, and cross-references. These four elements will be discussed in this chapter. The arrangement or presentation order of entries will be discussed in the next chapter.

INTRODUCTORY NOTE

An introductory note, also called a headnote, precedes index entries whenever the index deviates from standard index presentation formats or when the scope of indexing is not complete. Certain situations automatically trigger the necessity for an introductory note: the presence of more than one index; special handling of reference locators; nontraditional arrangement of index entries; use of special abbreviations; or limitations on the scope of indexing. Following are some sample notes for these situations.

Multiple indexes: "Two indexes are provided for your use: a Subject Index and a Names Index. The Subject Index presents all topics discussed in this book; the Names Index lists all persons discussed in this book."

Special reference locators: "All page numbers appearing in bold type refer to locations in the text where a term is defined." Or, "Page numbers appearing in italic type refer to pages that contain illustrations."

Nontraditional arrangement of entries: In a Product Number Index for a microprocessor book the following note appeared: "Devices are listed under their root number without prefixes, except when the prefix is an integral part of the number (e.g., Z80)."

Abbreviations: "Throughout this index the abbreviation *WF* will be used to indicate references to William Faulkner."

Scope limitation: "None of the information contained in footnotes has been indexed." Another example of a note outlining limited scope might be, "This index contains references to the main body text of the book; the material in the appendixes has not been indexed."

Introductory notes are necessary whenever there is a possibility that readers will not understand the arrangement or presentation of information in the index. The note will clearly and concisely explain any special devices used in the index.

Main Headings

The main headings in an index are the primary access points for readers. When looking for information about a topic, readers will attempt to locate the topic at the main heading level. Thus, the terms selected as main headings are crucial to the overall access to information within the index. The nature of main heading terms also determines the nature of subentry terms. For example, a main heading that is very general may be followed by not only subentries but also sub-subentries. In some indexes, such broad main headings will be eliminated and the subentries will become main headings themselves to provide more useful access points within the index.

Choice of Headings

It is always important that the indexer provide main heading terms that reflect the concepts in the text and terms that readers will be likely to look up. Main headings are often nouns, or nouns preceded by an adjective. A main heading should never be composed of an adjective or adverb standing alone. The structure of the following entry is not correct:

```
public
    affairs policy, 56
    health, 33
    information services, 43
    speaking, 98
```

These subentries, taken from a course catalog, are not related to each other. They have been forced into a hierarchical relationship based on the adjective *public*. The subentries should appear as main headings, separate and distinct from one another.

```
public affairs policy, 56
public health, 33
public information services, 43
public speaking, 98
```

Indexers should refrain from creating inappropriate relationships between terms. When a hierarchical relationship emerges in an index through the use of subentries, the indexer must carefully evaluate the nature of the relationship. It is not the indexer's job to create artificial relationships that do not exist in the text. Artificial relationships are misleading to readers and unfair to the text.

In the previous chapter, term specificity was discussed in relation to exhaustivity and depth of indexing. Recall that Gerard Salton wrote that "term specificity refers to the degree of breadth or narrowness of terms" (Salton 1988: 277). In regard to the choice of headings in an index, examination of the breadth or narrowness of terms leads naturally to a discussion of classification in indexes. A classification scheme is often presented in a hierarchical form with broad terms subdivided into narrower terms. We often see such arrangements in the natural sciences, where genus-species relationships cascade down a list from very broad to very narrow terms. The Dewey decimal system is another well-known classification scheme.

Indexers have been instructed to avoid classification in book indexes. Wellisch issues such a warning when he writes:

> Classification is in many respects fundamental to indexing as well as to any other information retrieval technique, but it ought not to be employed in the arrangement of topical index headings. The main reason for this is that, however "logical" or "natural" a classified arrangement in hierarchical form may seem to be to the classifier, it may not be so to other people who are not privy to the principles of division and subdivision employed by the maker of the classification. (Wellisch 1991: 39)

Wellisch also tells us that "under no circumstances should an alphabetical arrangement of headings be interspersed with a classified array of subheadings," as we shall see in the example below.

Classification schemes are often used in periodical and database indexing. One purpose of such schemes is to ensure some level of vocabulary control when indexing large, and often open-ended, collections of material. Bella Hass Weinberg (1988: 3) wrote, "The predetermined lists of subdivisions in subject catalogs and periodical indexes do not permit exact specification of the aspect or point-of-view of the topic." While it is possible to identify what a document is about in a general sense, Weinberg argues that "indexing which is limited to the representation of aboutness serves the novice in a discipline adequately, but does not serve the scholar or researcher, who is concerned with highly specific aspects of or points-of-view on a subject." Weinberg's article offers an excellent description of what we should not find in book indexes.

Main headings should be specific; they should be directly related to the concepts in the text. In a book about twentieth-century transportation, a discussion about automobiles and trucks is best represented by using the entries "automobiles" and "trucks," instead of "vehicles." Surely this book will be filled with references to many types of vehicles. If "vehicles" were chosen as a main heading, undoubtedly there would be a long list of subentries accompanied by some sub-subentries. For example,

```
vehicles
  automobiles
    diesel-powered autos
    four-door autos
    four-wheel drive autos
    station wagons
    two-door autos
  buses
  mopeds
  motorcycles
    with four-stroke engines
    with two-stroke engines
  trucks
    with double trailers
    flat beds
    height restrictions and
    refrigerated trailers
    with twin axles
  vans
    commercial use of
    private use of
```

The main entry, "vehicles," is not specific. While it can be argued that "vehicles" is a general term or broader term for the various subentries, it is not the job of an indexer to classify information by applying an external taxonomy to the language of the text. In a classified listing such as the one above, the subentries can be located only if the reader first looks up "vehicles." There is no direct access to "automobiles," "buses," or "trucks." These subentries are buried under the broad term "vehicles." If readers do not understand the classification scheme, they will not be able to locate relevant information.

When choosing main headings, indexers must always consider the reader and the nature of the text. Generally speaking, when index entries become extremely complex, going down to sub-subentry and sub-sub-subentry levels, the choice of the main heading is often far too general; the main heading lacks specificity. For a thorough and entertaining discussion of classification and classified headings, see G. Norman Knight's book *Indexing, The Art of* (pp. 96–100).

Despite the history of admonishment against classification in book indexes, it is important to maintain a reasonable perspective about this matter. There are those who would have indexers eliminate any index entry that has the appearance of classification, that is, any entry that embodies a genus-species relationship. Some of the entries used as examples in this book would be candidates for elimination, such as:

> dogs, 10–18; clumber spaniels,
> 75–83; collies, 1122–29; dalma-
> tians, 243–49; English setters,
> 35–42; Gordon setters, 282–89;
> Great Danes, 1541–49; Irish setters,
> 700–712; rottweilers, 342–56

This entry is composed of a broad term as the main heading ("dogs") and narrow terms as the subentries (types of dogs). If the only entry for "Gordon setters" were here, under "dogs," I too would argue that this is not a helpful way to present the information in the index. It would be best if each of the subentries also appeared as main headings in the index. That way the reader looking up "Gordon setters" would find the entry in the G's. But to suggest that the types of dogs be entered only as main headings and that the entry above be eliminated because of its classified nature is quite short-sighted.

Remember that the BS 3700 encourages the indexer to "group together information on subjects that is scattered by the arrangement of the document." Gathering together related information will sometimes result in the development of headings that appear to be classified. It is not difficult to imagine a context where the "dogs" entry above could prove very useful. For example, someone reading my autobiography might know that dogs played an important role in my life. If the "dogs" entry were eliminated from the index, the reader would have to know exactly what breeds of dogs to look for. Lacking this knowledge, the reader would be unable to locate any information about my dogs.

Imagine another book whose subject is using personal computers in a small business. We might find the following classified headings in the index:

> spreadsheets
> Excel
> Lotus 1-2-3
> Quattro
> SuperCalc

word processors
Ami Professional
Word for Windows
WordPerfect
WordStar

Again, we will assume that all the subentries above also appear as main headings in the index. These classified headings gather together related information for the readers. If these entries were eliminated, readers would have to read the entire book to find out which spreadsheet and word processing programs were discussed, or they would have to scan the entire index and locate the programs by name.

To blindly follow the rule that insists that there be no classified entries in indexes is not only short-sighted; it is often a disservice to the users of indexes. While an index should not rely solely on classified arrangements, the needs of readers must always come first. The thoughtful indexer will recognize the needs of readers and provide a balanced mixture of broad and narrow terms in the index.

At the main heading level, readers should be able to locate references for all the major topics in the document. Within the index structure, main headings are the primary access points. The choice of words and phrases as main headings will be informed by the language of the text and the anticipated language of the readers. Specific aspects of major topics are often treated at the subentry level, which will be discussed in the next section.

Double-Posting

Given the importance of the main heading level as the primary access point for information, the indexer must consider the need to provide multiple access points for the same information. Again, the needs of readers are crucial. It is reasonable to assume that readers may look up a topic in more than one way. While one reader may look up "automobiles," another reader may be just as likely to look up "cars." The indexer may decide to double-post the information by using both terms:

automobiles, 55–60
. . .
cars, 55–60

The phrase *double-post* is borrowed from bookkeeping. In a double-entry accounting system it is necessary to post account information twice, as a debit and as a credit. In this sense, *post* means to enter in the correct form and place—not always an easy task in either accounting or indexing!

When case law is cited in an index, it is often double-posted. The reason is that one reader may remember the defendant's name in a case, while another may remember the plaintiff's name. When double-posting a case law citation, retain the correct placement of the names so that the inversion makes clear who is the plaintiff and who is the defendant:

> *Roe* v. *Wade*, 78
> . . .
> *Wade*, *Roe* v., 78

Double-posting of index entries may take the form of direct inversions:

> book contracts
>   of trade publishers, 34–39
> trade publishers
>   book contracts of, 34–39

Sometimes the double-posted information is not a direct inversion of terms; instead, it is more subtle.

> concatenation of files
>   COPY command parameter for, 56–59
>   printing concatenated files, 93
> COPY command, 12–14, 56–59

In the example above, specific information (the COPY command parameter) about the COPY command has been double-posted at the subentry level and at the main heading level.

The advantage of the double-posting of information is that it gives readers multiple access points for information. But there can be disadvantages as well. First, double-posting of entries may take up too much space in an index. Second, when an entire entry is double-posted, both entries must contain the same information; the reference locators and subentries must be the same. While it may be easy to maintain this consistency when double-posted terms appear only once, as in the "automobiles/cars" entry above, it can be difficult for the indexer to remember to double-post all the cited information scattered throughout the text.

In the early stages of writing an index, many indexers do not double-post terms. Instead they create a *See* cross-reference at the main heading level, as in "automobiles. *See* cars." Later, during the editing stage, the indexer may decide to double-post information rather than use a *See* reference. Later in this chapter the use of the *See* cross-reference will be compared to the double-posting of entries.

Here, the important thing to keep in mind is that the main heading level is what provides the primary access to information in the index. The choice of main heading terms should be guided by the text itself and by the anticipated needs of the index users.

SUBENTRIES

A main heading followed by a lengthy sequence of page numbers should be broken down into subentries. Generally, when there are more than five reference locators for a heading, subentries should be added to enhance the usability of the index. The following main heading is in need of subentries:

> wildlife losses from pesticides, 83–85,
> 87, 88, 100–107, 114–117, 116–
> 117, 121–122, 125–129

Without subentries, readers will spend far too much time attempting to locate the information they seek. The index should provide quick and easy access to information. It should not place an excessive burden of locating specific information about a topic on the readers. The index should help readers narrow their search in order to retrieve information from the text quickly.

Subentries are always related to the main heading they modify. Often the subentries represent subdivisions or more specific aspects of the main heading. The entry above can be easily broken down as

```
wildlife losses from pesticides, 83–85
    Dutch elm disease spraying, 100–107
    in England, 114–117
    forest spraying, 121–122, 125–129
    Japanese beetle spraying, 87, 88
    in rice fields, 116–117
```

Subentries can also be action-oriented, as in the following example:

```
files
    copying, 52
    creating, 10–12
    deleting, 43
    editing, 35–38
    moving, 88
```

Subentries frequently present related aspects of the main heading. The purpose of subentries is to filter information about a topic further so readers can perform a more refined search for information. The following example from the index of the 13th edition of *The Chicago Manual of Style* shows subentries as filters that present specific information about the main heading:

```
Title page
    author's name on, 1.11, 1.13, 19.47
    content of, 1.9–13, 1.29
    copyediting, 2.111
    placement of, 1.1, 1.9
    type specifications for, 1.9–11, 19.47
```

Subentries can be overdone, however. As noted earlier, space in an index is a precious commodity. The usefulness of subentries must be carefully evaluated. A list of subentries, all with the same page number, should be condensed. The following entry from a college course catalog is an example of an overdone list of subentries:

```
accounting courses
    advanced, 14
    beginning, 14
    intermediate, 14
```

These subentries provide no substantive information. In this case the main heading, "accounting courses, 14," would have been sufficient. An index is not intended to be an outline of the entire contents of the document. The indexer's job is to present useful and efficient access points to information in the text. Readers should not have to sort through and read excessively long lists of subentries that over-analyze the heading they modify.

FORM OF MAIN HEADINGS AND SUBENTRIES

Main headings and subentries are usually nouns, nouns preceded by adjectives, or gerunds. They should be as succinct as possible without sacrificing clarity. Because most indexes are alphabetized, it is important to pull the crucial term in a phrase forward so that it can be alphabetized.

Inversion. When personal names are cited in an index, the name is often inverted so that the surname will be the keyword for sorting. If we wish to index Virginia Woolf, we invert the name, as in "Woolf, Virginia." This way the important portion of the phrase, "Woolf," is pulled forward for alphabetizing. Other types of terms are also often inverted. For example, the text may refer to a "holographic will." In the index this term may appear as "wills, holographic."

The following example, taken from Microsoft Press's *Running MS-DOS* (2d edition, 1985), illustrates the problems that arise when the important term in a phrase is not pulled forward for alphabetizing:

A Look at Files and Diskettes
A Tree of Files
. . .
More command
More on Redirection
. . .
Some Advanced Features
Some Important Keys
   Alt
   Backspace
   Break
   Ctrl
   . . .
   Shift
Some More Useful Batch Files

> . . .
> Some Useful Batch Files
> Some Useful Commands
> . . .
> The Backspace Key
> The Current Directory
> The Debug Program
> The Directory
> The Enter Key
> The Find Filter Command
> The Path to a Command
> The Path to a Directory
> The Sort Filter Command
> The System Prompt
> . . .
> What Do You Need for a Network
> What Is a Diskette
> What Is DOS

It is unlikely that someone looking for information about batch files will think of looking up "Some More Useful Batch Files" or "Some Useful Batch Files" in the *S*'s. All the information about batch files should be gathered together under the heading "batch files."

Singular versus plural. A question that often arises is whether headings and subentries should be expressed in singular or plural form. Those nouns that we can count numbers of and ask "how many?" are often expressed in plural form:

> rocks
> dogs
> mice
> books
> politicians

Those nouns that we do not count individual numbers of, but of which we ask "how much?" are generally expressed in the singular form:

> air
> fertilizer
> pepper
> tea
> wine

One should avoid the use of the plural form attached in parentheses to the noun, for example, "cake(s)" or "bicycle(s)." In both of these, we can ask "how many?" so the plural form should be used. Excessive use of punctuation in an index can make the index look busy and dense when printed and so make the index more difficult to use.

Consistency within the index is important to maintain. If the indexer uses *cakes* as an entry, then *breads*, not *bread*, would be used to ensure consistency. Consistent handling of singular/plural forms of entries is an aspect of parallel construction which will be discussed next. Indexers who resolve problems with singular versus plural forms of entries during the initial term selection process will find that there will be less editing needed later. Also, it is good to remember that singular and plural forms of terms not only are a matter of style but also can denote different meanings:

> writing (an activity)
> writings (artistic works)

Parallel construction. Throughout the index it is desirable to maintain parallel construction within entries. If gerunds are used in most of the subentries, a participle would look out of place.

> Words
>   capitalizing
>   dividing
>   hyphenated
>   spelling

The subentry "hyphenated" should be "hyphenating" in order to maintain parallel construction within this entry. Parallel construction can, of course, be overdone. An index is not an outline or other type of list. Parallel construction within entries is desirable, but one should be careful not to interfere with the meaning of subentries by forcing parallel construction.

Homographs. Homographs are terms with different meanings that have the same spelling. If there is any chance that readers may misinterpret the meaning of a homograph, the indexer can add a qualifying phrase to the term. But do note that capitalization can clear up some misinterpretations.

> Bourbon (a European ruling family)
> bourbon (an American whiskey made from corn)
> bow (front part of a boat or ship)
> bow (a device for shooting arrows)
> perch (a fish)
> perch (a resting place often for birds)
> rubber (tropical tree latex)
> rubber (slang for condom)
> Turkey (the country)
> turkey (the bird)

Multiple terms in an entry. There is no prescribed limit on the number of terms in a heading or subentry. Although entries should be as succinct as possible, additional terms are often needed for clarity. Frequently two distinct topics are discussed in tandem, and it may be appropriate to combine the terms and use a cross-reference.

> replace operations. *See* search and replace operations
> . . .
> search and replace operations, 56–60
>
> crime and punishment, 69
> . . .
> punishment. *See* crime and punishment

Adjectives and adverbs. Generally, an adjective or adverb should not stand alone as an index entry. An exception to this rule is when the term itself is the subject, as in a usage or style guide. Adjectives are often combined with nouns to form main headings and subentries in an index.

> lodgepole pine
> Indian names
> medical training
> metropolitan newspapers
> Ponderosa pine

The indexer must decide how readers are likely to look up information. In a general book about western pine trees, the indexer can reasonably assume that readers will look up the types of trees by their common names that usually begin with an adjective.

Articles, prepositions, and conjunctions. At the main heading level, articles, prepositions, and conjunctions, frequently referred to as function words, are not used as the first term in a common phrase. The only time they do appear as the first word is when they are part of a formal name, as in a book title or geographic name. In the next chapter the alphabetizing rules for function words will be discussed.

A casual review of a variety of indexes reveals that articles, prepositions, and conjunctions are heavily used as the first term in subentries in some indexes and not used at all in other indexes. Clearly, there are two schools of thought regarding the use of these terms.

It was noted earlier that subentries must have a direct relationship with the main heading they modify. This relationship can be described as a logical relationship. The following entry is an example in which the subentries could be described as subsets of the main heading. Thus, there is a direct logical relationship.

> breed groups
> herding group, 75–80
> hound group, 38–43
> non-sporting group, 25–30
> sporting group, 132–37
> terrier group, 90–95
> toy group, 50–55
> working group, 110–15

All subentries must be logically related to their main headings. However, there are some who feel that the subentries must have a grammatical relationship with their main headings as well. The idea here is that the main heading and the subentry can be read as a complete phrase. The following example from the index of *The Chicago Manual of Style* illustrates subentries that have a grammatical relationship with the main heading.

> Indention
> in bibliographies
> of block quotations
> of chapter openings

```
of footnotes
in indexes
marking for
with poetry
after subheads
in tables
```

Notice how each subentry can be combined with the main heading to form a sensible phrase: "indention in bibliographies," "indention of block quotations," "indention of chapter openings," and so on. Those favoring the logical approach would very likely structure the same entry in this way:

```
Indention
    bibliographies
    block quotations
    chapter openings
    footnotes
    indexes
    marking for
    poetry
    subheads
    tables
```

Proponents of the logical style would argue that the relationships expressed with the leading prepositions are implied and do not need to be formally included in the subentries. Anyone looking at the entry above would *know* that the "bibliography" subentry refers to "indention in bibliographies"; this does not need to be stated explicitly.

If we compare the two "Indention" entries, we notice that the sorting order of the subentries is the same. The leading prepositions have not been alphabetized in the first example. This alphabetizing oddity is another reason, some argue, that there is no need to impose grammatical relationships on subentries. Alphabetizing will be discussed in more detail in the next chapter.

A more pedestrian concern is the space used by leading prepositions, articles, and conjunctions in subentries. When an index is printed in narrow columns, a leading preposition may create a line that is too long for the column width; the line will break and carry over to another line. It can be argued that this will add unnecessary length to an index—a particular concern when space is limited.

An uncritical use of leading prepositions can easily lead to unsightly lists of the same preposition being repeated in each subentry.

recipes
  for beef
  for chicken
  for fish
  for pork
  for shellfish
  for turkey
  for veal
  for vegetables

It is important to remember that function words may be necessary as the leading term in a subentry for clarity. When the lack of a preposition creates an ambiguous subentry, the preposition should definitely be included even if entries appear to be unparallel. In the example below, the subentries clearly have two different meanings.

management
  by computers
  of computers

Heated discussion goes on in indexing circles about leading articles, prepositions, and conjunctions in subentries—see Wellisch's (1993) article "Function Words in Subheadings" for an overview of the purpose of function words, their use in indexes, and the alphabetizing debate. We must not lose sight of the important role that these parts of speech can play to clarify meaning. The trouble with these terms is primarily related to whether or not they should be alphabetized. Indexers wishing to sidestep this problem should consider using leading articles, prepositions, and conjunctions in subentries only when absolutely necessary for clarity.

Reference Locators

ANSI Z39.4-1984 defines a locator as "the device, such as a page or a file number, that indicates the place where material relating to the item or concept identified in an entry may be found." In printed media a reference locator can take many forms: a page number, a section number, a line number, and so on. In electronic media a reference locator might be a filename, a physical pointer to the actual text, a set of coordinates, or a filename–screen number–line number sequence.

Regardless of the type of locator, long series of undifferentiated locators after an entry are not desirable. The general rule is that an item should have no more than five locators. If there are more than five locators, the entry should be further qualified with subentries or sub-subentries.

Locators indicate the beginning and end of the discussion. Those indexes that cite only the beginning of a discussion eliminate a useful reference device. The entry below does not allow the reader to discern where the main discussion of this topic occurs.

> voodoo, 13, 22, 38

Far more helpful is the following entry:

> voodoo, 13, 22–29, 38

Page Numbers as Locators

Many books are numbered sequentially with Arabic page numbers (1, 2, 3, . . .). Often the front matter is numbered with sequential Roman numerals. The locators for a term should be presented in ascending numeric order with Roman numerals preceding Arabic numbers. For example,

> glaciers, iv, 45–52, 134, 140–42

Continuous discussion of a topic. Continuous discussion of a topic that traverses two or more pages is indicated by a page range: 23–29. Often the page range concatenator, the character between the page numbers, is the typographic symbol known as an en dash. An en dash is slightly longer than the hyphen used within a word and shorter than the em dash. *Words into Type* defines an em as "a unit of measurement equal to the space occupied by the letter *M* in the given font." An en is defined as "a unit of measurement equal to half of an em."

Whenever possible, page ranges should be expressed in full; that is, all digits should be used. Page ranges expressed in full leave no doubt regarding the numbers indicated. However, as we know by now, many editors are concerned about space requirements for the index. Expressing three- or four-digit page ranges in full can take up considerable space.

Many style guides request that page ranges be compressed or elided. There are various rules regarding which digits in a page range are repeated and which digits are dropped. The most common set of rules are those found in *The Chicago Manual of Style* (13th ed., 8.67):

First Number	Second Number	Examples
Less than 100	Use all digits	3–10; 71–72
100 or multiples of 100	Use all digits	100–104; 600–613; 1100–1123
101 through 109 (in multiples of 100)	Use changed part only, omitting un-needed zeros	107–8; 505–17; 1002–6
110 through 199 (in multiples of 100)	Use two digits, or more as needed	321–25; 415–532; 1536–38; 11564–68; 13792–803
	But if numbers are four digits long and three digits change, use all digits	1496–1504; 2787–2816

These rules are essentially repeated in the 14th edition of *The Chicago Manual of Style* (8.69), with the following modification: in the case of four-digit numbers, when the last three digits change, it is no longer necessary to repeat all digits; thus, 1496–504, 2787–816.

The style guide *Words into Type* (p. 77) provides another description of how to compress page numbers. Although this method results in the same type of compression as that recommended by the *Manual of Style*, the description is a bit more succinct.

> There are several styles of elision; whichever is chosen, the indexer should be consistent. The following is a suggested way: Omit from the second number the digit(s) representing hundreds, except when the first number ends in two zeros, in which case the second number should be given in full. If the next-to-last digit in the

first number is a zero, only one digit is necessary after the en dash.

8–10, 22–23, 100–102, 107–9, 119–21, 133–34, 1074–76

One last example, which differs slightly from those above, is drawn from *Webster's Standard American Style Manual* (p. 258).

1. Never elide inclusive numbers that have only two digits: 33–37, *not* 33–7.
2. Never elide inclusive numbers when the first number ends in 00: 100–108, *not* 100–08 *and not* 100–8.
3. In other numbers, omit *only* the hundreds digit from the higher number: 232–34, *not* 232–4.
4. Where the next-to-last digit of both numbers is a zero, write only one digit for the higher number: 103–4, *not* 103–04."

Noncontinuous discussion of a topic. When discussion of a topic is not continuous, but scattered throughout a range of pages, a page range is not generally used; an exception to this rule found in the *McGraw-Hill Style Manual* is discussed at the end of this section. The locators for noncontinuous discussions are separated by commas.

Scotch whiskey, 33, 34, 35

If passing mention of a topic spans many pages, some publishers allow the use of *passim* (meaning "here and there"). For example,

Scotch whiskey, 33–42 passim

Do keep in mind that most publishers discourage the use of *passim*, and many forbid its use. Trivial passing mentions of a topic are generally not indexed. However, if the scattered references are deemed indexable, *passim* is a convenient device to use as an alternative to a long string of page numbers if its use is allowed. It also helps distinguish a truly continuous discussion from a slighter mention of a topic. In the example above, had *passim* not been used, the entry would have been quite lengthy:

Scotch whiskey, 33, 34, 35, 37, 39, 40, 41, 42

Indexers may be tempted to use *passim* to indicate a long series of scattered references to a topic. It would be easy to imagine an entry in this book such as:

exceptions to indexing rules, 40–150 passim

When the use of *passim* is allowed, many indexers do not use *passim* if there is a break of more than three pages in the scattered discussion. Assume that a topic is mentioned on the following pages:

merlot wine, 20, 21, 23, 28, 29

Using the rule of no more than a three-page break, this entry would not qualify as a *passim* entry because of the five-page break between page 23 and page 28.

One of the main complaints about the use of *passim* is that it lacks precision, and indexers by nature desire precision. Although the use of *passim* in an index is discouraged, there are times when the use of *passim* may indeed provide additional and appropriate information for index users. In 1992, Andre De Tienne, an editor at the Peirce Edition Project, offered the following argument in favor of *passim* use during a discussion on the INDEX-L electronic conference.

> Many claim the primary problem with the use of *passim* in an index is the lack of precision. How far this is a real shortcoming is worth studying, since it is mainly a matter of interpretation. If *passim* is affixed to a big group of pages, like "25–60 passim," very little help is indeed given to the reader, no matter the meaning of the term. If, however, *passim* is affixed to a small cluster of pages, like "25–30 passim," the word becomes useful, because it gives to those page numbers a different tone, and thereby increases the information given to the reader. We may well imagine, for instance, a case where an author talks about objective idealism. If the entry reads "idealism, objective, 25–30," the reader will know that those pages address the topic somewhat fully. If it reads "25–30 passim," the reader will immediately know that those pages

talk intermittently about objective idealism, or make implicit references to it, in a manner that may well be worth a look (at least a diagonal reading). We may even imagine that the phrase "objective idealism" occurs on each of those six pages in a way that is more than a mere "mention," and less than a focused discussion. This may occur when objective idealism serves, not as a central topic of discussion, but as an important context of discussion, or as a secondary topic, or as a regular point of reference.

Another problem often cited about the use of *passim* is that *passim* means different things to different people. Well, this is a truism. Any word can be understood and used differently by different people, be they indexmakers or index-users. The point is that no matter how varying the meaning is, it will retain a common core, "here and there throughout," or some such. It may lack precision, but in a way that's exactly what the word is about: "the entry is worth looking up on pp. 25–30, but please know, dear reader, that it is not the central topic of discussion—its various occurrences lack definite precision." Adding *passim* to hyphenated numbers, in this regard, amounts thus to an increase of information, since it tells the reader that pages 25–30 are worth looking at, though they don't deserve the same degree of expectation as regular page numbers.

Andre De Tienne reminds us that we can add additional meaning to a reference locator with the judicious use of *passim*. Indexers often add additional information value to reference locators with the use of annotations or different type enhancements such as bold or italic. However, without a doubt the use of *passim* is discouraged by many publishers. Unfortunately, as we try to make indexes more "user friendly," we often abandon some of the finer details of the art of indexing.

In this day and age, many readers will not know the meaning of *passim*. If it is used in an index, particularly in a nonscholarly book, the meaning of *passim* should be included in an introductory note.

Other devices in addition to *passim* are used by some publishers to indicate separate references. The abbreviations *f.* and *ff.* are sometimes placed after the locator to indicate noncontinuous discussion on a very specific range of pages. Be warned that most publishers forbid the use of these abbreviations in an index. If your publisher's style guide does not describe the use of these abbreviations, do not use them.

The word *folio*, a printing term for the page number on a page, is abbreviated as *f.* (plural: *ff.*). Publishers who do allow the use of such abbreviations may have very specific rules for their use.

The 1991 "Notes on Indexes and Indexing" from Stanford University Press (SUP) requests that *f.* be used to mean "and the page following" and *ff.* be used to mean "and the two pages following."

> The problem "f" and "ff" solve is how to indicate, in a compact way, individual references to a subject on successive pages. This is a very common feature of any index. In our style, "35f" replaces "35, 36" with identical meaning of separate references on pages 35 and 36; "35ff" means separate references on pages 35, 36, and 37. (Continuous discussions over spans of pages take the form "35–36" or "35–37.")

SUP also allows the use of *passim* in situations where there is "a cluster of references not necessarily on every page but within *three* pages of one another." Indexes in SUP books contain a headnote that describes for the readers the use of these conventions that indicate noncontinuous discussion of a topic. In this context, *f.*, *ff.*, and *passim* have very specific meaning and will often save space in an index.

If a publisher provides no rules for the use of these abbreviations, the indexer should not use them. One reason that publishers discourage their use is that there is no universal agreement about what they mean and they often confuse readers.

It is not always easy for the indexer to distinguish continuous and noncontinuous discussion of a topic. The problem can be exacerbated by poor book editing. An experienced book editor will see to it that discussion of tangential matters does not interfere with the continuous presentation of a topic. The careful editor will remove such material, thus ensuring that information is provided in a cohesive manner.

In a departure from traditional practices regarding the handling of continuous and noncontinuous discussion, the *McGraw-Hill Style Manual* (p. 290) provides indexers with the following guidelines:

> Use inclusive page numbers for three or more consecutive page references, regardless of whether the discussion is continuous or interrupted:
> 236–238 (*not* 236, 237, 238)
> If only two consecutive pages are listed, use an en dash between them if the discussion is continuous from one page to the next; use a comma for two separate mentions.

Do note that the McGraw-Hill style distinguishes between noncontinuous discussion on two consecutive pages and on three consecutive pages or more. It has become common at some presses, including the University of Chicago Press, not to make any distinction between continuous and noncontinuous discussion of a topic on consecutive pages. It is thought that using a page range for an entire discussion is an aid for the readers because a page range is easier than a string of separate page numbers to read. Although indexers may find this practice disturbing because of its lack of precision, it is an important element to look for in a publisher's style guide. If no mention is made in the style guide of the distinction between continuous and noncontinuous discussion on consecutive pages, the indexer is safe to assume that a page range can be used for noncontinuous discussion on consecutive pages.

Multipart page numbers. Some documents are paginated with multipart page numbers rather than consecutive page numbers. A common example is the separate pagination of chapters in a document. Each chapter begins with a page 1. The actual folio is a combination of the chapter number and the page number. Page 3 in chapter 5 may be paginated as 5-3.

This type of pagination is often found in documents that are frequently revised—for example, an end user software manual. When future changes in the software affect only one chapter of the manual, the changes can be made to that one chapter without affecting the pagination (and indexing) of the remainder of the manual.

When chapter–page number pagination is used, the correct way to indicate a page range is by use of the concatenator *to*. If an entry cites discussion on pages 10 through 15 of chapter 3, the page range should look like this:

directory structure, 3-10 to 3-15

Notice that a hyphen, not an en dash, is used between the chapter number and the page number. Unfortunately this locator format takes up a lot of space. Although some may be tempted to change the format to something like

directory structure, 3.10–15

this is not permissible because the locators must be in the same format as that used in the text. Designers of documents with nonconsecutive pagination should consider what impact their pagination scheme will have on the index, but all too often this matter is never considered during the design process.

Multipart page numbers may be alphanumeric. Instead of numbered chapters or sections, there are letters. Appendixes are commonly numbered in this way. A document may have four appendixes, A through D. The pagination for the appendixes is of the form A-1, B-1, and so forth. Such references follow the same format as the numbered chapters above. If there is an entry that contains locators for both a numbered chapter and a lettered appendix, the appendix locators follow the chapter locators.

directory structure, 3-2, B-7 to B-10

In this example, the order of the locators follows that of the document itself. Matters become more complex when alphanumeric pagination in a document is not in ascending alphabetic order. Take another software manual that has three sections: "Getting Started," "General Reference," and "Utilities." The following pagination is used for the first page of each section.

Getting Started: STR-1
General Reference: REF-1
Utilities: UTL-1

The problem with this type of pagination arises when an entry has locators from more than one section. A sorting order has to be chosen. There is a tendency to sort multiple references alphabetically regardless of their order in the document:

> file conversion, REF-10, STR-23, UTL-4

Sorting these locators alphabetically implies that the STR-23 reference will be found after the REF-10 reference in the document. This is, of course, not correct. The "Getting Started" section precedes the "General Reference" section. Readers looking up a series of references should be able to work from the front of a document to the back without the need to flip back and forth in the document. Alphanumeric locators should be sorted in the sequence of their appearance in the text.

There are many other complex variations on the handling of multipart locators. See chapter 6, "Special Concerns in Indexing," for a discussion of locator format in multivolume works.

Annotated page numbers. An index often points out illustrative material in a book. One way to accomplish this is to add an annotation to the locator. In an architecture book that contains many photographs and drawings, distinguishing a discussion of a building from the page number of an illustration may be helpful:

> Palace of Fine Arts, 32–38, 40fig, 75–78

Rather than using an annotation like *fig,* some publishers ask the indexer to make page references to illustrative material italic. This technique saves space and reduces the density of the reference locator.

Books with a variety of illustrative material often distinguish annotations for photographs, maps, and tables. A scheme like the following may be used.

> References to photographs: 45(ph)
> References to maps: 45(map)
> References to tables 45(t)

In a heavily illustrated book, say, one that contains photographs, maps, and tabular material, the use of annotated page references can create a very dense and visually "busy" index. Instead of using annotated page references, descriptive subentries can convey the same information in clear manner:

> Palace of Fine Arts, 32, 38
> architectural drawing of, 40
> photographs of, 75–78

Pages that contain several illustrative items may be cited. If the items are numbered, the number may be added to the annotation. For example, reference to table 12 on a page that contains three other tables may be expressed as

> gross national product, 56(t12) or 56t.12 or 56t12

A similar format is followed when a footnote has to be referenced by number. A reference to footnote number 13 on page 68 can be cited as 68n13 or 68n.13. Endnotes, whether at the end of the chapters or the end of the book, are always cited by note number; otherwise, they would be difficult to find because there are many notes on one page.

When there is more than one note cited by number on a page, the note numbers are separated by a comma. Some publishers require that the *n.* annotation be changed to *nn.* when multiple notes are referenced. For example,

> Gordon setters, 55nn 23, 27 or 55nn. 23, 27

One might consider the use of parentheses in such a situation, as it is not hard to imagine a note number in the above format being confused with a page number. For example, Gordon setters, 55(nn 23, 27) or 55(nn. 23, 27)

Or the *n.* can be repeated and attached to each note reference:

> Gordon setters, 55n23, n27 or 55n.23, n.27

If there is only one footnote on a page, it is not necessary to include the footnote number as part of the reference locator. The addition of an *n* (with no period) is sufficient:

web presses, 45, 84n

Endnotes can pose a problem regarding context of a discussion. Let's suppose we find the following in the body text of a book on page 135:

> Several studies[18] have found that the kiwi fruit is an excellent source of Vitamin C. As a matter of fact, the kiwi contains twenty-six times the amount of Vitamin C per ounce as the orange.

Then in the endnotes section on page 387, we find note 18:

> [18] Perhaps the best-known study of the Vitamin C content of kiwi fruit is that of Mary Smith, "Vitamin C and Kiwis," *Journal of Australian Nutrition* 15, no. 4 (1987): 234–47.

The problem for the indexer is that Mary Smith is mentioned by name only in the note reference on page 387. If the only reference to Mary Smith is "Smith, Mary, 387n18," there is no convenient way for readers to locate the context where Mary Smith is actually discussed. The following reference would be misleading:

Smith, Mary, 135, 387n18

Mary Smith's name does not actually appear on page 135. Unless readers ascertain that note 18 refers to Mary Smith, they would likely be unable to discern the relevant context.

One solution to this vexing problem evolved during correspondence between myself and Hans Wellisch. To provide readers with the context of a referenced name that does not appear verbatim in the text, use a special locator format for the page number. Using the *Mary Smith* example above, and adding a few additional page references, such a format would look like:

Smith, Mary, 45–49, [135n18], 228, 387n18

An introductory note would explain the use of square brackets: "Page references enclosed in square brackets indicate textual references to endnotes." This format clearly indicates to readers that note 18 on page 135 references Mary Smith even though her name does not appear in the text.

The 14th edition of *The Chicago Manual of Style* offers the following recommendation (17.28):

> If the subject discussed in the endnote is not directly identified in the text, citation of the context in which the note reference occurs is nevertheless sometimes helpful. In that case the text page may be added in parentheses following the endnote citation:
>
> synergy, 224, 238–39, 364 n. 12 (193)
>
> If such contextual citations are used, they must be explained in a headnote at the beginning of the index.

The indexer, in consultation with the production editor, should devise a scheme for handling visually complex references in a way that will be readable. When choosing a format for annotated reference locators, it is best to work with a sample entry that contains both annotated references and "regular" references. Given the widespread access to desktop publishing equipment, it is an easy matter to try out different formats. It is worth the effort to take a little time before indexing begins to choose a format that will be easy to read. The problems that arise with reference locators that include table numbers or note numbers may become apparent when sample entries are formatted for review. For example,

Gordon setters, 23, 55nn 23, 27, 135
Gordon setters, 23, 55(nn 23, 27), 135
Gordon setters, 23, 55n23, n27, 135
Gordon setters, 23, 55nn23, 27, 135

gross national product, 35, 56(t12), 121
gross national product, 35, 56t.12, 121
gross national product, 35, 56t12, 121
gross national product, 35, 56T12, 121

As we can see in the first sample entry above, multiple note references attached to the same page number pose problems. The second note reference (note 27 on page 55) is not visually attached to the page reference; it floats on the line and could easily be mistaken for a page reference. It is always best to keep the reference locator as simple as possible, using a minimal amount of punctuation or type changes. But clarity is also important. The entirety of a locator should be unambiguous. Often it is only through trial and error, trying out different formats, that we can arrive at the best solution.

As we have seen, many variations are possible in annotated page references. For example, some publishers drop the period following *n.* and *nn.* (*n* and *nn*); some use italic for annotated page references while others do not. Regardless of which scheme is used, the format should be clearly explained to readers in an introductory note.

Column or quadrant identifiers. In large format books, such as encyclopedias, adding a column or quadrant identifier to the locator may be helpful. For example, a book with large pages and two columns of text per page may benefit from a quadrant identifier. Each page would be divided into four imaginary quadrants, identified by letters. Quadrant *a* would be the upper left quadrant, *b* would be the lower left quadrant, *c* would be the upper right quadrant, and *d* would be the lower right quadrant. A reference to 235b would refer to text that appears on page 235 somewhere in the lower left section of the page.

Column identifiers are used when there are multiple columns of usually dense text per page. In a book with three columns of text per page, a column identification scheme could start with column *a* on the left side and run to column *c* on the right side of each page.

This type of reference locator lends itself fairly well to the use of page ranges that indicate a continuous discussion of a topic. To indicate a discussion that begins on page 40, column *a*, and ends on page 43, column *b*, the page range would be 40a–43b.

It is also important to keep in mind that this type of notation can become quite confusing if other alphabetic identifiers are being used for footnotes or illustrations.

The use of either a column or quadrant identifier in an index requires mention in the introductory note for the index. Readers must be clearly told what scheme is being used, particularly when the locator includes imaginary elements that are not discernible by looking at a page of text.

Locators That Are Not Page Numbers

The primary benefit of using locators that are not page numbers is that the index's locators are not tied to the pagination of the document. Usually this means that indexing can begin before final page proofs have been produced. At other times, this locator format is chosen because extensive revision of the document is anticipated. These revisions will change the pagination. However, if the locators are not tied to the original pagination, the impact on the index entries will be minimized.

Section or paragraph numbers. In many reference books, paragraphs within each chapter are numbered. Most of the index entries are tied to the paragraph numbers. This scheme enables index users to quickly find the particular piece of text that is referenced. This numbering scheme works well in reference books in which the content is presented as discrete units.

Legal books are commonly indexed by section number. Sometimes the section numbering is quite straightforward. The first section in each chapter or division begins with the chapter/division number expressed in hundreds. For example, the first section in chapter 2 will be §200; the first section in chapter 6 will be §600, and so on. In some legal material the numbering scheme is very elaborate. It may begin with a Roman numeral article number and move down several levels using both Arabic numbers and letters. A complex legal reference locator may look like IV:2.3.1(a). Such detailed numbering schemes are also common in engineering reports.

When reference locators are lengthy and complex, the index will appear dense. Sometimes there is nothing one can do about this. However, the indexer should not hesitate to suggest a more compact locator format if it is feasible. Small changes can go far to increase the usability of an index. For example, many legal indexes are by their nature dense. They often are composed of entries that are several subentry levels deep. The index can be "lightened up" a bit by simply omitting the section number symbol (§) as part of the reference locator.

Line numbers. In some documents every line of text is numbered. The line numbering may be consecutive throughout the document, as in a legal brief. In other situations the line numbering may be consecutive throughout a chapter or division. Or the line numbering may start anew on each page. When the line numbering is not consecutive throughout the document, another locator will have to be added to the line number locator.

In the case of line numbering that is consecutive through each chapter, the chapter number will precede the line number in the reference locator. One way to reference line 435 in chapter 2 would be to cite it as 2:435.

If line numbering starts again on each page of text, the page number will have to be part of the reference locator. This format defeats the goal of not tying reference locators to final page proof pagination. But it may prove useful in text that is very dense.

Electronic media. Indexers working with online, book-length material will find that they must deal with a very different locator system than that which has already been discussed. While file structuring and pointer formats are outside the scope of this book, a few general comments may be helpful.

Online documents present the same indexing challenges as printed media documents. The indexing process and principles described in this book can be applied to online documents. The presentation of a structured index as a front end to an online document provides users with a familiar and useful gateway to information contained in the text.

The online index will very likely look like a printed index without the familiar reference locators. Users will be able to select the index terms and be taken directly to the referenced text. Indexers working with online material will physically mark the beginning and end of the discussion of a topic. In some systems, the pertinent discussion will appear highlighted, distinguishing it from surrounding text.

The demands on the indexer for exact and detailed reference locator assignments are potentially much greater in the online environment. However, the same guidelines we use when working with printed media documents apply in the online environment. It is still important to distinguish between continuous and noncontinuous discussion of a topic. Accuracy is still important. When these principles are applied properly, the rewards to online readers will be great. The book *Indexing Electronic Images and Text* (Bellardo et al. 1993) is an interesting collection of papers related to the design of information access structures for the electronic environment.

CROSS-REFERENCES

Unlike main headings and subentries that provide access to locations in the text itself, cross-references are internal navigation guides within the index itself. Instead of containing reference locators to information in the text, cross-references tie together related information within the index. Cross-references are a vital part of any index. They are the links between various nodes in the index network. Proper use of cross-references greatly enhances the usability of an index.

There are four types of cross-references used in book indexes:

See

See under

See also

See also under

This chapter discusses the use of cross-references. The actual format and placement within the entry of cross-references will be discussed in chapter 8, "Format and Layout of the Index."

See and *See under*

The primary function of the *See* cross-reference is vocabulary control. A *See* cross-reference directs users from a term not used in the index to the term that is used as a heading. *See* cross-references serve three important functions:

1. They *control* the scattering of information in an index.
2. They *anticipate* the language of index users.
3. They *reconcile* the language of the document with the users' language.

A *See* cross-reference is used whenever it may be reasonably assumed that a reader will look up a topic using terminology that is not used in the index. The text may use several different terms to describe the same thing—this is especially true in multiple-author works such as a collection of research papers. The indexer must choose one term or phrase as an entry. *See* cross-references are used to guide the readers from the terms not chosen to the chosen term. The *See* cross-reference can also relate synonymous terms or nearly synonymous terms:

> American Civil War. *See* Civil War
> War between the States. *See* Civil War

A *See* cross-reference can merge antonyms into one phrase:

> unemployment. *See* employment and unemployment

See cross-references are often used to handle slang or other popularized terms:

> grass. *See* marijuana

See references lead the reader to organizational names used in the text:

> Catholic church. *See* Roman Catholic Church

Or they direct a reader from an abbreviation or acronym to the spelled-out version of the term:

> ABA. *See* American Bar Association

See references are commonly associated with geographic names. The judicious use of this type of cross-reference is particularly important when place names have changed. For example,

> Burma. *See* Myanmar
> McKinley National Park. *See* Denali National Park

Personal names often require the use of *See* cross-references. When an individual has been mentioned under a pen name or pseudonym, it is good practice to cross-reference from the individual's real surname:

Clemens, Samuel. *See* Twain, Mark

Western women's names pose particular problems because the surname often changes with marriage. The text itself will most likely indicate to the indexer which name to use in the index. If the discussion in the text refers to a woman after she has married, then her married name is the likely choice for the index. But the indexer should provide a cross-reference from the woman's maiden name to the married name.

Nicolson, Vita. *See* Sackville-West, Vita

Conversely, if a woman is better known by her maiden name than by her married name, the indexer should use the maiden name. The situation becomes even more complex when a woman has been married more than once. It is the indexer's job, through the use of cross-references, to tie the various names together.

Burton, Mrs. Richard. *See* Taylor, Elizabeth
Warner, Mrs. John V. *See* Taylor, Elizabeth

Gorsuch, Anne M. *See* Burford, Anne M. Gorsuch

When a *See* cross-reference refers to a term that is a subentry, some indexers use the phrase *See under* followed by the main heading. Using the example below, we might find the cross-reference "silver coins. *See under* currency" in the index. The use of "under" indicates that the term will be found explicitly as a subentry below the main heading indicated. This convention may save space in the index because the indexer need not repeat the entire main heading and subentry elsewhere.

currency
    dollar bills
    silver coins

Alternatively, a cross-reference to a subentry may take the form of "silver coins. *See* currency, silver coins." This format repeats the main heading and the subentry text in full.

While *See* references are a vital part of an index, they can be over-done. Although many terms have synonyms, it is not the indexer's job to anticipate each and every one of them. To prevent an index from becoming cluttered with directional signs that send the reader back and forth in the index, the indexer must exercise common sense and anticipate terms that readers are likely to look up. The text itself may provide hints for possible cross-references. Such a hint may take the following form: "Introductory notes, also known as headnotes, play an important role in complex indexes." The following cross-reference would be appropriate:

headnotes. *See* introductory notes

The indexer must look carefully for such hints in the text. Many authors will provide synonymous terminology when a topic is first introduced and indicate which is the preferred term. Synonymous terms should be cross-referenced. However, the indexer must often go beyond the text and consider other ways that readers may look up information. Authors will not always provide the terminology.

See cross-references should be evaluated in terms of their use-fulness. It can be very irritating for readers to be sent from one place in the index to another only to pick up one or two page references. It is often kinder to provide quick access to information by double-posting a term rather than using a *See* cross-reference. For example, instead of using "cars. *See* autos" the indexer may decide to provide both terms because there are so few page references:

autos, 54, 89
. . .
cars, 54, 89

Double-posting information can save the index user time. But if "autos" were followed by subentries, posting the information one place and cross-referencing it from the other term would save space. Frequently the indexer will not know the complete form of an entry until the entire text has been indexed. To maintain term consistency, the indexer may decide initially to use a *See* reference. Later, during the editing phase of the index, the indexer can make a final determination on the benefit to the readers of double-posting the terms instead.

See also and See also under

The primary function of a *See also* cross-reference is to guide users to related and additional information at another heading, as in the following example:

> drug trafficking. *See also* narcotics
> narcotics. *See also* drug trafficking

See also cross-references may be "two-way" as above. The important point to remember is to guide users to closely related additional information. The indexer uses *See also* cross-references when users may be expected to miss additional and related information. The important word to keep in mind here is *additional*.

diskettes	FORMAT command
care of, 12	for floppy disk, 18–20
formatting of, 18–20	for hard disks, 35–39
	parameters summarized, 42
	See also diskettes

In the example above there is no additional information about the FORMAT command under the "diskettes" heading. The time of readers who look up "diskettes" for new, related information will have been wasted. Thus, the example above is an inappropriate use of the *See also* device.

Within an index there will be many related topics. It is not the indexer's job to make all these relationships explicit. In many situations it is fair to assume that readers have enough savvy to discern obvious relationships. A woodworking book most likely does not need a cross-reference like "hammers. *See also* nails." Indexers must be careful not to clutter the index with condescending cross-references. The indexer's good judgment will anticipate related information that readers might miss if a cross-reference is lacking.

While there is no hard and fast rule about the number of *See also* cross-references that may be associated with a particular entry, an excessive number suggest a structural problem with the entry itself.

In such cases, the main heading is often too general or vague. In other situations the indexer needs to refer readers to an entire class of terms without naming each and every term. Here a general cross-reference can be used. For example,

> commands
>   error messages associated with, 135–41
>   parameters, 28
>   syntax, 25–27
>   *See also individual command names*

or

> dogs
>   breeding of, 75–80
>   feeding of, 35
>   registration rules, 90
>   whelping of, 81–83
>   *See also breed names*

In both of the examples above the indexer has guided readers to specific types of entries without listing them verbatim. In a book on dogs where more than 120 breeds are discussed, the indexer can avoid listing each and every breed ("*See also* Afghans; cocker spaniels; collies; . . .").

Note that the words that form the general cross-reference are set in italics. The use of italics in this situation indicates to the reader that the terms referenced are general in nature; they are not specific terms that will be found in the index. For instance, there will be no entries in the *I*'s for "individual command names."

General cross-references are very useful devices. In the "commands" entry above, the indexer has chosen to post all the commands as main headings rather than listing them as subentries under "commands." In a technical index such as a computer manual, where one is likely to find many commands discussed, the usability of the index will be enhanced by posting individual commands as main headings. Most users wanting information about a particular command will look up that command by name. A user looking for "FORMAT command" will likely go to the *F*'s before going to the *C*'s. The use of the general cross-reference allows the indexer to post general information that applies to all commands under the "commands" entry. The *See also* cross-reference neatly guides readers to more specific information.

Completeness of Cross-references

The form that cross-references should take has fueled much debate among indexers and editors. Should the heading pointed to be cited in its complete form? The complete form includes all punctuation and all parenthetical phrases that may be associated with the term. The argument in favor of complete citation is that there will be absolutely no ambiguity regarding the term referred to. However, in the case of a lengthy main heading, one must exercise some common sense. For example, "labor unions. *See also* AFL-CIO" is no less clear than "labor unions. *See also* AFL-CIO (American Federation of Labor and Congress of Industrial Organizations)." Providing this cumbersome cross-reference in full adds unnecessary length to the entry.

Clarity, however, should never be sacrificed to succinctness. Given the sample entries below, a cross-reference such as "*See* LIST" would be inappropriate. The parenthetical phrase is needed so that the readers will know exactly which term is being referenced.

LIST (command)
LIST (text tag)

Because there is disagreement on whether cross-referenced terms can be shortened, the indexer would be wise to check with the publisher before shortening cross-references.

Directness of Cross-references

Cross-references should always provide direct access to information. They should be "one-step links." They should not send the reader on a cross-reference trail, as in "hunting dogs. *See* Gordon setters," and then only to find, "Gordon setters. *See* setters." In this case, the "hunting dogs" reference should direct the reader to "setters."

Multiple Cross-references

When more than one term is referred to in a cross-reference, it is necessary to separate the terms with semicolons.

books. *See also* reference books; trade books

A comma is never used to separate two referenced terms. However, a comma may be used to reference a subentry. For example,

whelping. *See* dogs, whelping of

Here, "whelping of" is a subentry under the main heading "dogs." This format is an alternative to

whelping. *See under* dogs

Blind and Circular Cross-references

The indexer should make sure that there are no cross-references that refer to terms that do not exist in the index. These are called blind cross-references; they send the reader nowhere. "Chicken. *See also* poultry" would be a blind cross-reference when there was no entry for "poultry."

Of equal bad form is the circular cross-reference. These are *See* cross-references that reference each other, resulting in no information being found. For example,

autos. *See* cars
. . .
cars. *See* autos

Reference Locators and Cross-references

A cross-reference never has a reference locator associated with it. Remember that the cross-reference is a navigation guide around the index itself. The purpose of a cross-reference is not to send readers to a particular location in the text. The main headings and subentries are the access points to the text itself. The cross-reference sends readers to locations within the index. It is not a device for directing readers to anything outside the index.

5

ARRANGEMENT OF ENTRIES

THE ARRANGEMENT OF ENTRIES refers to the order in which the entries are presented. In most indexes this order is alphabetic. However, there is more than one way to get from *A* to *Z*. There are two alphabetic orders, word-by-word order and letter-by-letter order. Main headings are alphabetized following one of these sorting orders. Although subentries generally follow the same alphabetizing scheme as the main headings, there are exceptions, which will be discussed shortly.

When as children we all learned to sing the so-called alphabet song, we were surely left with the impression that the order of the alphabet was a straightforward matter. Not so when it comes to alphabetizing index entries! The problem is that terms in an index often include elements that are not letters of the alphabet:

> Woolf, Virginia
> New York City
> !du command
> War of 1812

All four terms include spaces. The first and third terms have punctuation marks, the comma and the exclamation point. The last term includes numbers. Any sorting scheme must take nonletter characters into consideration. For the purposes of this discussion, each separable entity in a term will be referred to as a character. Characters include letters, numbers, symbols, and spaces.

WORD-BY-WORD ALPHABETIZING

When alphabetizing word by word, we sort the letters up to the end of the first word and then stop. The second and following words are sorted only when two or more entries begin with the same word. For example,

New Hampshire
New Jersey
New York
Newark
Newton

In this example, the space character is sorted. The sort value of the space character is lower than the value assigned to letters. Frequently a word-by-word sort gathers together like terms. However, a word-by-word sort can also create strange sequences such as that noted in the 13th edition of *The Chicago Manual of Style* (18.93):

Type font
Type metal
Typeface
Typeset

Every index should be evaluated individually to determine the most reasonable sorting method for its terms.

So far we have looked at relatively simple illustrations, with only letter and space characters. The variations on word-by-word alphabetizing become apparent when other characters are included in the terms. The common characters, in addition to spaces, that are often found in index terms are dashes, hyphens, and diagonal slashes. Some publishers assign these characters a sorting value equal to the space character; other publishers ignore these characters. This confusion is problematic not only for indexers, but also for index users and programmers of indexing software. It is therefore important to note that various international indexing standards assign these common characters the same value as the space character.

It is best to illustrate the difference in a word-by-word sort when these characters are sorted like the space character and when they are ignored.

Sorted like a Space	Ignored
TYPE-ADF command	type font
type font	type foundry
type foundry	type metal
type metal	TYPE-ADF command
Type/Specs Inc.	typeface
typeface	typeset
typeset	Type/Specs Inc.

In a short listing like this, such sorting differences may not seem important. But in a lengthy index, they may mean variations of many column inches in the placement of terms. A decision about the sorting method may mean the difference between a reader locating a term, or not locating a term and giving up in confusion. These sorting differences are not trivial.

The alphabetizing principles adopted in the British indexing standard (BS 3700:1988) can guide us here. The British standard recommends that spaces, dashes, hyphens, and diagonal slashes all have an equal sorting value (6.2.1.2(a)). In a word-by-word sort this means that these characters are treated in the same way as the space character.

Another character that is common within an index heading is the comma, as in "Woolf, Virginia." In a word-by-word sort the comma is ignored and the sort pauses at the space character following the comma. When these sorting principles are applied, a word-by-word sort looks like this:

> TYPE–ADF command
> Type, Alice Mary
> type font
> type foundry
> Type, James
> type metal
> Type/Specs Inc.
> typeface
> typeset

Letter-by-Letter Alphabetizing

In a strict letter-by-letter sort, only letters and numbers are sorted; spaces and other kinds of characters are ignored. The words are sorted as though they were run together:

> TYPE–ADF command
> Type, Alice Mary
> typeface
> type font
> type foundry
> Type, James
> type metal
> typeset
> Type/Specs Inc.

Many publishers, however, have added a curious variation to the straightforward letter-by-letter sort. The exception noted in many publishers' style guides applies to particular types of commas in entries. The 14th edition of *The Chicago Manual of Style* states this variation most clearly:

> In the letter-by-letter mode, alphabetization continues across spaces between words and stops at the first comma preceding a modifying element or an inversion. Serial commas, however—that is, commas used to separate items in a series—are ignored. Parentheses enclosing definitions, alternatives, explanations, or cross-references also interrupt letter-by-letter alphabetization. But as in the word-by-word mode, alphabetization continues across hyphens, slashes, apostrophes, and, as already mentioned, serial commas. (17.97)

If we add a book title with serial commas to the "type" list above and sort it letter by letter following the guidelines of the University of Chicago Press, the result looks like this:

> Type, Alice Mary
> Type, James
> TYPE-ADF command
> typeface
> type font
> type foundry
> type metal
> typeset
> Type/Specs Inc.
> *Type, Substance, and Form*

The apparent reason for this hybrid form of the letter-by-letter sort is to keep similar names together. But keeping similar names together is why one might choose a word-by-word sort rather than a letter-by-letter sort! Always consider the user. Most people believe that letter by letter means just that—letter-by-letter sorting. Many users are unaware that inverted headings may be treated differently than other terms.

Any time we apply obscure rules—and this is only one of many—to the arrangement of index entries, we must consider the impact on the index user. The present book must point out these quirks because many indexers will see them listed in an indexing style guide and will be expected to follow them. It is my hope, however, that the revisers of indexing style guides will consider eliminating these oddities in the future.

Unfortunately, the rule requiring the special handling of particular types of commas is found frequently in the style guides of publishers who prefer a letter-by-letter sort. This is not the recommended way to sort letter by letter. The American index standard (ANSI Z39.4-1984) recommends that punctuation be ignored in a letter-by-letter sort. Note the following letter-by-letter sequence from ANSI Z39.4 (6.4.1):

> Blackstone, William
> Black tern
> Black, William
> Blackwood, Algernon

The 1993 revision, draft 3, of ANSI Z39.4-1984 is explicit about the basic filing order of characters. Section 9.2 states that

The basic order of characters is:

a. spaces, punctuation marks, and symbols other than letters and numerals: All characters in this group have equal filing value and file before any numeral or alphabetic letter. All are treated as if they were a space. Multiple consecutive spaces and their equivalents are to be considered equal to a single space.

b. numerals: 0 through 9. All headings beginning with numerals are arranged before headings beginning with letters. Numbers are filed in numerical order. Roman numerals are filed with their Arabic counterparts.

c. alphabetic letters: A through Z. Lower-case and upper-case letters have equal filing value. Modified letters are treated like their plain equivalents in the English alphabet.

If non-alphanumeric symbols are prominently featured and must be filed, a filing system for them must be devised and explained, because no standards exist for the filing of non-alphanumeric symbols.

Optionally, the ampersand (&) may be filed as its spelled-out language equivalent.

Section 9.7 of draft 3 explains that word-by-word alphabetizing sorts a space character before it sorts a letter, whereas letter-by-letter alphabetizing disregards the space and symbols that have the same filing value as a space. In section 9.7 we find the following examples of the application of these sorting rules:

Word-by-Word	Letter-by-Letter
New, Agnes	New, Agnes
New Brunswick	Newark
new journalism	New Brunswick
new moon	Newfoundland
New, Thomas	new journalism
New York	new moon
Newark	news *see* network news
Newfoundland	news agencies
news *see* network news	news (journalism)
news agencies	news-letters *see* newsletters
news (journalism)	newsletters
news-letters *see* newsletters	newspapers
news photography	news photography
newsletters	New, Thomas
newspapers	New York

A PLEA FOR STANDARDIZATION

If I could wave a magic wand and be granted one wish regarding indexing, I would wish for universal agreement about word-by-word and letter-by-letter alphabetizing. It is a ridiculous state of affairs when publishers' alphabetizing rules result in different sequences of entries. We have enough confusion due to the fact that there are two distinct ways to alphabetize; certainly, we muddy the waters further by introducing variations within these two sorting methods.

In regard to word-by-word alphabetizing, I would begin by eliminating exceptions based on usage rather than straightforward alphabetizing rules. Some publishers treat hyphenated words in different ways in a word-by-word sort. The *McGraw-Hill Style Manual* makes the following recommendation (p. 293):

Words in which a hyphen is used after a prefix are alphabetized as one word:

Panama Canal, 172–183
Pan-American Exposition, 194
Panel discussions, 78–80

Hyphenated adjectives preceding a noun (sometimes called *unit modifiers*) are treated as two words:

Voltage-regulator tubes, 48
Voltage saturation, 96

Such distinctions will not play a role in word-by-word alphabetizing. I would also eliminate the instruction found in the 14th edition of *The Chicago Manual of Style* (17.97), and adopted by many other publishers, to stop a letter-by-letter sort at all commas except serial commas.

The following alphabetizing rules are adapted from the British standard (BS 3700:1988, section 6). After the discussion of the rules there is a list of terms sorted word by word and letter by letter.

Alphabetizing applies to each level in the index separately. First, the main heading is alphabetized; then subsequent levels, such as subentries and sub-subentries, are alphabetized individually if they are present.

There is a basic order of filing characters that applies to either type of alphabetizing (BS 3700:1988):

> 6.2.1.2 *Basic order of filing characters.* The basic order of filing characters should be:
> (a) spaces, dashes, hyphens, diagonal slashes, all of which have equal filing value; *followed by*
> (b) ampersands, unless it is considered more useful to file as spelt out in the appropriate language; *followed by*
> (c) Arabic numerals and Roman numerals; *followed by*
> (d) Roman alphabet letters
> 6.2.1.3 *Other characters.* Other characters should be treated as follows.
> (a) The apostrophe should be disregarded and the word in which it occurs treated as one word.
> (b) Punctuation marks other than those listed in 6.2.1.2 (a) should be disregarded unless given a

function by the indexer, as, for example, to separate a surname from a forename or to enclose a qualifier. They then acquire a filing value imposed by the indexer.

(c) Signs and symbols should be treated according to their importance in the text and the likelihood of their being found in an alphabetical sequence. If they are few, they may be arranged as if spelt out. If many, a conventional order may be used as demonstrated in 4.3 in BS 1749:1985.

Notice that the characters above are presented in ascending order, from lower values to higher values. Punctuation marks other than those listed in section (a) are disregarded unless given a function by the indexer. Note that the comma is disregarded. The following sets of terms are sorted in the same way:

"books" and books
publisher's and publishers'

The filing order of symbols is discussed in chapter 6. A special sorting sequence is used for the *See* cross-reference. Also as recommended in the 14th edition of *The Chicago Manual of Style* (17.97), I suggest that letter-by-letter alphabetizing be interrupted by the parentheses that enclose modifying terms or cross-references. For example,

file. *See* text file
FILE (First Integrated Linear Encoder), 107

precedes

file access, 56

In this case the alphabetizing stops after *file;* the characters, *s-e-e,* are not sorted. Regardless of the format of the *See* cross-reference, the alphabetizing stops at the end of the term preceding the *See.* All of the following cross-reference forms,

file. *See* text file
file *see* text file
file (*see* text file)

precede

filenames, 56

When a period appears in an entry, it is disregarded. For example, the periods in *N.E. Zenith Co.* are ignored.

Word-by-word alphabetizing. This sorting method follows the basic order of characters noted above without modification. Spaces, dashes, hyphens, and diagonal slashes all have an equal sorting value, which is lower than either numbers or alphabetic characters. When alphabetizing word-by-word, characters are sorted until a space, dash, hyphen, or diagonal slash is encountered. Additionally, the parentheses enclosing a qualifying expression have a sorting value higher than the space character but lower than either numbers or alphabetic characters. The following sequence results:

> N.E. Zenith Co.
> new. *See* original
> NEW (New England Whistle)
> New, Arnold
> new-fashioned devices
> New Hampshire
> new/old continuum
> New York
> New, Zachary
> Newark
> Newton, Isaac

Letter-by-letter alphabetizing. This sorting method ignores the characters in section (a) above (space, dash, hyphen, diagonal slash). The *See* cross-reference is handled in the same manner as in the word-by-word method. Additionally, letter-by-letter sorting stops when a parenthesis is encountered. The alphabetizing resumes if there are two or more entries that are the same up to the first parenthesis. In that case, the characters inside the parentheses are sorted. This method produces the following sequence:

> new. *See* original
> NEW (New England Whistle)
> Newark

New, Arnold
new-fashioned devices
New Hampshire
new/old continuum
Newton, Isaac
New York
New, Zachary
N.E. Zenith Co.

It is important to note that the alphabetizing sequences described in this section are a departure from the rules presented in the 13th and 14th editions of *The Chicago Manual of Style,* which have been adopted by many publishers. But these methods of alphabetizing do conform to international standards.

Following is a listing of the terms used earlier in this chapter sorted alphabetically word by word and letter by letter using the rules described in this section:

Word-by-Word	Letter-by-Letter
Black tern	Blackstone, William
Black, William	Black tern
Blackstone, William	Black, William
Blackwood, Algernon	Blackwood, Algernon
N.E. Zenith Co.	new. *See* original
new. *See* original	NEW (New England Whistle)
NEW (New England Whistle)	New, Agnes
New, Agnes	Newark
New, Arnold	New, Arnold
New Brunswick	New Brunswick
new-fashioned devices	new-fashioned devices
New Hampshire	Newfoundland
New Jersey	New Hampshire
new journalism	New Jersey
new moon	new journalism
new/old continuum	new moon
New, Thomas	new/old continuum
New York	news *see* network news
New, Zachary	news (journalism)
Newark	news agencies
Newfoundland	news-letters *see* newsletters
news *see* network news	newsletters
news (journalism)	newspapers
news agencies	news photography
news-letters *see* newsletters	New, Thomas
news photography	Newton, Isaac
newsletters	New York
newspapers	New, Zachary

Newton, Isaac
Pan-American Exposition
Panama Canal
panel discussions
TYPE-ADF command
Type, Alice Mary
type font
type foundry
Type, James
type metal
Type/Specs Inc.
Type, Substance, and Form
typeface
typeset
voltage-regulator tubes
voltage saturation
voltages

N.E. Zenith Co.
Panama Canal
Pan-American Exposition
panel discussions
TYPE-ADF command
Type, Alice Mary
typeface
type font
type foundry
Type, James
type metal
typeset
Type/Specs Inc.
Type, Substance, and Form
voltage-regulator tubes
voltages
voltage saturation

For comparative purposes, following is a listing of the same terms sorted letter-by-letter according to the guidelines of the 14th edition of *The Chicago Manual of Style* and the 1993 (draft 3) recommendations in the *Proposed National Standard Guidelines for Indexes in Information Retrieval (ANSI/NISO Z39.4-199x):*

Letter-by-Letter
(Chicago style, 14th ed.)

Black, William
Blackstone, William
Black tern
Blackwood, Algernon
new. *See* original
NEW (New England Whistle)
New, Agnes
New, Arnold
New, Thomas
New, Zachary
Newark
New Brunswick
new-fashioned devices
Newfoundland
New Hampshire
New Jersey
new journalism
new moon
new/old continuum
news *see* network news
news (journalism)
news agencies

Letter-by-Letter
(ANSI Z39.4-199x, draft 3)

Blackstone, William
Black tern
Black, William
Blackwood, Algernon
new. *See* original
New, Agnes
Newark
New, Arnold
New Brunswick
new-fashioned devices
Newfoundland
New Hampshire
New Jersey
new journalism
new moon
NEW (New England Whistle)
new/old continuum
news *see* network news
news agencies
news (journalism)
news-letters *see* newsletters
newsletters

news-letters *see* newsletters	newspapers
newsletters	news photography
newspapers	New, Thomas
news photography	Newton, Isaac
Newton, Isaac	New York
New York	New, Zachary
N.E. Zenith Co.	N.E. Zenith Co.
Panama Canal	Panama Canal
Pan-American Exposition	Pan-American Exposition
panel discussions	panel discussions
Type, Alice Mary	TYPE-ADF command
Type, James	Type, Alice Mary
TYPE-ADF command	typeface
typeface	type font
type font	type foundry
type foundry	Type, James
type metal	type metal
typeset	typeset
Type/Specs Inc.	Type/Specs Inc.
Type, Substance, and Form	*Type, Substance, and Form*
voltage-regulator tubes	voltage-regulator tubes
voltages	voltages
voltage saturation	voltage saturation

Basic Rules Affecting Both Alphabetizing Orders

Almost every "rule" that follows has significant exceptions that will be discussed in chapter 6. These rules, however, can be followed for many indexes that do not include the use of specialized terminology.

Apostrophes are disregarded when sorting a word. A contracted word is treated as one word. Quotation marks are also ignored when alphabetizing a word.

When Arabic or Roman numerals appear in entries either at the beginning of the entry or within the entry, and are sorted numerically, they are sorted in ascending numeric order. Arabic and Roman numerals within entries are interfiled according to their numeric order. Entries beginning with numbers are generally placed before the alphabetic listing of entries:

5th Avenue
XX Century Gazetteer
2001: A Space Odyssey

Symbols in an index, if they are few, may be sorted as they are spelled. But if there are many symbols, it may be preferable to arrange them in accordance with special rules (see chap. 6).

Diacritical marks are usually ignored in alphabetizing; a *ü* sorts as a *u*. When possible, letters with diacritical marks are sorted like their English equivalents.

An introductory note will be necessary if the indexer has chosen to use a nontraditional arrangement sequence. The note will explain any convention used by the indexer that might confuse users of the index.

NONALPHABETIC ARRANGEMENT IN INDEXES

Readers expect indexes to be arranged in alphabetic order. The decision to arrange entries in a nonalphabetic order should not be made lightly. The important factor to consider is whether the nonalphabetic arrangement will make entries easier for readers to locate. Generally, main headings are arranged in the alphabetic sequences noted above. Nonalphabetic arrangements occur at the subentry levels.

Articles, prepositions, and conjunctions. By far the most common nonalphabetic arrangement encountered in indexes is when leading articles, prepositions, and conjunctions in subentries are not alphabetized. Instead, the word following the article, preposition, or conjunction is sorted.

> books
>> for adult readers
>> the autumn market for
>> mass market sales of
>> and movie options
>> in production during May

As noted earlier, the best way to handle leading articles, prepositions, and conjunctions in subentries is a subject of debate. Many publishers' style guides instruct the indexer not to alphabetize these terms. Here are some arguments on both sides of this issue.

Those in favor of not alphabetizing these terms argue that the attention of the index user should be on the important keyword that follows the introductory term. Readers should not be burdened with figuring out which, if any, introductory term an indexer may have used to begin the entry. Furthermore, ignoring these terms when alphabetizing has been standard practice for years, so readers are familiar with it.

Those in favor of alphabetizing the introductory terms point out, quite correctly, that we alphabetize everything else in the index and that readers expect index entries to be alphabetized. They remind us that these structural terms should not be used frivolously in the index. They should be used only when absolutely necessary for clarity. So, the argument goes, if the terms are necessary, why not alphabetize them?

Clearly both schools of thought have strong arguments. See Hans Wellisch's (1993) article in the ASI newsletter, *Key Words*, and letters to the editor in subsequent issues for a discussion of ways to handle introductory terms in subentries. Chances are that your publisher will not want the introductory terms alphabetized when they appear in subentries. The rules regarding these terms in main headings are much clearer.

When articles, prepositions, or conjunctions appear as the first term in a main heading, the phrase is probably a title of a book, an article, a play, or a painting. If the first term is an article, such as *A* or *The*, the term is not alphabetized. For example, the book title *A Tale of Two Cities* would appear in the *T*'s, sorted on "Tale." The actual entry could appear in the *T*'s in one of three ways:

> *Tale of Two Cities, A,* or
> *A Tale of Two Cities,* or
> *Tale of Two Cities*

In the last example above, the *A* has been dropped entirely from the entry. This practice is common and preferred when it is necessary to economize on the length of index entries. The absence of the article does not compromise the meaning of the entry. Unlike in a bibliography, it is not required that titles in an index be entered in their complete form.

If the first term in a main heading is a preposition or conjunction, the term is alphabetized. For example, the book title *Of Mice and Men* appears in the *O*'s, sorted on "Of."

If an article, preposition, or conjunction appears in any other position besides as the first term in an entry, it is always alphabetized. The *and* in the phrase "dogs and cats" is alphabetized.

Words that are spelled alike. Many style guides recommend that terms that are spelled alike be arranged in the following sequence: person, place, and thing. Some style guides go one step further: they require filing a title after a thing. This arrangement results in a listing such as

> London, Jack
> London, England
> *London, an Antique Shopper's Guide*

The major problem with this odd rule is that most index users have no idea that it exists. Readers looking at the list above will probably think that the indexer made an alphabetizing mistake. And in a lengthy index, readers may miss index entries entirely because the entry they are looking for is not in alphabetic order. This type of arrangement is not recommended by any national or international standard on indexes. The 14th edition of *The Chicago Manual of Style* specifically recommends (17.99) that

> when a person, a place, and a thing have the same name, they are arranged in normal alphabetical order:

> London, England   hoe, garden
> London, Jack   Hoe, Robert

Words that are spelled alike are to be arranged in alphabetic order like all other entries in the index. If there are two words that are spelled alike but have different meanings, a qualifier must be added to distinguish the two entries.

Chronologic/page number order for subentries. In some books readers may be aided by subentries arranged in a chronological order. In the biography of a naval officer the following type of subentries might be helpful, for example:

<pre>
military career
  ensign
  lieutenant
  lieutenant commander
  commander
  captain
</pre>

Subentries in a geology book might be arranged in the order of geologic epochs:

<pre>
sedimentary strata
  pleistocene
  pliocene
  miocene
  cretaceous
</pre>

But all too often, chronologic order is confused with page-number order. A handful of publishers require all subentries to be sorted in page-number order. Apparently the reasoning is that the entries will be in chronologic order. As the example below will demonstrate, this is often not the case. Chronologic order is not synonymous with page-number order. This entry is taken from the book *China Builds the Bomb* (Stanford University Press, 1988). As originally published, the entry was in run-in style. Indented style is used here because it is easier to read. Also, only the first few page-number sequences have been included in the excerpt.

<pre>
Tests, 234, 244–45
  arms control negotiations and, 1, 12
  first atomic bomb (Oct. 16, 1964), 1–2, 182–89
  U.S., 18, 20
  plutonium bomb (Dec. 27, 1968), 113, 114n
  atomic bomb detonation process (Nov. 20, 1963; June 6, 1964), 156–60
  "cold," 201
  "fundamentals of a thermonuclear explosion" (Dec. 28, 1966), 201
  hydrogen bomb "booster" (May 9, 1966), 201
  DF-2 missile (Oct. 27, 1966), 202–3, 209
  hydrogen bomb (June 17, 1967), 205–6, 267
  weapon, 207, 290
  air-dropped atomic bomb (May 14, 1965), 208
  liquid-fueled missile (Nov. 1960), 212
  DF-3 missile (Dec. 1966), 213
  underground, 285
  British, 290
  French, 290
  Soviet, 290
</pre>

Because the indexer has included dates as part of some of the subentries, we are able to analyze the order of the entries. Moving down the list, which is in page-number order, the first date is 1964, the next date is 1968, the following date is 1963, and so on. Although these subentries are in page-number order, they definitely are not in chronologic order. Moreover, like items ("hydrogen bomb," for example) are separated. The reader must read the entire list because of the nonalphabetic arrangement. Without a doubt, the usability of an index arranged in this manner is severely compromised.

However, chronological subentry arrangement is frequently found in histories and biographies. Hazel Bell (1989: 169, 170) makes a strong case for chronological arrangement in subentries:

> It seems generally agreed that alphabetical arrangement of subheadings should give way to *chronological* for biographies. For one thing, alphabetical arrangement is helpful only if you know what the entries are likely to be: climate/history/population of a country. But it is at best confusing, at worst ridiculous, to list for a person:
> death, dental problems, divorce, marriage, meets future wife, schooldays
> and chronological arrangement will coincide roughly with the events of the book, producing a minor narrative in itself, easy to follow.

Bell clearly acknowledges the problems of arranging entries in simple page-number order when she writes:

> Some take the easiest way of all to arrange entries—in order of occurrence, no messing. This will not help the reader who does not know where to look for them; nor where entries occur where one would not expect them— the funeral of the character anticipated in the introduction, for instance—even his entire career there summarized.

Bell goes on to suggest other ways of collating entries in the index of a biography. Biographies challenge the indexer in a most demanding way. Indexers wishing to index biographies will benefit from consulting Hazel Bell's articles (1989, 1990) and booklet (1992) on the subject.

To return to the matter of page-number order for entries in books other than biographies, this arrangement can be difficult to use. In order to access specific information, readers must possess a good amount of prior knowledge about when the information might have appeared within the particular time spectrum for the book. The less specialized the knowledge required of index users, the greater will be the access to information in the index to a greater number of readers.

When subentries are sorted in page-number order, the demand for clear and structured term selection disappears. Since the entries will not be sorted alphabetically, the wording of the entries is less important. The subentries still must convey a clear sense of the material cited, but the demand on the indexer to pull the most important term forward for sorting is eliminated. But the demand on the reader, who must stumble through often long lists of subentries, is greatly increased.

In this section the most common examples of nonalphabetic arrangement have been discussed. Chapter 6, "Special Concerns in Indexing," will present a more specialized discussion of this matter.

How to Choose an Arrangement Order

Ideally every index will be arranged in such a way that readers can easily and quickly locate information. The indexer cannot conclude that one way of alphabetizing is always better than another way of alphabetizing.

The easiest way to decide on an alphabetizing scheme is to view the index in word-by-word order and also in letter-by-letter order. Thanks to dedicated indexing software, this is an easy task.

Here are some general guidelines for determining which alphabetic order may be most applicable to certain types of documents. If an index has a lot of names, word-by-word alphabetizing may be the best way to keep groups of similar names together. In disciplines in which many entries will be related, multipart phrases, word-by-word alphabetizing may be the best way to keep groups of these terms together. Legal and medical indexes are frequently sorted this way.

Many technical indexes, particularly those dealing with "high tech" topics, will benefit from a letter-by-letter sort. This is particularly true in fields in which the language is not standardized. Take the following terms as examples:

data base	on line
database	on-line
	online

Of course, a given index would not contain all these variant spellings. In the text, one of the spellings would be used consistently, it is hoped. But a reader might easily assume that the term is spelled differently than the usage in the text. These terms will all be sorted in the same location if a letter-by-letter sort is used. However, a word-by-word sort will place the variant spellings in quite different locations. This certainly can be an issue in a lengthy index.

Remember that advocates of word-by-word order argue that this scheme gathers like terms together. Those in the letter-by-letter camp suggest that readers are more familiar with letter-by-letter sorting because it is used frequently in dictionaries, encyclopedias, and directories.

In many indexes there will be little, if any, discernible difference between the two alphabetizing orders. But if the indexer or editor feels that an entry is out of place, it is time to consider sorting the index in a different way.

The decision to arrange subentries in a nonalphabetic sequence should be made thoughtfully. Common sense will be the best guide in this matter. If a true chronological listing is desired, do not confuse chronological order with page-number order for subentries.

An indexer can do an excellent job of isolating concepts that need to be in an index; however, if the arrangement of the index entries is not sensible, readers will have a difficult time using the index. Whatever arrangement order is selected for an index, the selection should be based on the needs of the readers.

6

SPECIAL CONCERNS IN INDEXING

THIS CHAPTER IS A collection of disparate topics that require special consideration in indexing. Even in the most straightforward text, indexers sometimes confront oddities they are not quite sure how to handle. This chapter offers some guidance to those who strive to present a systematic (and sensible) arrangement of index entries.

ABBREVIATIONS AND ACRONYMS

Quite often lengthy names of organizations and companies are referred to in the text in a shortened form. The indexer must decide whether to post information at the shortened form or at the spelled-out form of the term. The general rule is that organizations that are "widely known" by their shortened forms should be entered in the index in the shortened form (*The Chicago Manual of Style*, 13th ed. 18.87; 14th ed. 17.92). Undoubtedly we can agree on certain abbreviations and acronyms that fall into this category—such as NATO or UNICEF. Such terms can be entered in the index in their shortened forms without cross-references from the spelled-out versions of the names.

As we deal with more specialized texts, the question "widely known to whom?" arises. Then it becomes very important that the indexer have a good sense of the audience for the book. The indexer must decide not only which form of a term to use for the entry in the index but also whether cross-references are necessary. Inserting cross-references for every abbreviation or acronym used in the index can add a great deal of length to the index and possibly cause space problems. The indexer must decide how much cross-referencing is appropriate for the audience.

An introductory book about programming languages will refer to terms such as ASCII, BASIC, COBOL, and FORTRAN. All of these terms are acronyms. When the terms were introduced in the text, the author undoubtedly provided the spelled-out versions from which the acronyms were derived. However, a complete list of cross-references such as those below is not necessary. It would add length to the index out of all proportion to the other important concepts included in it.

American Standard Code for Information Interchange. *See* ASCII
Beginner's All-purpose Symbolic Instruction Code. *See* BASIC
COmmon Business-Oriented Language. *See* COBOL
FORmula TRANslation. *See* FORTRAN

The decision on whether to provide cross-references does not rest solely on whether a term is widely known. We may not be able to make that assumption about the reader of an introductory programming book, who may have never heard of FORTRAN. But FORTRAN is a term the readers of this book will learn; they will be likely to look it up as FORTRAN, not as FORmula TRANslation.

Some acronyms have enjoyed wide usage, and the original meanings of the terms have been forgotten by most readers. Such acronyms should be entered directly in the index. There is no need for cross-referencing from the spelled-out version of the term.

modem, *not* MOdulator DEModulator
laser, *not* Light Amplification by Stimulated Emission of Radiation

An index that posts information at abbreviations or acronyms may benefit by including the spelled-out version of the terms after the shortened version.

SLA (Special Libraries Association)
SLA (Symbionese Liberation Army)

This way readers can be certain that they have indeed located the term desired.

In a book that contains many shortened forms of names, the indexer's job will be made slightly easier if the author has provided the indexer with a list of these names in both shortened and spelled-out forms. Indexers not blessed with working with such an organized author can pick up the full form of a shortened name when it is first introduced. The name may not be mentioned for another 200 pages, and it is quite time-consuming to return to the text in order to locate the full version of a name.

As with any type of multiple postings, all information should be gathered in one place or else completely double-posted. The indexer must decide the exact form of the organization name entry and use it consistently. Do not split references between more than one form of the entry.

Alphabetizing of Abbreviations and Acronyms

Abbreviations and acronyms should be alphabetized in the same way as the other entries in the index, whether letter-by-letter or word-by-word. They are not usually alphabetized as if they were spelled out. An exception that many publishers allow is that the abbreviation U.S. may be alphabetized as though spelled out. This allows a term like *U.S. Bureau of Reclamation* to interfile with other U.S. entries such as *United States Coast Guard.*

UPPERCASE AND LOWERCASE LETTERS

The case of letters in an entry is generally disregarded when entries are sorted. An uppercase *A* has the same sorting value as a lowercase *a*. However, in certain odd situations entries may be the same except for case. In the 24th edition of *Stedman's Medical Dictionary* we find the following two entries in this order:

> M.u. Abbreviation for Mache unit.
> m.u. Abbreviation for mouse unit.

It would seem from this example that uppercase precedes lowercase when the entries are the same except for case. Given the widespread use of computers, such a sorting precedence would make sense (see chap. 10 for a discussion of computers and sorting). But one must decide whether uppercase or lowercase has precedence and apply the rule throughout the index when two entries are spelled the same except for case.

International Characters

In English language indexes international characters are sorted according to their English equivalents. For example, *à* sorts as *a,* *ç* sorts as *c,* and *ü* sorts as *u.*

Numbers, Symbols, and Other Nonalphanumeric Characters in Entries

Frequently nonalphabetic characters appear within index entries, as in "War of 1812." In the case of numeric terms, many scholarly publishers require that the numbers be alphabetized as though spelled out. Many style guides and even indexing standards offer little or no guidance regarding the arrangement of symbols in entries. Indexers who work with technical material will surely have entries that contain symbols as terms—for example, the "!mv command." To ensure efficient access to entries containing nonalphabetic characters, a consistent sorting procedure must be adopted for these types of entries.

Numerals in Entries

Numerals may appear at the beginning or in any other position within an entry. When an entry begins with a numeral, the filing sequence is of greater importance than entries that include numerals within the text of the entry because of the reader's need to find the main entry. There are two ways to sort numerals. One approach is to sort them as though spelled out. The second method is to arrange the numerals in ascending numeric order.

As noted above, many scholarly publishers require that numerals be alphabetized as though spelled out (*The Chicago Manual of Style,* 13th ed. 18.98). For example:

10 Downing Street (alphabetized as Ten)
2001: A Space Odyssey (alphabetized as Two thousand one)

The British Indexing Standard (BS 3700, 6.2.1.4) suggests that "in indexes where few numerals occur as entry words they may be arranged as if spelt out in words in the appropriate language." The following examples are provided by the British Standard:

5% (as if Five per cent)
800 m (as if Eight hundred meters)
1001 Nacht (as if Tausend und eine Nacht)
1001 nights (as if Thousand and one nights, A)

BS 3700 qualifies the suggestion to arrange the terms as though spelled out only when there are "few numerals" as entry words. This is sensible advice. When there are many terms beginning with numerals, the indexer should consider arranging the terms in ascending numeric order. The 14th edition of the *Chicago Manual of Style* also suggests a numeric arrangement "when there are many such entries or when the numbers are complicated" (17.102). Draft 3 of the American index standard (NISO 1993: 9.8) recommends that "in indexes where few headings begin with numerals, they may be arranged as if spelled out in words."

It is important to keep in mind that the "alphabetize-as-though-spelled-out" rule can create rather strange sorting sequences when consistently applied to entries.

Route 66 (alphabetize as Route sixty-six)
Route 33 (alphabetize as Route thirty-three)

War of 1812 (alphabetize as War of eighteen twelve)
War of 1037 (alphabetize as War of ten thirty-seven)

Sorting sequences can become even stranger when a term can be spelled in a variety of ways. The following term is the name of a CPU chip for a computer:

80486 CPU

How should this term be spelled out? There are several options:

eight oh four eight six CPU
eight zero four eight six CPU
eighty four eighty-six CPU
eighty thousand four hundred eighty-six CPU

Then what does one do about the common nomenclature? This chip is commonly referred to as the "486" (four eighty-six).

The alphabetize-as-though-spelled-out rule is fraught with problems when more than a handful of entries contain numerals. A more sensible approach is to arrange numerals in ascending numeric order and, if there are only a few of these entries, to provide either double-posted entries or cross-references at the spelled-out version of the terms.

Entries that begin with numerals and are sorted in ascending numeric order are placed either at the beginning of the index before the *A*'s or at the end of the index after the *Z*'s. The general preference is the first alternative and is the placement recommended in the NISO index standard (1933: 9.8).

When numerals are sorted in ascending numeric order, the rule applies to all numerals within an entry, regardless of their placement within the entry. It is important to note at this juncture that unsophisticated computer sorting programs will not sort numbers in correct ascending order. The following is likely to result from sorting by these programs:

> 80486 CPU
> 8088 CPU

The indexer must be prepared to remedy such incorrect arrangements.

When numbers are sorted numerically, a decimal point is treated as a decimal point, not as a period. When a comma is used as a visual aid in large numbers, it should not be sorted.

> 5 version
> 5.01 version
> 5.12 version
> 5.2 version
>
> 10 widgets
> 100 widgets
> 1,000 widgets
> 10,000 widgets

There are occasions when the indexer may choose to arrange numeric entries by size which may not follow a strictly numeric order. For example, the following list of memory chips is arranged by size:

16 Kb DRAM
64 Kb DRAM
256 Kb DRAM
1 Mb DRAM
4 Mb DRAM
64 Mb DRAM
1 Gb DRAM

This arrangement begins with the smaller unit of measurement, kilobytes, then continues with megabytes and gigabytes. Notice that within each category the entries are sorted in ascending numeric order.

Alphanumeric terms. As noted above, entries that begin with numbers are placed either at the beginning or end of the index when they are sorted in numeric order. On the face of it, the decision about where to place such entries may seem to be a layout decision. However, an order of precedence is being established; numbers either precede or follow letters. This order of precedence is of particular importance in regard to alphanumeric terms.

ANSI Z39.4 (1984, 6.4.1) points out:

Alphanumeric indexes may be sequenced with numbers preceding or following letters:

1	or	A
2		B
A		Z
B		1

The same sequence should apply throughout the index:

LA-6352	or	LA-UR-76-09
LA-UR-76-09	or	LA-6352

In both examples, the items in the left column are sorted with numbers preceding letters. The items in the right column are sorted with letters preceding numbers. As noted earlier, it is common to place entries that begin with numbers at the beginning of the index, before the *A*'s. Thus, numbers precede letters.

Roman and Arabic numerals. When numbers appear in both Arabic (1, 2, 3) and Roman (I, II, III or i, ii, iii) form, and the entries are sorted in numeric order, the Arabic and Roman numerals should be interfiled and sorted by their numeric values.

> test 2
> test III
> test 5
> test X

Numbers in chemical names. Subscript and superscript numbers that occur in chemical compound names are sorted by numeric value with numbers preceding letters. BS 1749:1985 (*Alphabetical Arrangement and the Filing Order of Numbers and Symbols*) provides the following example (4.3):

> C_3H_8
> $CaCO_3$
> cadmium
> CO
> CO_2
> CS_2

However, when a number forms the prefix to a chemical name, the number is at first ignored.

> cadmium
> 4-chlorophenol
> CO
> CO_2

If there are two chemical compound names that are identical except for the numeric prefix, the prefix is taken into consideration after the alphabetic portion of the term is sorted. For example:

> 3-chlorophenol
> 4-chlorophenol

(See the discussion below for information on Greek letters and other symbols as prefixes in chemical names.)

Symbols in Entries

What is meant here by a symbol? On a very basic level, in this discussion, a "symbol" shall mean anything that is not a letter or number. Symbols come in such a variety of forms that dealing with every possible symbol would be impossible. Symbols will be discussed in terms of their function or use: as punctuation, as representations, as literals.

Symbols as punctuation. Indexes frequently contain symbols that are used as punctuation within an entry. For example, the comma in *Smith, Mary* is used as punctuation. Commas are also used to separate a main heading from a subentry; for example, *horses, nutritional requirements of.* As we saw in the previous chapter, the word-by-word and letter-by-letter sorting methods guide the sorting of the space character, the hyphen, and the diagonal slash. All other punctuation marks are ignored in the alphabetization of entries. Such marks include the following:

apostrophe	Harry's Diner
colon	*The Geography of Strabo: Books I–II*
comma	Woolf, Virginia
double quotation	"Crisis at Noon"
exclamation point	On! Corporation
semicolon	books. *See also* media; publishing

Symbols as representations. Symbols are often used to represent words; the ampersand (&) is a good example. Frequently such symbols are arranged in the index as though spelled out:

business & management certificate programs
business law

In this example the ampersand is sorted as if spelled "and."

In medical or chemistry indexing it is common to encounter terms that begin with Greek letters, such as alpha (α) or beta (β). Sometimes such prefixes are not sorted, but the keyword following the prefix is sorted. Other times the prefix is sorted as though spelled out as the name of the letter. If the prefix is sorted in this way, the following would result:

α-dog
β-cat

The arrangement of medical and chemical terms is not a straight-forward matter. Often the same term is spelled in different ways by different authors. While it is the indexer's job to provide the most direct access to a term through sensible arrangement of the index, that task can become quite complex in medical texts. Furthermore, terminology can change over time.

For example, α-fetoprotein frequently used to be indexed in the *F*'s as "fetoprotein." Nowadays this protein is widely known by its abbreviation, AFP. Today's indexers, as a result, generally file the term in the *A*'s, as if spelled alpha-fetoprotein.

A common rule is to produce an entry in the index just as it is provided in the text. If the Greek letter is used in the text, the Greek letter is used in the index. The interpretation of the Greek letter is of little consequence if the Greek letter is ignored and the sorting begins with the keyword that follows. However, the indexer must be very careful when interpreting the meaning of such symbols. For example:

μ (micro)
μ (micron)
μ (mu, the twelfth letter of the Greek alphabet)
μ (mean daily motion in astronomy)

The indexer must know that μg will sort as "microgram," whereas μ circuit will sort as "mu circuit." It is beyond the scope of this book to explore the nuances of the arrangement of entries in medical, chemistry, or engineering books. These specialized disciplines have various conventions that the index must follow. Companies that publish material in these disciplines will have indexing style guides that resolve some questions regarding the sorting of entries that contain symbols. There are also subject-area dictionaries that may help the indexer understand the nomenclature. But all too often the indexer will be confronted with terms that appear in neither the publisher's style guides nor the special dictionaries. This is when the experienced indexer's judgment is so crucial.

In many texts names are followed by the trademark, service mark, or registered mark symbol.

Widgets To Go ®

Generally such terms are entered in the index without the symbol. If an editor wishes to have the symbols present in the index, a generic code will have to be used to represent the symbol, because there is no standard way to represent these symbols. Generic coding is discussed in chapter 8.

Symbols as literals. In many texts, especially in computer documentation, symbols are intended to be used quite literally. As noted above, we often treat commas, hyphens, or diagonals as punctuation. But when these symbols are used in a literal sense, we must apply a standardized sorting sequence to them. For example, let's say we have the following entries in a technical index:

mv command
-p parameter
/p parameter

The hyphen and the diagonal above are characters that the user would actually type as part of the command; they are used literally. The indexer must decide which comes first, the hyphen or the diagonal. Luckily we can to turn for guidance to a standard that assigns a decimal code value to 128 characters. The decimal code value is "understood" by a great many computers, enabling the exchange of information among those computers. For our purposes, the decimal codes provide an ordering sequence; they start at 000 and end at 127. This standard is called the American Standard Code for Information Interchange, better known as ASCII (pronounced "as-key").

Following is a partial ASCII table that includes the characters we would be most likely to encounter when indexing computer documentation. In appendix B there is a complete ASCII table.

Decimal Code	Character
032	(space character)
033	!
034	"
035	#
036	$
037	%
038	&
039	' (apostrophe)
040	(
041	)
042	*
043	+
044	, (comma)
045	- (hyphen)
046	. (period, decimal point)
047	/
058	:
059	;
060	<
061	=
062	>
063	?
064	@
091	[
092	\
093	]
094	^
095	_ (underscore)
096	` (grave accent)
123	{
124	| (vertical bar, logical OR)
125	}
126	~ (tilde)

If you refer back to the example of the "mv command," you will see that the subentries appear in the correct order. The hyphen, used in the "-p parameter" subentry, has an ASCII value of 045 while the diagonal, used in the "/p parameter" subentry, has an ASCII value of 047.

Use of the ASCII table is appropriate for many types of computer manuals. But if the text is written for the IBM mainframe environment, the EBCDIC table must be used instead. EBCDIC is an acronym for Extended Binary Coded Decimal Interchange Code. In EBCDIC the sorting order for the various symbols is quite different.

When an entry begins with a symbol as a literal character, these entries should be placed at the beginning of the index, preceding any entries that begin with numbers or letters. When there are only a few symbols as literal characters, the indexer may wish to double-post the entry—as a symbol and also in the spelled-out version:

> * (asterisk), as a wildcard character, 56
> ? (question mark), as a wildcard character, 57
> asterisk (*), as a wildcard character, 56
> question mark (?), as a wildcard character, 57

When these symbols appear within an entry, the sort order precedence is the same as when they appear at the beginning of an entry. That is, symbols precede numbers, which precede letters:

> Control-!, 67
> Control-", 12
> Control-*, 35
> Control-1, 89
> Control-9, 45
> Control-A, 76
> Control-C, 55

In technical documentation different entries may be preceded by the same symbol. For example, in some programs all commands are preceded with a "control" character, as in ^B or ^C. When there will be many entries of this type in the index, the indexer may decide to ignore the special character when sorting the entry. This way an entry such as ^B *command* would appear in the *B*'s and ^C *command* in the *C*'s. Should the indexer decide to ignore the special character when sorting entries, an introductory note at the beginning of the index should explain the sorting method.

It is commonplace that indexers working with technical material must cope with several types of symbols in entries. Often the symbols are ignored and the entries are sorted in a letter-by-letter sequence. This type of arrangement may not require an explanatory note since the interfiling of entries with and without symbols is immediately obvious to the index users. The 1992 edition of the *Microsoft Windows Resource Kit for Operating System Version 3.1* contains an index where entries often begin with or contain various symbols. In the following example, note how the indexer has interfiled these types of entries:

Default
_DEFAULT.PIF
Deleting files
. . .
DLL (dynamic-link library)
.DLL filename extension
. . .
Network Assistant
Networks and Windows 3.1
[Network] section
[Network_Specific] section
[Network_Version] section
[New.groups] section
NewSpace
Nonmaskable interrupts (NMI)

Readers scanning this index will quickly ascertain the arrangement used by the indexer.

Other Nonalphanumeric Characters in Entries

Many disciplines use special symbols and signs that have particular meaning within the discipline. In astronomy we find symbols for the sun, moon, and planets. There are special symbols that represent the signs of the zodiac, and aspects and nodes of stellar objects. While these special characters may appear in the index, they are unlikely to appear as the first character in an entry. They probably would appear in parentheses after their name in the index. The key here is that they all have names. The name would be used as the alphabetizing term in the index. For more information about the indexing of stellar object names, see the *Deep-Sky Name Index 2000.0* by Hugh Maddocks. As with registered marks, service marks, and trademarks, special symbols of this type will need a generic code if they are going in the index (see the discussion of generic coding in chap. 8).

The graphical user interface (GUI) that has become so prevalent in computer software poses special problems for the indexer of GUI documentation. Software with a graphical interface is characterized by the presence of icons that represent particular functions or tasks.

Before discussing icons, we should note a rather important characteristic of computer documentation in particular and technical documentation in general. A computer software manual, for instance, is part of a larger package that includes the program itself. In this sense the manual does not exist in and of itself; rather, it exists in relation to the software product. Many software manuals are intended to be used for reference purposes. Instead of reading them from front to back, readers turn to the manuals for information about particular aspects of the program. The software manual and its index attempt to provide a path from the program, or what is seen on a monitor, to specific information in the text.

When programs were character based rather than graphically oriented, many functions had a name that appeared on the monitor. The technical writer would use that name in the documentation, and the indexer would include the name in the index. It was quite simple; for example, the *Edit Fields command* would appear in the index in the *E*'s.

Today, however, we find that GUI-based software often presents users with images on their monitors that have no names. Some of these images, or icons as they are called, suggest their own names. But the names of many of the icons are impossible to figure out by just looking at them. The technical writer will undoubtedly write about how to use the icon and will use the icon name in the text. The challenge for the indexer is to provide access to the discussion about the particular icon when the readers may have no idea what the icon is called.

While some have suggested that the icons appear as small graphic representations in the text of the index, this still does not solve the problem of how to provide access to them. If the icon appeared immediately after its name, for example, we still would have the problem of readers not necessarily knowing its name. If the icons appeared at the beginning of the index, how would we order them? If there are only a few icons, the order may not make much difference since the short list can be easily scanned. But some of the more complex programs have many, many icons. It would not be easy to scan such a long list.

One solution used by some software publishers is to provide an appendix that includes all the program's icons along with their names. Once the users know the name of the icon, they can look up information about the icon in the index. Another solution that is far more efficient is to provide a way for users to get the name of the icon while online.

The bottom line is that readers need to know the icon name. The index in a printed book is text oriented. Users of indexes look up words. Technical writers and technical indexers use words. Users of GUI-type software need to be provided with a way to access the words used by the writers and indexers.

MULTIAUTHORED WORKS

Multiauthored works come in a variety of forms. From an indexing perspective, the easiest type of multiauthored book to work with is one on which the authors have collaborated closely with an editor to help make the text a seamless, one-voice discussion. Working with a book of this type is similar to working with a single-authored text.

Far more indexing challenges are posed by books that contain submissions by multiple authors where content editing has not been performed on the book as a whole but, instead, the individual submissions have been edited for internal consistency. Such books are fairly common in specialized subject areas. Often collections of papers are solicited on a specific topic and published as graduate-level textbooks. Another common example is the publication of proceedings from a conference as a collection of papers delivered at the conference.

The primary problem for the indexer with this type of multiauthored publication is vocabulary control. Even when the collection of writings is about a narrow subject, multiple authors will use a variety of terms in writing about the same topic. The indexer will need to identify synonyms carefully and gather related information together under one term. Without careful vocabulary control, information in the index will be scattered.

As an example, different authors may refer to a hard disk drive in a computer in different ways. The indexer must decide on a term of choice, post all relevant information at that term, and cross-reference to the preferred term from the other terms. The following example illustrates scattered information:

    hard disk drives, 34–37
    rigid disk drives, 125
    Winchester drives, 223

A reader looking up *hard disk drives* would miss the information on pages 125 and 223. A better method would be for the indexer to consolidate the entries in the following way:

> hard disk drives, 34–37, 125, 223
> rigid disk drives. *See* hard disk drives
> Winchester drives. *See* hard disk drives

Often the content of multiauthored works is dense. Given the need for vocabulary control, the indexer should refrain from extensive double-posting of information during the initial indexing work, postponing double-posting until later, during the editing stage. When the indexer anticipates a vocabulary control problem, it is best to focus on gathering together related information rather than running the risk of scattering information. Making decisions about double-posting will be far easier after related information has been gathered together and one can assess the merits of double-posting by actually looking at what has emerged from the text after it has been indexed.

Collections of papers are frequently highly technical. Such collections often represent the "cutting-edge," or most current work, in a field. New theories and new terminology will often be introduced. Ideally the indexer will be extremely fluent in the language of the discipline and able to cope effectively with such technical material.

Some editors offer to send the indexer author-highlighted page proofs. Authors highlight the terms in their papers that they think should go in the index. Earlier in the book there was discussion of author highlights in general, with a single author highlighting terms in the text. Multiple-author highlights are generally not too helpful because of the absence of vocabulary control. Some authors will be far too detailed, while others will highlight only a few terms, not wishing to be involved in the process at all!

These days many conference proceedings are available at the time of the conference. Papers are submitted in camera-ready form months in advance of the conference dates. While it is still rare for such proceedings to contain an index, more and more proceedings are appearing with alphabetical subject listings in the back. Authors are asked to submit index terms along with their papers; then these terms are collated and matched with the appropriate page numbers.

This type of author-selected topic index is probably better than nothing and certainly provides ample evidence of the need for proper subject indexing in multiauthored works.

MULTIVOLUME WORKS

A range of books may appear in multivolume editions: biographies, histories, technical manuals, and so on. Sometimes the volumes are published one at a time, with several years in between; other series are released all at once. It is common for individual volumes to be indexed individually. Then a cumulative index, or master index, is issued for the entire series after all volumes have been published.

The indexing of multivolume works can be manageable (at best) or a dreadful nightmare (at worst). The worst-case scenario is the collection that has missed every production deadline; instead of taking five years to publish, it has taken fifteen years. Each volume was indexed by a different person. None of the indexers were given much guidance regarding term selection and vocabulary control. And now it's time to produce a cumulative index to the series. The editor in charge of the cumulative index believes that the individual volume indexes can be merged and gently massaged by an index editor in a short time. The resulting cumulative index is a hodgepodge of scattered information with cross-references that go in seemingly endless loops.

Diane Ullius, formerly copy chief at Time-Life Books, managed the production of many of the Time-Life Books series. Each series generally averaged twenty volumes. The average length of each volume was approximately 160 pages, or around 60,000 words. During the production life of the series, a volume was produced every two months. With few exceptions, an index was produced for each volume and some of the series did have a cumulative index which typically appeared about two months after the publication of the final volume.

Ullius points out that the ideal arrangement was to contract with a single indexer for an entire series.

> An individual indexer is more likely to maintain consistent terminology and a consistent conceptual approach to the index. The problems we discovered when mul-

tiple indexers worked on a series were more than differences in term selection. There were also significant
differences in the depth of indexing and the conceptual
design of the indexes.

Not all Time-Life series have a cumulative index for the entire
series. Ullius feels that the amount of topical overlap between the
volumes is the key determinant of the need for a cumulative index.
Volumes that are arranged in discrete topical or chronological units
may not benefit from the production of a cumulative index.

Once the decision to produce a cumulative index has been made,
Ullius points out,

> it's not just a matter of merging the individual volume
> indexes. We put as much time and effort into a 160-page
> index as we put into a 160-page narrative book. Work on
> the cumulative index begins long before the last volume
> in the series has been published. It is extremely im-
> portant to budget an adequate amount of time for editing
> the cumulative index. Even if a single indexer has pro-
> duced all the individual indexes, there will still be term
> consistency problems that must be resolved during the
> editing phase. Ideally, the indexer will be heavily in-
> volved with the preparation of the cumulative index.
> However, even with the best of planning it's still a chal-
> lenge.

Three tenets to keep in mind when dealing with multivolume
indexes are (1) planning for indexing is necessary, (2) your plans
will be incomplete, and (3) every step will take longer than anticipated.

Multivolume works, even when written by one author, pose some
of the same vocabulary control problems that we find in multiauthored works. The maintenance of term consistency is crucial in
multivolume works. It is important to identify any type of terminology that can be standardized. For example, in a ten-volume series
about plants, there should be a uniform set of guidelines about how
to post plant names.

When a large series of volumes is being indexed by a team of indexers, the team will work best with a formalized vocabulary. Pre-
indexing activities may include the development of a thesaurus for

indexing. The use of a classified set of terms may result in more consistent indexing. For more information about thesaurus design see NISO Z39.19, *Guidelines for the Construction, Format and Management of Monolingual Thesauri.*

The indexing team needs a leader—one person the indexers can turn to for guidance and resolution of indexing problems. Ideally, the index project manager/editor will be involved in the crucial planning stages as well. It is folly to believe that eight competent indexers working independently without supervision will produce eight indexes that will cumulate flawlessly.

Even if a cumulative index for a series is not being produced, the individual-volume indexes need to be as consistent with each other as possible, because readers will use indexes from various volumes. Readers should be able to look up the same topic in the same way in each index. Readers will be frustrated if they must rethink how a term might be posted as they move from one index to another.

Reference locator format for cumulative indexes. Often the reference locator format for cumulative indexes is not as straightforward as the format for a single-volume index. If each volume in a series begins pagination anew, the volume number and page number for each entry will need to be identified. Each volume is likely to be numbered, with the number visible on the spine of the book. Whatever numbering system is used by the publisher to identify the volume should also be used in the cumulative index. If a publisher has used Roman numerals for the volume numbers, Roman numerals should be used in the cumulative index. A reference for page 35 of volume II and page 78 of volume V may look like the following:

> term, II:35; V:78
> term, *II*:35; *V*:78
> term, (II)35; (V)78
> term, *II* 35; *V* 78

The design of the reference locator format should be kept as simple as possible. Cumulative indexes tend to be dense and lengthy. A simple locator format that provides readers with the necessary information should not add significantly to the density of the index text.

When planning the locator format, it is important to consider how continuous discussions in the form of page ranges will be handled. Will it be necessary to repeat the volume number?

term, II-35 to II-39

Or can the locator be designed in such a way that the volume number is not repeated? The latter alternative will save space.

term, II:35–39

In the case of multiple references from the same volume, will the volume number be repeated?

term, II:35–39, II:68, II:235

Ideally, the volume number should not be repeated, as it is in the example above. This format takes up a lot of space and will surely create more turnover lines. However, we must also assume that there will be entries with not only multiple references from the same volume but also multiple references from multiple volumes. Readers need to be able to easily distinguish references from various volumes without becoming confused. Repeating the volume numbers with each locator is perhaps the most accurate approach. But careful design of the locator can provide accurate results while producing an easily read line of text:

term, *II:*35–39, 68, 235; *V:*78, 123; *VIII:*78–85, 97
term, *II* 35–39, 68, 235; *V* 78, 123; *VIII* 78–85, 97

Notice that in the examples above, commas are used to separate references from the same volume while semicolons are used to separate references from different volumes. If bold or italic typefaces are used in the text of the index itself, one should be careful about using such typefaces in the reference locators. Index pages that are dense and cluttered with various typographical elements are difficult to use.

Are cumulative indexes necessary for all multi-volume works? Just because a group of books form a series it does not necessarily follow that a cumulative index for the entire series will be useful or worth the time and expense of producing. When the individual components of a series stand on their own, quite independent of other titles in the series, a cumulative index is probably not necessary. Let's take the example of a nature series that includes titles such as *Rocks, Mammals, Plants,* and *Climate.* Readers interested in locating information about hurricanes will turn to the index in the *Climate* book. Likewise, readers interested in bears will probably go immediately to the *Mammals* book. Such readers are unlikely to need the cumulative index to find the proper volume. Assuming that each volume has its own index, most readers will find the use of a cumulative index a cumbersome extra step.

On the other hand, when the individual books in a series are closely interrelated, a cumulative index to the series may prove extremely useful. A five-volume collection of a writer's diary entries would be enhanced by a cumulative index to all five volumes. Undoubtedly there will be people and places that are referred to in all five volumes. A cumulative index will save readers time by gathering together all these related references. Without a cumulative index, readers will have to look up particular entries in five separate indexes.

MULTIPLE INDEXES

Most books are published with a single index that contains all references in one index. The primary benefit of a single index is that readers need look in only one index for information. In some situations, though, the readers' needs may be better served by multiple indexes. In legal works, for instance, the subject index is frequently preceded by a table of cases.

Multiple indexes can be useful with discrete types of entries that can stand alone in their own index. Quite often a secondary index is a specialized subset of the general subject index. The different indexes are designed for different types of users, with one group having more specialized subject knowledge than the other group.

A subject index and a command index might be quite appropriate for a computer software manual. The subject index contains entries for the "plain English" version of the commands. The command index contains entries for the commands themselves. For example, the subject index may have an entry for "saving a file" while the command index may cite the same information as "^KD (save a file)" and "Alt-F7 (save a file)."

Entries for plant names in a gardening book may appear in their vernacular form in the subject index while a separate botanical name index cites the formal names.

Subject Index	Botanical Name Index
English ivy	*Hedera helix*
redwood	*Sequoia sempervirens*
scrub oak	*Quercus dumosa*

It is sometimes useful to put names of people in a separate index. When a book has references to many names, a separate name index can help make a subject index easier to use because it is not cluttered with names. In the same vein, a book that contains many references to authors and titles of works may benefit from the inclusion of a separate index of authors and titles cited.

The decision to provide multiple indexes should not be made lightly. As Booth (1988: 17) points out, "If it is thought that the users are not likely to anticipate or even recognize the difference between the kinds of entries, then all entries are put into a single sequence—perhaps using typographical distinctions to indicate the differences (italic for botanical names, for example)."

If there is more than one index, each index should be titled in a clear manner so as to distinguish it from the other index. It is good practice to reference the other index in the introductory note: "Following the Subject Index is a Command Index." And "Preceding the Command Index is a general Subject Index."

The decision to provide multiple indexes is ideally made before indexing begins. The indexer will need to maintain multiple sets of index entries. While this is not too difficult to do, it is best done right from the start.

Another matter to keep in mind in regard to multiple indexes is that they are more difficult to revise in the future than are single indexes. If a book and its index will definitely be revised in the future, it is best to approach multiple indexes for this type of text with some caution. During the index revision process, revising a single group of index entries will be much easier than revising multiple groups of entries.

Translations

As the publishing industry becomes much more global, many more books will be translated from one language to another. There will arise the matter of what to do with the index. There are two options: translate the original index, or index the translation.

Because a properly written index is so intimately tied to the language of the audience, the most viable solution would seem to be to reindex the translated text. A simpleminded, word-by-word translation of the index could easily result in a loss of the nuances of the index. For example, the double-posting of synonymous terms that make sense to an American audience may make no sense to a German audience. An index that anticipated the vocabulary needs of an American audience may appear quite chauvinistic to a French audience if translated verbatim.

Another argument in favor of indexing the translation is that the process will probably take no more time than translating an existing index and changing the page numbers to match the new text. A more thorough discussion of indexes in translated books can be found in "Myths about Indexing," a paper presented by AnnMarie Mitchell at the Annual Conference of the American Translators Association. There are far more indexers with multilanguage skills than there are translators with indexing skills. Both the American Society of Indexers and the (British) Society of Indexers maintain listings of indexers with language skills.

7

NAMES, NAMES, NAMES

AT FIRST GLANCE names in a text might seem to be easily handled. The first time I was asked to produce a separate name index for a book, I thought it would be a simple task. The book, which was about the Italian section of San Francisco, contained many Italian names, with amazing combinations of vowels. The task proved to be quite tedious. There were the usual typos, making it difficult to discern who was who. Many of the women mentioned in the text were married, and therefore their names had changed. Various devices had to be used to distinguish two people with the same name. This first experience with a name index made me suspicious of future requests from editors to "throw together a simple name index."

One of the problems with names is that they often change. This is true not only of personal names but also of organization names and geographic names. The rule of thumb regarding names is to post the entries in a way that readers are most likely to look up. Keep this important rule in mind as we discuss the nuances of personal names, geographic names, and organization names.

The American Library Association's *Anglo-American Cataloging Rules* (2d ed.) has been used as a primary reference source for personal names. Particular references to this tome will be cited as follows: (AACR2 section number). When appropriate, more specialized reference sources will be mentioned. One of the most comprehensive sources of reference information is K. G. B. Bakewell's *Information Sources and Reference Tools,* particularly chapter 3, "Reference Tools for the Indexer."

PERSONAL NAMES

Many Western names are composed of at least two elements: a forename (first name) and a surname (last name). Such names are inverted in the index so that the surname is the element that is first alphabetized. Thus, "Virginia Woolf" is entered in the index as "Woolf, Virginia."

The way names are presented in the text will often determine how they are presented in the index. If an author discusses "John F. Kennedy," the name should be indexed as "Kennedy, John F.," not as "Kennedy, John Fitzgerald."

It is not uncommon in texts or scholarly works to find a name given only as a surname. When only a surname is given, it may be that the individual is well enough known within the context of the book that no forename need also be given. For example, we often see references to Freud or Columbus or, in a book about indexing, to Knight. In situations like this, when the author has provided only a surname, the indexer must add the forename or initials to the surname when posting the entry. It is very bad form to have a surname standing alone as an entry. The examples above would be posted as:

> Columbus, Christopher
> Freud, Sigmund
> Knight, G. Norman

Indexers who expect to encounter personal names in their work will benefit from having reference sources at hand. Library catalogers who must decide upon the form of names for catalog entries are apt to look up how the name is handled in the *Encyclopedia Britannica* (15th ed.), *Academic American Encyclopedia,* and *The Encyclopedia Americana.* If the name is entered the same way in all three of these sources, then that is the form used. If the form varies in these sources, the form in the *Encyclopedia Britannica* generally takes precedence.

For general purposes another reference choice is *Webster's New Biographical Dictionary.* There are also many specialized references for different fields, such as the *Who's Who* series, the *New Catholic Encyclopedia, The Encyclopaedia Judaica,* and *The Oxford Classical Dictionary,* to name a few.

In a book that contains many references to individuals, the indexer may be able to find in the bibliography the full names of the people mentioned in the text of the book by their surnames only. For this reason, indexers should always request a copy of the bibliography, even though the actual contents of the bibliography are not being indexed. Make it clear to the editor that you need the bibliography for reference. It need not be typeset; manuscript copy is better than nothing!

There is some debate regarding how far the indexer should go to provide a complete, full citation for a name. Let the treatment of the name in the text and common sense be your guide. In the case of Columbus, if the author has made reference to the explorer's Spanish name, Cristobal Colon, or the Genoese name, Cristoforo Colombo, the indexer should provide cross-references.

> Colon, Cristobal. *See* Columbus, Christopher
> . . .
> Columbo, Cristoforo. *See* Columbus, Christopher

But if the author has made no reference to Columbus's other names, there is no need for the indexer to insert these lesser-known variations in the index.

Pseudonyms. Often pseudonyms are pen names used by authors or stage names used by actors. Or, as Knight points out, a pseudonym might be used "to court obscurity after disgrace, as Oscar Wilde ended his days in Paris under the name of Sebastian Melmoth."

Whatever the reason for the use of a pseudonym, if the text does not make mention of the real name, the indexer need not provide a reference to it. For instance, a book about American authors that discusses Mark Twain with no mention of his given name, Samuel Clemens, needs only an entry for "Twain, Mark."

If the text provides both the real name and the pseudonym, both variations must be in the index. Whichever form is predominantly used in the text is the form in which the entries should be posted. A discussion of George Orwell that includes an initial reference to the writer's real name would be handled in this way:

> Blair, Eric Arthur. *See* Orwell, George

All the index entries for George Orwell would be gathered together under "Orwell, George."

Likewise, if most of the discussion in the text refers to a real name, the pseudonym would provide a cross-reference.

Cross, Amanda. *See* Heilbrun, Carolyn G.

It may be helpful in some indexes to add the pseudonym in parentheses after the real name. Such a descriptor may assure readers that they have indeed located the proper reference.

Heilbrun, Carolyn G. (pseudonym: Amanda Cross)

The addition of such descriptors, however, should be left to the discretion of the indexer. An entry for as well known a writer as Samuel Clemens would not necessarily need such a descriptor. As with any entry, name entries are best kept as short as possible without sacrificing clarity.

Names that change. Personal names can change for a variety of reasons. An individual entering a religious order may replace a secular name with a religious name: a woman named Mary Jackson, say, becomes Sister Anthony. Some individuals may legally change their names: Delbert Hodgepuss, say, petitions the court to change his name to Mack Turner. Many immigrants to the United States changed their names so that they would sound less "foreign": Bohimer Veverka changes his name to Bruce Vevera, for example. By far the most common instance of name changing in patriarchal societies occurs when a woman marries and takes on her husband's surname.

In any situation where a name has changed, the indexer must decide whether it is necessary to provide a cross-reference from an earlier name to the name currently used. The text itself often provides guidance in this matter. If the author has referred to a name that is not currently used, then the indexer must provide a cross-reference.

Bouvier, Jacqueline. *See* Onassis, Jacqueline
. . .
Kennedy, Jacqueline. *See* Onassis, Jacqueline

The matter of cross-referencing is very much determined by the text. The index should not be a vehicle for the indexer to demonstrate prowess in tracking down the genealogical roots of every individual mentioned in a text. Nor should the index attempt to compensate for less than thorough research by the author. On the other hand, through the use of simple devices, the indexer can add depth to an entry. In historical or genealogical works indexers may cross-reference from a woman's maiden name to her married name and include the maiden name in parentheses:

> Agee, Victoria (Powers)
> . . .
> Powers, Victoria. *See* Agee, Victoria

Compound names. Names that are composed of three or more name elements, sometimes with the last two joined by a hyphen, are compound names. Do note that a distinction is made between a compound surname and a surname that includes articles or prepositions. Ascertaining which element to use for alphabetizing can be difficult.

If there is a preferred or commonly known form of a compound name, it should be alphabetized under the preferred element. For example, the paternal surname for David Lloyd George is "George." However, he is known as "Lloyd George" and is entered in the index in that manner:

> Lloyd George, David

Knight's discussion (p. 69) of the alphabetizing of Sir Winston Spencer Churchill is another example of indexing under a preferred form. The name was originally presented as "Spencer-Churchill." But most readers, and indeed Sir Winston himself, would expect and prefer references at "Churchill" instead.

Again, hints from the text can guide the indexer. If the element preceding the last surname element is usually presented as an initial, this is an indication that the shortened element should not be used for alphabetizing. If Mary Daley Stanton is commonly referred to as Mary D. Stanton, then Stanton is the element used for indexing.

Familiarity with the subject matter is of course a great asset. Someone indexing material that is not their specialty may easily misinterpret a reference to the English composer Vaughan Williams. Instead of entering the name as "Vaughan Williams, Ralph," the indexer may post it in the *W*'s, which would be incorrect. Referring to a biographical dictionary would be wise in situations like this. When there is doubt about which element to alphabetize first, the indexer should pay careful attention to the way the author has handled the name. Of course, the name may not be used again until much later in the book. However, the careful indexer will maintain a query list so that sorting problems such as these can be resolved. As a last resort, the book editor can be consulted. But indexers should keep in mind that it is their job to solve such problems and only particularly troublesome name problems should be referred back to the book editor.

When a compound surname is hyphenated, the name is alphabetized under the first element:

> Dalton-Smith, George
> Hills-Fenworth, Alice

When a name appears in compound form without hyphenation, the indexing task becomes more difficult. The indexer must then decide how to enter the name in the index. Again, the first place to turn for guidance is the text itself. Let's say that Thomas Parsons Brinkerhoff is formally introduced using the complete name and later is referred to as Parsons Brinkerhoff. The indexer would pick up this clue from the text and enter the name in the index as

> Parsons Brinkerhoff, Thomas

Unfortunately, the indexer is not always provided with such guidance in the text. The next recourse for the indexer is to check the reference sources mentioned earlier in this chapter. If the name cannot be located in reference sources, and the person's language is English or one of the Scandinavian languages, AACR2 (22.5C6) recommends entry under the last part of the name:

> Davenport, Susan Grissom
> Eklund, James Swann

Married women's names sometimes take the form of compound surnames composed of a maiden name and a husband's surname. The husband's surname is the element generally recommended for entry. For example,

Frequently it is assumed that the maiden name precedes the husband's surname in an English married woman's name, and indeed, this is often the case. But the arrangement of a married woman's compound surname is not always predicated on the "maiden name first, husband's surname last" rule. These days the names may be arranged on the basis of aesthetics, on which arrangement sounds better or looks better. Let's say that Susan Smith marries Harry Jackson; she decides to be called Susan Jackson Smith because to her that arrangement sounds better. The indexer who may know nothing of the marriage can safely enter the name in the index as *Smith, Susan Jackson.* The indexer can dispense with the patriarchal rule regarding husband's surname first and instead follow the guidance in AACR2 22.5C6 and enter the name under the final element.

Note that if the compound surname is Czech, French, Hungarian, Italian, or Spanish, AACR2 (22.5C5) recommends that the first element of the compound be used as the entry element.

Names with "Saint." Many publishers' style guides recommend that personal names in the form of a saint's name be alphabetized as if the "St." were spelled out as "Saint." However, the names retain their original spelling, whether Saint or St. This rule results in alphabetized lists such as

> St. Albans, Marie
> St. George, Francis
> Saint Thomas, Claire

Sorting abbreviated "St." names as if they are spelled out is yet another quirk that has become common practice. Anytime an alphabetic list is not sorted alphabetically we must take pause. We must consider the users' needs. Is it likely that index users intuitively know that names with *St.* will not be sorted as they are spelled? It should be noted that the 14th edition of *The Chicago Manual of Style* recommends that "such names are preferably alphabetized letter-by-letter as they appear" (17.107). Additionally, the British standard explicitly recommends that these names be alphabetized as they are given, not as if spelled out in full form (BS 3700:1988, 6.2.1.5). The three names above, when alphabetized as they are given, would appear as

> Saint Thomas, Claire
> St. Albans, Marie
> St. George, Francis

Christian saints. The names of Christian saints are not alphabetized in the *S*'s with the word "Saint" preceding their name. Instead, they are entered under one of the other elements of the name. The *New Catholic Encyclopedia* is a good reference for the form of name entries for saints and popes.

> Francis of Assisi, Saint
> Gonzaga, Luigi, Saint
> Teresa of Avila, Saint

Names with Mac, Mc, or M'. As with names with "Saint," some publishers' style guides recommend that abbreviated forms of "Mac," that is, "Mc" and "M'," be alphabetized as if spelled out as "Mac." Such a recommendation results in lists such as

> McBain, Sally
> McDougal, Jeremy
> Macintosh, George

We have here another situation in which entries are arranged out of alphabetic order. The 14th edition of *The Chicago Manual of Style* recommends that "personal names beginning with *Mac, Mc,* or *M'* are preferably alphabetized letter-by-letter as they appear" (17.109). The British standard, on the other hand, recommends that "in names, Mac and its contractions should be filed as given unless the nature, purpose or tradition of a list requires arrangement as if the contractions were spelt in full" (6.2.1.5). Knight rightly points out that "it should be noted that with African names the prefix M' is not a contraction for Mac. Thus the township of M'Baiki would have to be listed between, say, Mazgirt (Turkey) and Mbala" (p. 121).

In regard to the abbreviated forms of "Mac" and "Saint," the primary reason one might wish to sort these names as if they are spelled out is to gather these similar names together in one place. Most people, though, expect an index to be arranged in alphabetical order. Thus, names that are not arranged in alphabetic order can be confusing. Certainly, forms of names with "Mac" and "Saint" are not the only names that sound alike but are spelled differently. It is not unreasonable to ask how far we might go with this type of alphabetizing quirk. Should all names that sound like "Harrison" be placed in the same location in the index, including Harison, Harrisson, and Harisson?

Pat Booth and Mary Piggott, authors of the Society of Indexers Training Unit 2, *Choice and Form of Entries* (sec. 4.1.1.1, p. 27), offer a sensible solution.

> Where names that sound alike may be spelled differently, a reference from one form to the other will be necessary. If the name is of a single person or family, a *see* reference should be made, as Ussher *see* Usher. If more than one family's name appears in the index and alternative spellings could be overlooked, *see also* references should be made between the alternatives

> fford *see also* Ford
> Ford *see also* fford
> Philips *see also* Phillips
> Phillips *see also* Philips

The Booth and Piggott recommendation ensures that the index will remain in alphabetic order and that readers will be guided to alternative spellings of homophonous names.

Titles in names. Titles preceding names come in a variety of forms: Mr. John Smith, Dr. Lisa Jones, Msgr. Joseph Reilly, Lady Jane Maddocks, and Capt. Marcia Miller, to coin a few. While there is disagreement about whether to retain a title in the index, one general rule can be discerned. If two entries are identical, a title can be used effectively to distinguish between the two.

> Smith, John
> Smith, John (Capt.)

Some indexers place the title before the forename, as in "Smith, Capt. John." However, the title is not used as a secondary sort field.

The entry for Capt. Smith would still be adjacent to the other John Smith entry.

Some style guides require that clerical titles be retained in the index while others suggest that clerical titles be dropped. One problem with many titles, including clerical titles, is that they can indeed change during the course of discussion. For example, when Joseph Reilly is introduced on page 35, he may be a monsignor. But by the time we reach page 278, Joseph Reilly may be an archbishop. If there is more than one Joseph Reilly in the index, then it will be necessary to distinguish one from the other. In a case like this, the highest ranking title should be used:

> Reilly, Joseph (Archbishop of Kensington)

If there is only one Joseph Reilly in the index, the title may be safely dropped without grave consequences.

Titles of nobility present indeed a tangled web for indexers living in societies lacking a formal tradition of peerage. Indexers who must deal with titles of nobility should consult appropriate reference sources. Section 22.12 in AACR2 provides a simple overview of titles of nobility. In regard to British titles, the Society of Indexers Training Unit 2 by Booth and Piggott provides useful examples that may meet the needs of many indexers. These authors also recommend the following references: the current edition of *Who's Who* (London: Black); Valentine Heywood's *British Titles: The Use and Misuse of the Titles of Peers and Commoners; with Some Historical Notes* (London: Black, 1951).

Titles of nobility are not restricted to British names. Indexers working with names of nobility from other countries should consult appropriate references for the particular country.

Though British titles of rank are complex, a simple overview, drawn from Booth and Piggott, can offer guidance. Titles are often retained in the index entry; however, the placement of the title within the entry can vary. The recommendation regarding "Dame," "Sir," "Lord," and "Lady" is to place the title in front of the forename:

> Maddocks, Lady Jane
> Shelton, Sir James

Note that the "Lord" and "Lady" above are used as courtesy titles. The handling of the title is different when the wife of a knight or baronet is given the title "Lady." In this situation, the title is placed after the forename:

Hunt, Mary, Lady

But if the woman is also the daughter of a duke, duchess, marquess, marchioness, earl, or countess, the title is placed before the forename. The daughter of a countess would be entered in this way:

Hunt, Lady Mary

If an individual does have a title of honor, but does not use the title, the title should be omitted:

Christie, Agatha, *not* Christie, Dame Agatha

According to Booth and Piggott, "If the predominant name is the title of nobility, then the entry is under that, with a reference from the form of entry under the surname" (4.1.1.5). As they illustrate, the text is likely to refer to the individual by a term of address such as "Lord Sandwich." They suggest indexing the name as

Sandwich, Edward Montagu, Earl of

and providing a cross-reference from the surname:

Montagu, Edward, Earl of Sandwich. *See* Sandwich, Edward Montagu, Earl of

AACR2 provides suggestions for handling persons who acquire new titles or disclaim titles (22.6B3).

Names with suffixes. When names are followed by abbreviations for degrees, such as Ph.D. or M.D., the abbreviation is not retained in the index. If a name includes a suffix like "Jr." or "Sr." or "III," the suffix is retained in the index but placed after the forename.

Roosevelt, Theodore, Jr.
Tittwillow, James R., III

Not only can people whose names have titles and suffixes be troublesome; animals can also pose problems. Take the example of a 350-page book that chronicles the history of a particular breed of dog. The indexer will undoubtedly be confronted with hundreds, if not thousands, of dog names. Many of these names will be composed of titles, both preceding and following a kennel name. Also, many of the dogs will be best known by their "call names" (the name they are called at home). The indexer may need to devise an unorthodox arrangement. For example, the introductory note to the index may point out that the designation for "Champion" (Ch.) that precedes many names will not be alphabetized and that names in parentheses following kennel names indicate the call names. If the "Ch." preceding the name were sorted, there would be hundreds of names listed in the C's. However, it is important to retain the "Ch." in the name, and, because other titles are placed after the kennel name, the "Ch." must remain in front. The name index for this dog book may contain entries in the following order:

Ch. Aberlon's Catch the Hawk, CD, JH, WD (Gavin)
Ch. Aberlon's Catch the Wind (Macy)
Ch. Aberlon's Daring Dazzler, CD, JH (Daz)
Afternod Ember of Gordon Hill
Ch. Afternod Robena of Aberdeen
Ch. Afternod Yank of Rockaplenty, CD
Ch. Blackthorn's Thistle of Kymry, CD (Tulip)
Hacasak Grand Ute
Ch. Harvest Going in Style (Questor)
Hugh's Sir Gordie of Windy Hill
Ch. Loch Adair Kate
Ch. Rockaplenty Hang Em High
Rockaplenty Inherit the Wind
Ch. Torrance of Ellicot

An important point to remember about names is that there is often more to the arrangement of names than at first meets the eye. Whatever devices an indexer uses, they must be used consistently. And decisions regarding the arrangement of names must be guided by the needs of the readers. Even though, in the kennel name listings above, the names are not in strict alphabetic order, a consistent method has been used to arrange the names so that dogs with the same kennel name are gathered together. Furthermore, a good indexer will have placed a headnote to the index explaining the arrangement conventions.

Names with only a forename. A name that does not include a surname can be indexed under the given name. Include modifying phrases that help distinguish the name from other names that are the same.

> Charles II, King of France
> Charles II, King of Great Britain
> John, the Baptist
> John XXIII, Pope

Roman names. AACR2 recommends that a Roman living before A.D. 476 be entered under the part of the name that is most commonly used (22.9):

> Cicero, Marcus Tullius

If the text is unclear or there is any doubt regarding the element to use for entry, the recommendation is to enter the name in uninverted order:

> Martianus Capella

Obscure names. Sometimes a text makes reference to an individual by only a forename or a surname. If such references are indexable and the full name cannot be ascertained, the name is entered as given in the text and further identified by a qualifying phrase:

> Sarah (Lady Jane's handmaid)

Names with Particles

Complete information regarding the nuances of indexing all types of names is beyond the scope of this book. It is hoped that enough information is presented here to guide the indexer through casual encounters with non-Anglo names. Far more detailed reference sources should be sought when the indexer confronts more than a handful of such names.

The primary reference for this section is *Anglo-American Cataloging Rules,* 2d edition, 1988 revision (AACR2).

General rules. If a surname contains articles or prepositions or a combination of the two, the portion of the name most commonly used should be the basis for alphabetizing. The author's use of the surname in the text will guide the indexer. If the use of the name in the text is not clear, the indexer may wish to refer to an appropriate biographical dictionary. If the name cannot be located in a reference source, the following rules for handling articles and prepositions in surnames, adapted from AACR2 (22.5D1), may be consulted. AACR2 differs greatly in some instances from the rules used in Webster's biographical dictionaries, particularly in relation to particles in European names. The AACR2 rules are presented because of their growing acceptance around the world. But regardless of how a name is posted in the index, if there is any doubt about readers' ability to locate a name, the indexer must provide cross-references from alternative posting locations.

Afrikaans. The Afrikaans name should be entered under the prefix.

> Du Toit, Stephanus Johannes
> Van der Post, Christiaan Willem Hendrik

American and English. American, Australian, Canadian, or British names should be entered under the prefix.

> De Havilland, Sir Geoffrey (British aeronautical engineer)
> de la Roche, Mazo (Canadian novelist)
> De Peyster, Abraham (American merchant and shipowner)
> Van Buren, Martin (American president)
> Van de Graff, Robert J. (American physicist)

Dutch. In Dutch names, if the prefix is *ver,* enter under the prefix. Otherwise enter under the name following the prefix.

Brink, Bernhard ten
Hertog, Ary den
Roos, Sjoerd Hendrik de
Ver Boven, Daisy

French. If the prefix in French names consists of an article or a contraction of an article and a preposition, the prefix should be used for alphabetizing. If the prefix is a preposition, the part of the name following the preposition should be used.

Aubigné, Théodore Agrippa d'
Du Bos, Charles
Du Guesclin, Bertrand
La Fontaine, Jean de
Musset, Alfred de
Toulouse-Lautrec, Henri de

In the case of a compound French surname, AACR2 recommends that the name be entered under the first element (22.5C5).

German. Enter German names under the prefix when the prefix consists of an article or a contraction of an article and a preposition. Otherwise, enter under the name following the prefix.

Am Thym, August
Beethoven, Ludwig van
Goethe, Johann Wolfgang von
Richthofen, Manfred von
Zur Linde, Otto

Hungarian. Although AACR2 makes no special mention of Hungarian names in section 22.5D1, many indexing guides (*The Chicago Manual of Style,* 13th ed. 18.109; 14th ed. 17.113) direct that Hungarian names be presented with the surname first, followed by a forename. The name is entered in the index in the same form, with a comma inserted after the surname. Thus, the text reference for Molnár Ferenc is cited in the index as

Molnár, Ferenc

Section 22.15B2 of AACR2 advises, "Include the enclitic *né* attached to the names of some Hungarian married women." Additionally, in the case of a compound Hungarian surname, AACR2 recommends that the name be entered under the first element (22.5C5).

Italian. Modern Italian names are sorted under the prefix.

> De Martini, Luigi
> Della Piane, Giovanni
> Di Maggio, Giuseppe
> Lo Schiavo, Fiorello

If the name is of medieval origin, the indexer must determine whether the prefix is part of the name. According to AACR2, "*De, de', degli, dei,* and *de li* occurring in names of the period are rarely part of the surname." For example, Lorenzo de' Medici is entered as "Medici, Lorenzo de'."

In the case of a compound Italian surname, AACR2 recommends that the name be entered under the first element (22.5C5).

Portuguese. The prefix of Portuguese names is not alphabetized, and the name is entered under the element following the prefix.

Romanian. The prefix of Romanian names is used for alphabetizing unless the prefix is *de.* If the name contains *de,* use the element following the *de* for alphabetizing.

Scandinavian. If the prefix is of Scandinavian, German, or Dutch origin, alphabetize under the name following the prefix unless the prefix is the Dutch *de* or is of other origin. In those cases, enter under the prefix.

Spanish. If an article is the only element in the prefix of a Spanish name, it should be used for alphabetizing:

> Las Heras, Manuel Antonio

Other names are entered on the element following the prefix.

> Figueroa, Francisco de

In the case of a compound Spanish surname, AACR2 recommends that the name be entered under the first element (22.5C5). Juana Sánchez Esquivel is entered as

Sánchez Esquivel, Juana

The *Chicago Manual of Style* (13th ed. 18.106; 14th ed. 17.110) adds that

> The two names that form the full surname are sometimes joined by *y* (and), but this does not affect use of the first element in alphabetization:

> Ortega y Gasset, José
> Leguía y Salcedo, Agusto

Non-European Names

Languages of non-European origin are not written in the Roman alphabet. Scholarly texts that include personal names and other terms from non-Roman alphabets will very likely indicate what transliteration system has been used. Problems arise for the indexer when the text uses more than one type of transliteration. For example, some books about China may contain both Wade-Giles and pinyin usage. The indexer should post names in the way that the author has cited them. Cross-references to alternative forms of a name should be provided when the author has used them in the text. It is not the indexer's job to impose a consistent transliteration system on the index when such consistency is lacking in the text.

For more information about various transliteration schemes see "Transliterated and Romanized Languages" in *The Chicago Manual of Style* (13th ed. 9.85–118; 14th ed. 9.86–126).

Many names of non-European origin are composed of several compound elements. As Knight says in regard to Arabic names, "These can present some difficulty." This is an understatement at best. Often with no guidance from the text, the indexer must determine which portion of the name should be used for alphabetizing purposes.

Readers are cautioned that the guidelines that follow are very, very general. Indexers confronted with a multitude of non-European names are urged to consult reference sources for the appropriate language. The applicable sections of AACR2 are cited with the various language groups. For more detailed treatment of names in other languages, AACR2 refers readers to *Names of Persons: National Usages for Entries in Catalogues.*

Arabic. Modern Arabic names often consist of two elements presented as a forename and a surname. These names should be inverted for alphabetizing. Anwar Sadat is entered as "Sadat, Anwar."

The AACR2 rules in section 22.22 apply to names that do not contain a surname or an element acting as a surname. Arabic names are frequently indexed under the first element, as in

Omar al Khayyám, *not* Khayyám, Omar al

If an individual is better known by the family name, often beginning with *al-*, the entry element should be the family name. But these names are generally alphabetized using the name following the particle *al-*. For example, Muhammad Hamid al-Jamal can be entered as

Jamal, Muhammad Hamid al-

or as

al-Jamal, Muhammad Hamid

In the latter case, the *al-* is not alphabetized. The indexer must recognize that the particle *al-* can precede not only a family name but also a place of origin or residence.

Often a forename is followed by connectives that indicate relationships, such as *ibn-* for "son of" or *abu-* for "father of." Some names contain both types of words. Abu Muhammad ibn al-Muqaffa, for instance, is commonly cited as

Ibn al-Muqaffa, Abu Muhammad

Likewise, the founder of Saudi Arabia is known (and alphabetized) as Ibn Saud, whereas his son is entered under his forename, Faisal. As should be evident, there is nothing straightforward about the indexing of Arabic names. The treatment of the name in the text should guide the indexer. Lacking guidance from the text, the indexer may turn to AACR2 (22.22) or *The Encyclopaedia of Islam.*

Burmese. Surnames are not used in Burmese. Occasionally a West-ern name precedes the Burmese name. If this is the case, the Western name should be moved to the end and the Burmese name used for the entry element. A term of address is often included in the name, quite often the term of respect *U*. These terms are retained in the index listings. The indexer must be careful to distinguish terms of address from the same words used in a name:

> Chit Maung, Saw (term of address)
> Nu, U
> Mya Sein
> Than Tun, Walter
> Thant, U
> U Shan Maung, Maung (term of address)

Chinese. Chinese names are usually presented with the surname given first. In the index, these names are presented as given, without inversion. No comma is used between the elements:

> Cheng Shifa
> Li Keran

If the name has been Westernized—that is, the surname is given last, preceded by the given name—the name should be inverted in the index:

> Tsou, Tang
> Wong, Thomas

Indian. Modern Indian names generally appear with the surname last. In the index these names are inverted. Mohandas Karamchand Gandhi is indexed as

> Gandhi, Mohandas Karamchand

AACR2 points out exceptions found in Kannada, Malayalam, Tamil, and Telugu names that do not contain surnames (22.25B2). In these cases, the recommendation is to enter under the given name. The given names in these languages are often preceded by a place name, sometimes by the father's given name, and sometimes by a caste name. It is important for the indexer to keep this arrangement in mind when attempting to ascertain the given name. For example, Tittai Kirusna Ayyankar would be entered as

> Kirusna Ayyankar, Tittai
> (given name = Kirusna)
> (caste name = Ayyankar)
> (place name = Tittai)

AACR2 recommends that persons living before the middle of the nineteenth century be entered under the first element of their personal name (22.25A1).

Indonesian. Javan names consist of only a personal name and should be indexed in that manner:

> Suharto
> Sukarno

Other Indonesian names frequently consist of more than one element. They are often entered under the last element of the name. For example, Idrus Nasir Djajadiningrat is entered as

> Djajadiningrat, Idrus Nasir

There are many exceptions to this rule. Some names include elements that denote filial relationships plus the father's name; other names include initials or abbreviations as the last element; still other names include titles or honorifics. Sometimes these names are entered under the first element rather than the last element. Indexers should see AACR2 22.26C–22.26F for further discussion. Additionally, Indonesian names may include titles and honorific words in the text. Indexers can consult AACR2 (p. 426n) for listings that may help distinguish a title from a given name.

Japanese. Generally two elements form a Japanese name. The surname is given first, followed by the forename. These names are entered in uninverted format. However, some authors present a Japanese name in Western order: forename first, followed by surname. If a Japanese name is presented in this fashion, it must be inverted in the index. The indexer must make certain which portion of the name is the surname.

If a name is presented in traditional format in the text, such as Yoshida Shigeru, it appears in the index uninverted:

> Yoshida Shigeru

Malay. The general rule for Malay names is to enter the name under the first element of the name unless the person uses another element of the name as a surname:

> A. Samad Said
> A. L. Bunggan
> Rejab F. I.

See section 22.27 in AACR2 for a more detailed discussion of Malay names. Note that AACR2 provides a list of Iban titles of honor, titles of office, and religious titles (p. 429n).

Thai. Although surnames are used in Thai names, the general rule is to use the forename as the entry element because most people are generally known by and addressed by this name. In the text the Thai name is usually presented with the forename first, followed by the surname. Thus, the name Dhanit Yupho is entered in the index as

> Dhanit Yupho

AACR2 provides recommendations for the citing of Thai royalty, nobility, Buddhist monastics, ecclesiastics, and supreme patriarchs. See AACR2 sections 22.28B through 22.28D3 for further discussion.

Vietnamese. Vietnamese names are usually composed of three parts, with the surname given first. What causes confusion with Vietnamese names is that persons are usually referred to by their forename.

For example, General Vo Nguyen Giap is referred to as General Giap. But the name is entered in the index as

Vo Nguyen Giap

A cross-reference can be provided from the more familiar part of the name for those individuals better known by their forename.

Many Cambodian and Laotian names follow the same pattern of usage and citation as Vietnamese names.

Geographic Names

More frequently than not, geographic names that appear in the text are indexable. Like personal names, geographic names can have various spellings and some do change over time. The way the name appears in the text should help the indexer determine the form of the name in the index.

Preliminary Expressions: Geographic

It is important to distinguish between a place name, such as the name of a town, and a name for a geographic feature, such as the name of a mountain or lake. When a geographic feature is preceded by a preliminary expression such as "Mt." or "Lake," the name is placed in the index in inverted format. For example, "Mt. Shasta" appears in the index as "Shasta, Mt."

But if the preliminary expression is part of a place name, the expression is retained in uninverted form in the index. "Mount Vernon, Virginia" would appear in the index as "Mount Vernon (VA)." The indexer must determine whether such a reference is to a town or to a mountain peak. Careful examination of the context of the reference in the text generally clears up any ambiguity.

On this distinction between preliminary expressions that refer to a geographic feature and those that are parts of place names, Wellisch (1991: 306) remarks:

> There is no good reason for this procedure other than perhaps to avoid an accumulation of too many entries beginning with the same word, and it is probably due to

the practice of inversion of many compound terms in a
misguided attempt to bring the "more important" term
to the fore. Since, however, geographical terms in foreign
languages, such as Golfe, Lac, Lago, Mare, Mont, or
Monte, are never inverted, the practice of inversion in
English place names is quite incongruous and inconsistent. Is the Isle of Man to be so entered or is the name to
be inverted to Man, Isle of?

Although the rule for inversion of preliminary expressions seems
clear-cut, there are exceptions. When citing the rule to invert preliminary expressions for geographic features, many style guides include
the "Cape of Good Hope" example. One style guide tells us to index
this term as "Good Hope, Cape of," while another style guide presents the term in uninverted form. *Webster's New Geographical Dictionary* provides the most sensible resolution to the "Cape of Good
Hope problem." That work posts the information at "Good Hope,
Cape of" and provides a *See* cross-reference from "Cape of Good
Hope" to "Good Hope, Cape of." It is always important to keep
the readers' needs in mind. When it appears likely that readers may
look up a term in a form not used in the index, provide a *See* cross-
reference to the preferred term.

There are times when one and the same index must distinguish
between a "real" cape and cape as part of a place name. For example,
a book about the Outer Banks of North Carolina may make reference
to Cape Hatteras and Cape Hatteras National Seashore Park. Strictly
speaking, these two terms would appear in the index in the following order:

> Cape Hatteras National Seashore Park, 38
> Hatteras, Cape, 28, 30, 35–42

In a moderately lengthy index, these two entries may be separated
from one another by several pages. Readers could look in the *C*'s and,
finding only the reference for the park, assume that the cape itself is
not discussed. These readers would miss all the references found at
the "Hatteras, Cape" entry. In such a situation, it is quite reasonable
for the indexer to insert a pointer (a cross-reference) to the actual
"Cape Hatteras" entries. The entries might then appear as

Cape Hatteras. *See* Hatteras, Cape
Cape Hatteras National Seashore Park, 38
Hatteras, Cape, 28, 30, 35–42

In the entries above, the indexer has handled the references correctly and at the same time has provided a reasonable cross-reference for readers who may not know the posting rules.

Preliminary Expressions: Articles and Prepositions

There are place names that begin with articles. A common example is The Dalles in northern Oregon, an exciting spot where the Deschutes River joins the Columbia River. Another well-known example is The Hague in the Netherlands. In both cases, the article *The* is part of the name. These names appear with the article on maps. Since the article is part of the formal name, the names are entered in the index in uninverted form, sorted on *The*. It might be very helpful to readers to also supply cross-references, as in

Dalles *see* The Dalles
Hague *see* The Hague
. . .
Thebes
The Dalles
Thedford
The Hague

Likewise, if the name begins with a non-English article or preposition, the preliminary term is generally alphabetized; the phrase is presented in uninverted form.

De Baca County (NM)
De Kalb (IL)
Del Mar (CA)
El Cajon (CA)
La Crosse (WI)
Le Mans (France)
Los Angeles (CA)

Identifiers for Geographic Names

It is often desirable to provide a clear identifier for a geographic name. This is especially true when the same name appears in several distinct contexts:

Los Angeles (CA)
Los Angeles (Chile)
Los Angeles County (CA)

If a common set of identifiers will be used in the index, such as abbreviations for states in the United States, the indexer must use the abbreviations in a consistent manner. It is not proper to abbreviate California as "CA" in one place and as "Calif." in another place.

References

Indexers who handle material that contains references to geographic names would do well to have a geographical dictionary at hand, such as *Webster's New Geographical Dictionary*. If a more detailed reference is required, in the United States information about the standard form of geographic names can be obtained from the United States Board on Geographic Names (U.S. Geological Survey, Reston, VA 22092).

The gazetteers that exist for many countries are generally the most reliable source for indexers who handle specialized material. A recent search of the online catalog at the University of California Berkeley Library retrieved 142 records of gazetteers listing names approved by the U.S. Board on Geographic Names. These gazetteers ranged from name listings for Antarctica to a gazetteer of Zambia.

On Britain, Bakewell (1988: 28) states that

> the standard gazetteer of Britain is *Bartholomew Gazetteer of Britain* compiled by O. Mason (Edinburgh: Bartholomew, 1977), which has about 40,000 entries compared with the 90,000 entries in the same publisher's earlier *Gazetteer of the British Isles* (Edinburgh: Bartholomew, 1970). The English Place-Name Society publishes separate volumes on the place names of each English county.

ORGANIZATION NAMES

The names of organizations, like other types of names, are not without their problems. It must be decided where to post an organization's name and whether to provide a cross-reference. In some cases the decision is an easy one. For example, the utility company Pacific Gas and Electric would be entered in its full form in the *P*'s. But since most customers of this utility company refer to it as "P.G.&E.," a *See* cross-reference should be provided from the abbreviation to the full name.

More troublesome are names that begin with what appears to be a forename, such as the John Deere Company. While inverting a name like this might seem natural, it is a sounder practice to enter the name in uninverted form in the index. When such a company name is well known, a cross-reference is usually not necessary.

Unfortunately, many business owners do not think of the alphabetizing consequences of the names they choose. Take a book that discusses both "Tony Roma" and "Tony Roma's," the latter being a restaurant. Tony, himself, would be indexed as "Roma, Tony." However, Tony's restaurant name would correctly appear in the *T*'s. In the *R*'s we might find the following:

> Roma, Tony, 35–39
> Roma's, Tony (restaurant). *See* Tony Roma's

Another type of business name is one that is pronounced differently from its spelling. In my town there is a local restaurant named Hs. Lordships. When the townspeople refer to this restaurant, they say "His Lordships." A cross-reference such as the following would be appropriate for a name like this:

> His Lordships. *See* Hs. Lordships

The general rule is that organizational names should appear in uninverted form; cross-references should be provided when necessary. But the topic of how to handle organizational names cannot be wrapped up without discussing some exceptions to the rule.

In some situations it would make more sense to double-post a name in both direct and inverted format rather than provide a cross-reference:

> American Society of Indexers
> American Translators Association
> Japanese Translators Society
> Society of Indexers

could be double-posted as

> Indexers, American Society of
> Indexers, Society of
> Translators Association, American
> Translators Society, Japanese

This advice applies when there are only a few reference locators at each of these entries. Thus, the double-posting of information saves space in the index.

When confronted with a text that has many organizations cited, many of which begin with the same title, such as "Association of . . .," the indexer may invert the names to pull the important portion of the name forward. Such a decision will help readers who are not certain of the formal name of an organization. They need not worry whether the name is Association of American Indexers or American Indexers Association or Society of American Indexers or American Society of Indexers.

If a decision is made to handle the index in an unusual way, the headnote to the index must explain the convention used. An example of a subject index that handled the names of organizations in an unconventional but useful way can be found in the 1989–90 edition of the *Washington Information Directory,* published by Congressional Quarterly Inc. *WID,* as the directory is fondly called, is a lengthy (more than a thousand pages) compendium of who's who in the greater Washington, D.C., area. It includes names and addresses of people from the executive branch, Congress, trade associations, and nonprofit groups. Agencies, subagencies, divisions, subdivisions, committees, and subcommittees are all included. There are thousands of organizational names. The following headnote precedes the subject index (p. 960):

> If the title of an agency or organization begins with one or more of the words listed below, it is not listed under those initial words. Rather, it is indexed under the next word in the title. For example, the National Gallery of Art is listed alphabetically not under "National" but under "Gallery of Art, National." In addition, agencies and

groups are indexed under KEY words. The National Gallery of Art will also have an entry under "Art, National Gallery of."

Academy
Advisory
Agency
American
Association
Bureau
Center
Coalition
Commission
Committee
Council
Department
Federal
Foundation
Fund
Institute
International
National
Office
Society
U.S.
United States

This introductory note makes quite clear the scheme that has been used in this index. Although a generally accepted indexing rule has been broken, the usability of the index has been greatly enhanced by this decision. The designer of this index clearly put the readers' needs first.

Changing of names. Even more than other types of names, corporate names seem to be in a state of flux. Some businesses have more than one formal, legal name. Others have one formal name but may also have other names that are protected by trademark or service mark.

Indexers working with a variety of names for a corporation will need to settle on one name and cross-reference from the others. Generally, the form of the name most frequently used in the text will be the name at which to post the information:

International Business Machines Co. *See* IBM

Some companies do file the necessary papers and formally change their names. If it is decided that information will be posted at the current name, then a cross-reference from the old name to the current name is appropriate. For instance, in a discussion about the changing world of computer retail sales, the author may point out that the Soft Warehouse changed its name to CompUSA because the company's inventory began to include a great deal of hardware in addition to software. The new company name, it is felt, better reflects the goods now being sold. The names may appear in the index as

CompUSA (*formerly* Soft Warehouse)
Soft Warehouse. *See* CompUSA

But if the author makes no mention of the old name, such a cross-reference is not needed. Again, the text should be the indexer's guide. The indexer need not research the posting of every company name and provide cross-references from former names to current names when the older names are not mentioned in the text.

Mergers and acquisitions of companies provide yet another indexing challenge. Take the example of the acquisition of NCR by AT&T. Prior to 1991, NCR had a distinguished history of its own, unrelated to AT&T. Even though NCR has been acquired by and is owned by AT&T, it still operates using its own name. Entries for NCR should not be merged under an AT&T main heading. Instead, the NCR entries should appear under NCR in the *N*'s. However, the relationship between the two companies should not be ignored. Each company should have a *See also* reference that refers to the other.

The main difficulty with organization names is determining how to post the name. While it may be comfortable to establish the rule that all such names will be posted at their formal spelled-out versions, this may not meet the needs of the readers. Readers may tend to look up "AT&T," not the "American Telephone and Telegraph Company." Ideally there will be entries for both "AT&T" and "American Telephone and Telegraph Company." But one of these entries will be a *See* cross-reference to the entry where information has been gathered. If readers of the book will tend to look up the shortened form of the name first, then that is where the information should be posted.

Alphabetizing of names. Names are alphabetized in the same way that the rest of the index is alphabetized. Be aware that word-by-word sorting and letter-by-letter sorting schemes will often place entries in very different positions in the index. Because of the space following the "U," "U S WEST" will fall at the beginning of the *U*'s, far removed from other entries such as "US Sprint" if word-by-word alphabetizing is followed

Most readers looking up this term will think of it as "us west" and look for it in the "us" portion of the index. A letter-by-letter sort would interfile this entry with the other "US" entries in the index.

This problem brings us back to the discussion of how to choose an alphabetizing method. If an index will contain many terms with spaces within entries, the indexer may wish to consider the use of a strict letter-by-letter sort. Fine examples of word-by-word alphabetizing that sorts the punctuation within an entry can be found in the "white page" name listings in phone books. Go to the beginning of any letter group and examine the names. In the G section of one phone book we find the following alphabetized list:

> G-Style Body & Sound
> G A Photography
> G & A Systems
> GAB BUSINESS SERVICES
> GE COMPANY
> GHL International
> GTE Cellular Communications
> G W Paving & Construction
> Gaal, Ronald P
> Gaar, Tony
> Gabato, Ronald

Admittedly, the list above is a hybrid. Upon close examination we find that it really does not follow any conventional sorting arrangement. Most of us who have had to use lists like this in the phone book are grateful that we can get directory assistance by dialing 411. The listing above does illustrate what happens when unconventional decisions are made regarding the sorting of terms. Indexers faced with many entries that contain spaces, punctuation, and other symbols must seriously consider the alphabetizing order that will help readers locate the entries. Improvising one's own arrangement scheme should be avoided simply because it will very likely confuse the readers (and readers cannot dial 411 for index assistance!). See chapter 6 for a discussion of nonalphabetic characters in index entries.

8

FORMAT AND LAYOUT OF THE INDEX

THE INDEXING STYLE GUIDE that is provided to the indexer will explain how the publisher wants the index formatted. The format of an index includes items such as

overall style: indented or run-in

format and placement of cross-references

special typography used within the index

Additionally, the style guide will outline the final submission format of the index. Sometimes the index is to be provided as manuscript only. But it is far more common to submit the index in manuscript form and on disk.

There is an important relationship between the layout and design of the index and its usability. Ideally all decisions regarding index format take into consideration the needs of index users. Unfortunately, we do not live in an ideal world. All too often indexes are squeezed into a limited number of pages and their usability is greatly compromised. But with a little advance planning and an understanding of index design issues, an index can be presented so as to enhance its usefulness.

If we agree that an index should provide quick and easy access to information, we cannot ignore the crucial role played by the format and layout of the index in this regard. Indexes are rarely "read" in a linear style, that is, from beginning to end. Index users jump into the index at various points. The overall design of the index should provide for easy scanning of index entries by the readers. Readers should be able to ascertain very quickly, at any place, where they are in the index. The index text pages should be clean, inviting, and easy to scan rather than dense and cluttered. In reference books, where the index is very likely the most heavily used portion of the book, the format and layout of the index are especially important.

This chapter will discuss format considerations and index submission formats, matters that directly involve the indexer. Once the index is submitted to the publisher, the production department must lay out the index. Although the indexer's dedicated indexing software can do much of this work, the production department must explain its needs to the indexer. Later in this chapter we will discuss issues related to the layout of indexes.

OVERALL INDEX STYLE

Indexes are printed in the same typeface as the text of the body of the book but often two points smaller. If the body text of the book is printed as 10 point Times Roman with 12-point leading, the index text will be printed as 8 point Times Roman with 10-point leading. In this context leading refers to the amount of space between lines of text.

Indexes are often printed in multiple columns on a page. In many books, the index is printed in two columns per page. Books with oversized pages can accommodate three or four columns of index text per page.

The alignment of the right-hand margin of the index is almost always *ragged right*. The body text for many books is set in a right-justified column. This means that the right side is straight and even. The ragged right alignment used in indexes allows the lines to break where they may—the effect is an uneven right margin. When the columns are narrow, such a format is easier to proofread, typeset, and read.

The two general formats for indexes are indented and run-in. The distinguishing feature of these two styles is the way subentries are formatted. In both formats, main headings are flush left—they are not indented—and runover lines are indented. This arrangement is what is known as flush-and-hang style. This simply means that subentries and "runover lines" (see below) are indented in some fashion under the main heading. Following is an example of an index entry formatted in indented and run-in style:

Indented Style	Run-in Style
dogs	dogs: breed clubs, 242–48; breeding
breed clubs, 242–48	of, 180–95; herding group, 135–42;
breeding of, 180–95	hound group, 67–72; non-sporting
herding group, 135–42	group, 23–29; obedience training

hound group, 67–72
non-sporting group, 23–29
obedience training for, 275–84
registration of, 210–15
showing of, 250–62
socialization of puppies, 198–206
sporting group, 56–60
terrier group, 125–30
toy group, 86–94
working group, 34–39
See also American Kennel Club

for, 275–84; registration of, 210–15; showing of, 250–62; socialization of puppies, 198–206; sporting group, 56–60; terrier group, 125–30; toy group, 86–94; working group, 34–39. *See also* American Kennel Club

INDENTED STYLE

In an indented-style index, each subentry begins on a new line with a specific measure of indentation, or indention. This type of layout is also referred to as setout, hierarchical, outline, or line-by-line style. The amount of indention for lines appearing under a main heading is a function of the level of the line in the hierarchy. Subentries could be indented 1 em, with sub-subentries indented 2 ems. Recall that an em is a linear measurement used in printing that is equal to the point size of the type. As an example, if the index is in 8-point type, then 1 em is 8 points wide, 2 ems is 16 points wide, and so forth.

The indented format allows for clear display of sub-subentries:

> dogs
>   breed clubs, 242–48
>   breeding of, 180–95
>   herding group, 135–42
>   Australian cattle dogs, 135
>   bearded collies, 135–36
>   Belgian Malinois, 136
>   Belgian sheepdogs, 137
>   Belgian Tervurens, 137–38
>   briards, 138
>   collies, 139
>   . . .
>   hound group, 67–72
>   non-sporting group, 23–29
>   obedience training for, 275–84

As the example above illustrates, the various levels in an indented-style index are easy to follow. When there are multiple levels in an index—that is, subentries, sub-subentries, sub-sub-subentries, and so on—this is the correct format to use.

When an indented index is set within narrow columns, there will be lines that do not fit within the column width. Lines that must be continued on the next line are called turnover, wraparound, or run-over lines. The indention of a turnover line must be different than the indention for subentries or sub-subentries. Turnover line indention will be discussed in more detail later in this chapter.

Run-in Style

There is one, and only one, reason to use a run-in format for an index: that reason is to save space. The two format styles shown at the beginning of this chapter illustrate the space-saving attribute of run-in style. But subentries formatted in run-in style are not as easy to scan or locate as in an indented format.

Run-in subentries follow one another with no line breaks in between. Subentries are separated from each other by a semicolon. Sometimes the subentries begin indented under the main heading and its locators. But since the purpose of this type of format is to save space, more often than not the subentries are run off from the main heading; they begin on the same line as the main heading.

The run-in format does not lend itself easily to the display of sub-subentries. The run-in format should be used only when the index is composed of main headings and one level of subentries. This format should not be used when the index contains more levels. Unfortunately, this advice is not always followed; some publishers have concocted ingenious punctuation schemes for further cluttering a run-in index with sub-subentries. The problem of sub-subentries and run-in format will be discussed shortly.

The only situation in which the run-in format saves a useful amount of space is where there are many main entries that have subentries. If an index is composed of mostly main entries, the space ultimately saved by the run-in style is negligible.

A run-in format should be considered only when there definitely is not enough room for an indented index. Sadly, many publishers routinely format indexes in run-in style regardless of space considerations. Choosing a run-in format should be a conscious decision that takes into consideration that to some extent the usability of the index will be compromised. The user of the index may find it particularly annoying to struggle through a run-in index of densely packed subentries only to discover several blank pages following the index that could have accommodated an indented style index. Given the powerful formatting capabilities of dedicated indexing software, it is a very simple matter to format an index in both indented and run-in style and see how much space is needed for the two formats.

Like the indented format, the run-in format also indents the runover lines under the main heading. The indention is generally 1 em. Since there are no sub-subentries, no further indention will be required.

More details regarding both types of formats will be presented in the layout section of this chapter. Subtle variations can be used with both formats to enhance the usability of an index.

OTHER STYLES

Any decision to set an index in a style other than the traditional flush-and-hang format should be made with caution. One common deviation from the standard indented format can be found in some legal books. In these books the indexes are printed two columns per page, main headings set in capital letters in bold type centered across the column width, with subentries set underneath, the first subentry level set flush left and the second, indented:

AFFIRMATIVE ACTION	**CIVIL ACTIONS**
Generally, 5:1	Age Discrimination in Employment Act
Bakke revisited, 2:29	EEOC civil actions, 5:17
EEOC guidelines, 2:34	Federal employee civil actions, 5:18
Rehabilitation Act	private civil actions, 5:16
Federal employment, 6:11	Equal Pay Act
Federal grants, 6:7	EEOC civil actions, 4:16
government contracts, 6:3	private civil actions, 4:15
Seniority relief, 2:30	
Voluntarily negotiated plans, 2:31	

Such a format is useful only in indexes in which every main heading has at least one subentry. A main heading would look quite odd standing alone centered within a column on a page. Setting the first subentry level flush with the left margin saves space by reducing the number of turnover lines.

Years ago it was not unusual to see indexes with their locators set flush right, preceded by leader dots. This format produced a right-justified index. In general, this format is frowned upon today. It is difficult to typeset and proofread. Also, the locator is separated from the entry so that the user must carefully follow a trail of leader dots to the locator. I have recommended the use of this format only once—when both the entries and the locators were cryptic. The index was easier to use with the locator physically separated from the entry. For example:

```
BDCHa....................3C:libpt:BDCHa
BDClear................3C:libpt:BDClear
BDCompare............3C:libpt:BDCompare
BDConv..................3C:libpt:BDConv
label
    create............3H:libpxio:LabCreat
    length....................4D:getInfo
    print..............3H:libpxio:LabPrnt
    read................3H:libpxio:LabRd
ldxep.................5H:stdio-libh:Xep
LFBuff................2C:libtool:LBuff
```

In general, though, right-justified indexes are more difficult for readers to use and should be avoided. For an interesting discussion of typography and the layout of indexes see Nan Ridehalgh's (1985) article, "The Design of Indexes." The article provides examples of many typographic and design elements in printed indexes and delves into the history of some of the design considerations in indexes.

CROSS-REFERENCE FORMAT
AND PLACEMENT

An indexing style guide will indicate the format and placement of cross-references within index entries. Many, many variations exist. Some of the more common examples will be presented here. See also table 3.1 for a synopsis of various publishers' styles for cross-reference format and placement. Designers of specifications for cross-reference format and placement should strive to enhance the readability of the typeset index.

It is important to distinguish between cross-references that refer from the main heading and those that refer from subentries. The format of main heading cross-references must be different from that of subentry cross-references. Readers should easily be able to ascertain whether a cross-reference leads to more information about a main entry or about a subentry.

"See" cross-references. Generally *See* cross-references for main headings are run off from the main heading in both indented and run-in style indexes. The *See* itself may or may not be capitalized. It is almost always set in italics. Sometimes the *See* reference is preceded by a period and space; other times the *See* and the term referred to are placed within parentheses:

> AKC. *See* American Kennel Club
> AKC, *see* American Kennel Club
> AKC (*see* American Kennel Club)

One problem with the format that places the cross-reference inside parentheses is the difficulty of using a parenthetical expression as part of the cross-reference itself. Earlier we discussed the debate about the completeness of cross-references. Many editors would like to see the full main entry, *American Kennel Club (AKC)*, cited in the cross-reference. When the entire cross-referenced text is placed inside parentheses, the result can be visually distracting:

> AKC (*see* American Kennel Club (AKC))

Such awkward arrangements are to be avoided when possible.

The cross-reference is occasionally placed as a subentry under the main heading. The problem with this format is that two lines are used instead of one. Many consider this a waste of space:

> AKC
> *See* American Kennel Club

The first example above—AKC. *See* American Kennel Club—is a more flexible format when there is a need to provide for *See* references from subentries. Using that *See* format and placement, we can place a *See* reference from a subentry within parentheses immediately following the subentry. Regardless of the format used for a subentry *See* cross-reference, such a reference is far easier to format and read in an indented index when compared with a run-in index. An indented index with a *See* reference for a subentry can be formatted in the following way. Notice the subentry "obedience training."

> dogs
>   breed clubs, 242–48
>   breeding of, 180–95
>   herding group, 135–42
>   hound group, 67–72
>   non-sporting group, 23–29
>   obedience training (*See* training)
>   registration of, 210–15
>   showing of, 250–62
>   socialization of puppies, 198–206
>   sporting group, 56–60
>   terrier group, 125–30
>   toy group, 86–94
>   working group, 34–39
>   *See also* American Kennel Club

The identical entry formatted in run-in style can use the same format for the subentry cross-reference:

> dogs: breed clubs, 242–48; breeding of, 180–95; herding group, 135–42; hound group, 67–72; non-sporting group, 23–29; obedience training (*See* training); registration of, 210–15; showing of, 250–62; socialization of puppies, 198–206; sporting group, 56–60; terrier group, 125–30; toy group, 86–94; working group, 34–39. *See also* American Kennel Club

In a run-in index, the situation that must be anticipated is the presence of a subentry cross-reference at the last subentry, which is then followed by a cross-reference for the main heading. Readers must be able to distinguish the two cross-references easily. If we take the entry above and create a cross-reference for the last subentry, "working group," the entry would look like the following:

> dogs: breed clubs, 242–48; breeding
> of, 180–95; herding group, 135–42;
> hound group, 67–72; non-sporting
> group, 23–29; obedience training
> (*See* training); registration of,
> 210–15; showing of, 250–62; so-
> cialization of puppies, 198–206;
> sporting group, 56–60; terrier
> group, 125–30; toy group, 86–94;
> working group (*See* Akitas; mala-
> mutes; rottweilers). *See also* Ameri-
> can Kennel Club

This format may not be pretty, but it does work. It distinguishes clearly between a subentry cross-reference and a main heading cross-reference.

In general, *See* cross-references from subentries should be avoided in an index. As pointed out earlier, the primary function of a *See* cross-reference is vocabulary control. Vocabulary control is done at the main heading level and not repeated at the subentry level. But there are situations where a subentry *See* cross-reference cannot be avoided. Careful formatting of these references will make the index easier to read and use.

"See also" cross-references. More elements are at work in the place-ment and format of *See also* references for main headings than there are in the format and placement of *See* references. Placement will be discussed first.

In both indented and run-in indexes, a *See also* reference that re-fers from the main heading can be placed either at the top of the entry or at the bottom of the entry as the last subentry. In an in-dented index the two placements may look like this:

dogs
> breed clubs, 242–48
> herding group, 135–42
> hound group, 67–72
> non-sporting group, 23–29
> registration of, 210–15
> sporting group, 56–60
> terrier group, 125–30
> toy group, 86–94
> working group, 34–39
> *See also* American Kennel Club

dogs. *See also* American Kennel Club
> breed clubs, 242–48
> herding group, 135–42
> hound group, 67–72
> non-sporting group, 23–29
> registration of, 210–15
> sporting group, 56–60
> terrier group, 125–30
> toy group, 86–94
> working group, 34–39

In the entry on the right, the placement of the *See also* reference at the top of the entry—run off from the main heading—eliminated a line, thus saving space. But keep in mind that, unlike here, main headings are often followed by page numbers. Placing the *See also* reference after the main heading page numbers may result in a turnover line and no saving in space:

dogs, 1–6, 39–42. *See also* American
Kennel Club (AKC)

Placement of *See also* references has proponents on both sides. Those who favor placement at the bottom argue that

1. Readers are not distracted by references suggesting that they look elsewhere in the index for information;
2. The overall appearance of the entry is neater because *See also* references placed at the top, running off from the main heading, often result in turnover lines that add unnecessary visual complexity to the printed page;
3. Since the index entry is a hierarchy, less important information within the entry should come last.

Those in favor of placing the reference at the top of the entry argue that

1. Readers should be immediately informed of related information that may be germane to their search.
2. When an index contains lengthy lists of subentries, readers might not see the cross-reference placed at the end of the list.

Regardless of which placement is chosen, the decision must be applied uniformly throughout the index. *See also* references must appear in the same place within all entries. When the *See also* reference is placed at the bottom as the last subentry in an indented style index, it is very important to maintain correct subentry indention regardless of the level of the entry preceding the cross-reference:

dogs
    breed clubs, 242–48
    herding group, 135–42
    hound group, 67–72
    non-sporting group, 23–29
    registration
        breeds registrable, 10–14
        forms, 210–15
        litter registration, 35–38
        refusal of registration, grounds for, 125–30
    See also American Kennel Club

Like *See* references, *See also* references may appear in a variety of formats. The *See* may be capitalized or lowercase; the entire reference may stand alone or be placed within parentheses.

See also American Kennel Club
see also American Kennel Club
(*see also* American Kennel Club)

Following are examples of formats and placements of *See also* references for main headings in run-in style indexes:

dogs (*see also* American Kennel Club): breed clubs, 242–48; breeding of, 180–95; herding group, 135–42; hound group, 67–72; non-sporting group, 23–29; obedience training, 275–84; registration of, 210–15; showing of, 250–62; socialization of puppies, 198–206; sporting group, 56–60; terrier group, 125–30; toy group, 86–94; working group, 34–39

dogs: breed clubs, 242–48; breeding of, 180–95; herding group, 135–42; hound group, 67–72; non-sporting group, 23–29; obedience training, 275–84; registration of, 210–15; showing of, 250–62; socialization of puppies, 198–206; sporting group, 56–60; terrier group, 125–30; toy group, 86–94; working group, 34–39. *See also* American Kennel Club

> dogs, 10–20 (*see also* American Ken-
> nel Club); breed clubs, 242–48;
> breeding of, 180–95; herding
> group, 135–42; hound group,
> 67–72; non-sporting group, 23–29;
> obedience training, 275–84; regis-
> tration of, 210–15; showing of,
> 250–62; socialization of puppies,
> 198–206; sporting group, 56–60;
> terrier group, 125–30; toy group,
> 86–94; working group, 34–39

> dogs, 10–20. *See also* American Ken-
> nel Club; breed clubs, 242–48;
> breeding of, 180–95; herding
> group, 135–42; hound group,
> 67–72; non-sporting group, 23–29;
> obedience training, 275–84; regis-
> tration of, 210–15; showing of,
> 250–62; socialization of puppies,
> 198–206; sporting group, 56–60;
> terrier group, 125–30; toy group,
> 86–94; working group, 34–39

General cross-references. A general cross-reference refers to a class of entries rather than a specific entry. The placement of this type of cross-reference follows the same format as the placement of other cross-references in the index. However, the general cross-referenced entries are usually set in italics to distinguish them from actual entries that are referenced:

> Southeast Asia. *See specific country names*

The use of italics for "specific country names" indicates to readers that this is a general instruction; there is no entry in the *S*'s for "specific country names." Instead, the reader is instructed to look up countries by name throughout the index.

Some publishers prefer that a *See* or *See also* be set in regular (nonitalic) type when it is followed by a reference in italics:

> dogs. See also *Travels with Charley*
> Twain, Mark. See *Life on the Mississippi*

SPECIAL TYPOGRAPHY

By their very nature, indexes tend to be dense. A good rule of thumb is that the more simple and plain the typography, the better. Most of the text in an index will be set in regular type. Italic will be used for *See* and *See also* references and titles of books. But in some situations the use of simple typographic devices can enhance the usability of the index and provide information at the same time.

Reference locators can be set in a different typeface when they refer to a particular type of entry. For example, a reference locator that refers to an illustration might be set in italic type:

Beef Wellington, 45, *54*

Without taking up extra space, the entry above indicates that a recipe can be found on page 45 and a picture of the dish can be found on page 54. This simple typographic device saves space in the index. Of course, a note explaining the use of italic page numbers must appear at the beginning of the index.

Often bold type is used with reference locators that indicate where the reader can find definitions or substantial discussion of a term:

random access memory (RAM), 35, **41–43,** 78–79

Readers looking at the entry above know immediately that pages 41–43 contain the definition and description of the term. Once more, space has been saved. The subentry "defined" is not needed to indicate the relevance of the material on these pages. Again, an introductory note must explain this particular use of bold type.

In some indexes the typeface used within the text for particular kinds of terms is retained in the index. For example, many software manuals use a monospaced Courier font to indicate commands that users type themselves. When the commands are index entries, the same monospaced font is used in the index:

FORMAT command, 56–58, 65–67
formatting disks
   floppy disks, 57, 78
   hard disks, 65–68, 79

It is easy to overdo the use of typographic variations. Too many changes in typefaces can make the index pages overly dense and busy. Some indexes use large and small caps for the names of authors to distinguish them from the names of other individuals in the index. Rarely is the use of such typography truly helpful.

On the other hand, setting the main headings in bold type may greatly enhance the usability of indexes with a preponderance of subentries. This method is frequently used in legal indexes. The bold type helps readers locate information on dense index pages; it helps to focus the eye. But in an index with many main headings and few subentries, the bold type in main headings can add annoying density to the index page.

When special typography is used in an index, the indexer usually needs to know what devices to use before the indexing begins. If pages that contain illustrations are to be set in italic, the indexer must code these entries for italic when the entry is written. It would be extremely tedious and time consuming to insert the coding after the index has been completed.

All too often the actual design of the index pages is given little forethought. Ideally, the design is set before the indexer receives final pages. The addition of typographic codes for particular types of entries will increase the time needed for indexing. First, the indexer must know what additional keyboarding is to be done. Second, any special typography that is called for in the design will have to be proofread carefully by the indexer and the book editor.

Indexers who suspect that special typography may be useful in an index should bring the matter up with the editor as early in the indexing process as possible. Experienced indexers, without even seeing pages of the book, can often anticipate when the use of special typography will be helpful. But if the matter is not discussed early on, the editor is unlikely to allow extra time for indexing so that the indexer can go back into the index and, for example, add italic codes to specific page numbers.

FINAL SUBMISSION FORMATS

Although beginning indexers may think their task will never end, there does come a time when the index is finished and must be turned over to the editor. Writing brilliant and robust indexes is certainly part of the indexer's job; submitting the index in the format desired by the editor is also an important part of the job. When the index is submitted, there is not a lot of time built into the publishing schedule. It is extremely important that the indexer understand at the beginning of the project exactly how the editor wants the index submitted. Two submission formats will be described: manuscript format and electronic format.

Manuscript Format

While an indexer will rarely be asked to submit an index as manuscript only without a disk, submission of an index in manuscript form along with a disk is common. Some editors do not edit from the indexer's printout; it is used only for reference or if there are problems with an index disk file. When the indexer's manuscript will not be used for editing, the indexer can submit a single-spaced printout. Many editors expect the index to be submitted as a typed, double-spaced manuscript so that it can be edited. The discussion that follows will assume that the manuscript will be used for editing purposes and may also be turned over to a typesetter for typesetting.

Many publishers' style guides include a section devoted to manuscript submission format. Some common submission guidelines follow:

1. Paper size is 8 1/2 inches by 11 inches.
2. Margins are at least 1 inch on the top, bottom, and right and left sides.
3. Typeface is monospaced, Courier font.
4. Double-spaced lines are used throughout the index, with one column of index entries per page.
5. Each manuscript page is numbered.
6. Italics are indicated by underlining the term.
7. Bold is indicated by actual bold type or manually by placing a wavy line under the term.

Variations on these guidelines of course exist. Some publishers will want larger margins; others will specify an index line length. Some will not require a monospaced type. Regardless of minor variations, it is important that the indexer understand the importance of following the submission guidelines.

Even though many indexers have access to printers that can print the manuscript in "fancy" proportional fonts, the use of a monospaced, serif font is sometimes regarded as critical. Experienced editors can estimate the approximate length of the typeset index by looking at the index manuscript. A monospaced, serif font is easier to read, edit, and proofread than, for instance, a sans serif proportional font such as Helvetica.

Double-spaced index lines allow space for the editor or proofreader to insert corrections.

The index manuscript should be very neat. The type should be dark and easy to read. Handwritten corrections made by the indexer should be minimal. Submitting a manuscript littered with corrections is unprofessional.

It is wise for the indexer to keep a copy of the index manuscript in case the original copy is lost in transit. The indexer will need a copy of the index manuscript for reference, in case the editor has questions about the submitted index. The indexer should also retain copies of the page proofs in order to answer any questions that may arise about the index.

Electronic Format

Two types of electronic format will be discussed—submission of the index on disk and transfer of the index by modem. Most publishers expect indexes to be submitted in electronic format on a disk. Publishers want indexes submitted on disk because (1) time is saved, and (2) the error-prone process of retyping an index is eliminated.

When an index is submitted electronically, the publisher must specify various details. These details can be divided into two groups—the preferred physical format of the disk and the type of index text file desired. When the index is transferred via modem, there is no need to be concerned with the disk format.

Physical format of the floppy disk. Disks that can be read by personal computers come in a variety of types, depending upon size of the disk, density of the disk, and whether the disk is single- or double-sided. Microsoft's MS-DOS 5 operating system, used on many IBM PCs and compatibles, accommodates no less than eight floppy disk formats. So it is important that the publisher indicate what size and density of disk can be read by the in-house computers. If there is any doubt about the compatibility of the indexer's disk and the publisher's computer system, the indexer may wish to send a sample disk to the publisher for testing.

Modem transmission. Transferring an index text file from one computer system to another over the telephone lines with the use of a modem eliminates the need for disk compatibility. Such direct, computer-to-computer transfers are also quite fast, even when compared to same-day or overnight courier service. At the time of this writing, many book publishers are not set up for modem transfer of index files; however, many typesetters do offer this capacity. Because at this stage in the production cycle time is critical, some publishers (or their typesetters) welcome the opportunity to receive an index via modem.

It is beyond the scope of this book to describe the details of telecommunications. Indexers who wish to offer modem delivery of their work will need to become familiar with modem hardware and communications software. As the use of telecommunications becomes more widespread, indexers may wish to prepare for more requests for modem delivery of index files.

Text file format. The next concern in electronic submission is the actual format of the index text file. Even if the publisher can read the indexer's disk, the text file will be of little use if it is not formatted correctly.

Many publishers, including the University of Chicago Press, request that the index be submitted in a format compatible with popular word processing programs or page design software. The indexer may be asked to submit the index as a WordPerfect, WordStar, Word, XyWrite, or Ventura Publisher file. When the indexer submits an index as a particular type of word processor file, many elements of text file formatting are automatically taken care of. For example, the indexer need not insert generic codes for italic in a XyWrite file; the XyWrite codes will work fine. It is important to understand that these types of files are proprietary text file formats. In their native state, these files can only be used by the program for which they are designed. Chaos ensues when a WordStar file is imported directly into WordPerfect because, for instance, WordStar uses a different set of codes to turn italics on and off than the codes used by WordPerfect. Neither program understands the other program's codes.

Indexers who work with dedicated indexing software are able to produce text files for a variety of popular word processing programs. Also, utility programs are available that will convert text files from one format to another and many word processing programs are able to convert text files to and from various formats. The indexer does not need to actually work with the text file in the word processing program preferred by the publisher. No matter what program is used to create the index, it is important to understand what elements in an index must be uniquely coded so that the publisher's (or typesetter's) computer system can manipulate the file.

Eventually, the index text file will be imported into a particular program for typesetting and layout so that final page proofs for the index can be produced. For our purposes, it does not matter what page design software will be used by the publisher. In many respects the general requirements of page design programs are the same. Although there are exceptions, the list of format elements that follow pertains to many indexes.

1. *Beginning and end of lines.* The publisher's computer system (hereafter the "target system") must be able to recognize when a new line begins and ends. This recognition is generally achieved with a unique end-of-line code. Often this code is a sequence of two characters, a carriage return/line feed sequence. In many word processing programs this sequence is referred to as a "hard return." When the target system encounters a carriage return/line feed sequence, it interprets this code as the end of a line and the next character encountered as the beginning of a new line.

2. *Indentions.* In the case of an indented style index, the target system must have a means of recognizing various levels in the index. For example, the target system must treat subentry lines differently from how it treats main heading lines or sub-subentry lines. Subentry indention levels are often indicated by the insertion of a unique code, such as [S1] for subentries and [S2] for sub-subentries. Some target systems use the tab character as an indention indicator. Subentries can be indented with one tab, sub-subentries with two tabs, and so on. The advantage of using a tab character is that the actual width of the tab space can be set on the target system. The tab character is a unique ASCII character with a particular value (009).

A run-in style index will not have the multiple indention levels of an indented index. A run-in index entry will undoubtedly have many lines that turn over. Until the index file has been formatted with particular font and leading instructions, it is not possible to know exactly where each line will break. Therefore, many target systems require that run-in subentries be strung off from the main heading and continue one after another until the end of the entry, which is terminated with a carriage return/line feed sequence. The target system will identify the text between the beginning of the line and the end of the line as a complete entry and will format it in run-in style appropriately.

3. *Typeface changes.* Any text in the index that changes from the regular typeface to another typeface must be indicated in some manner. For example, if the *See* and *See also* text in an index is to be set in italics, the target system must have a way of knowing when the typeface change begins and when it ends. Any typeface change, whether it be to italics, to bold, to small caps, or to monospaced font, must be indicated in a unique manner within the text file. The target system must be instructed to change from the regular typeface to the new typeface and then back again to the regular typeface.

4. *Special characters.* In appendix B you will find an ASCII table. This table reproduces the characters that have been standardized, along with their ASCII values. Any character that appears in this table will be correctly recognized by any computer system that reads ASCII text files. In this table you will find the letters of the Roman alphabet, numbers (0 to 9), and many punctuation marks and other symbols. You will not find any international characters, any of the Greek letters, an en dash, or many other symbols; these characters are not part of the ASCII standard. If any characters appear in an index that do not appear in the ASCII table, they will have to be coded for the target system in a special way.

Although many computer manuals list the international characters and various symbols as part of the ASCII character set, any character after ASCII 127 is not part of the International Standard 646. The only standardized text characters are those with an ASCII value between 32 (the space character) and 126 (the tilde character). Many word processing programs for IBM PCs and compatibles do handle characters beyond ASCII 127. But what ultimately matters is how the page design software on the target system will handle these characters.

Because characters after ASCII 127 are not truly standardized, it is often necessary to code each character individually. For instance, the actual typesetting code for many of the French and German characters varies according to which vendor's typeface is being used for typesetting. One method for handling such complexities that has emerged in recent years is generically coded ASCII text files. This type of text file will be discussed in a moment.

It is important for indexers to understand that special characters usually require special treatment. Even if indexers can see the special characters on their computer screens, it does not necessarily follow that their clients will enjoy the same view. In fact, it is very likely that the special characters will not appear in the same way on the target system's computer screen.

ASCII Text Files and Generic Coding

An ASCII text file with generic coding can be read and manipulated by any computer system that reads ASCII. An excellent resource for information about generic coding for indexes is the American Society of Indexers publication *Generic Markup of Electronic Index Manuscripts* by Hugh Maddocks.

To qualify as an ASCII text file, a file must, according to Maddocks (1988: 1), (1) contain "only those characters defined by the American Standard Code for Information Interchange (ASCII)," (2) be "structured into lines terminated by a carriage return character (decimal value 13) followed by a line feed character (decimal value 10)," and (3) be "terminated by an end-of-file character (decimal value 26)."

Most PC-based word processing programs and all dedicated indexing programs are capable of producing an ASCII text as described above. Maddocks describes generic coding as follows:

> Generic markup is nothing more than assigning groups of ASCII characters to label parts of an electronic manuscript such as headings, words in italics, sections (such as the index), and special characters not defined by ASCII. The generic marks (codes) placed in the electronic manuscript serve, in part, the same purpose as copyeditors' marks for typesetting placed on a conventional paper

copy of the manuscript. Generic codes are used in electronic manuscripts so that a typesetter does not have to search through the computer files and insert the required codes one at a time.

For a number of years publishers have been accepting or requiring the submission of index manuscripts on disk. Now many publishers require the use of a set of generic codes in their indexing style guides. A national standard for electronic manuscript preparation and markup has been developed through the joint efforts of the National Information Standards Organization (NISO) and the Association of American Publishers (AAP). The *Standard for Electronic Manuscript Preparation and Markup* was formally adopted as ANSI/NISO Z39.59-1988. This ANSI/NISO standard is an application of the Standard Generalized Markup Language (SGML) that was formally adopted in 1986 by the International Standards Organization (ISO) as ISO 8879.

The Electronic Publishing Special Interest Group (EPSIG) was established as a clearinghouse for information about ANSI Z39.59-1988 and other standards of interest to those involved in electronic publishing. Copies of the Standard and companion guides to the Standard are available from EPSIG. EPSIG also publishes an informative newsletter devoted to SGML applications and other items of interest to electronic publishers (see appendix F).

Another widely used set of generic codes are those of the University of Chicago Press. In 1987 the Press published, for authors and publishers, the *Chicago Guide to Preparing Electronic Manuscripts.* Although this guide addresses issues beyond the preparation of indexes, indexers would benefit from its excellent overview of the problems and advantages of electronic manuscript submission from both the author's and the publisher's perspective.

In the discussion that follows, examples of both ANSI/NISO coding (ANSI Z39.59-1988) and University of Chicago Press coding will be presented. Codes that do not appear in the *Chicago Guide* are drawn from Maddocks (1988). A summary of common generic codes needed in indexes is provided for both sets of codes in appendix C.

Heading levels. In an indented style index, the various levels of the index need to be coded. In the examples that follow, the final printed version of the index entries will be presented first, followed by the ANSI/NISO coded lines and the Chicago coded lines.

Final printed version

roses
   grafting, 19
   propagating, 67
   pruning, 56

ANSI/NISO Codes	University of Chicago Codes
`<itm>roses`	`<x1>roses</x1>`
`<sit2>grafting, 19`	`<x2>grafting, 19</x2>`
`<sit2>propagating, 67`	`<x2>propagating, 67</x2>`
`<sit2>pruning, 56`	`<x2>pruning, 56</x2>`

Notice that in both generic code examples all the index lines are flush left, without indention. In place of indention are codes that indicate the heading level for each line. Unlike the ANSI/NISO coding system, the University of Chicago Press system requires an end-of-line code for each type of heading level.

En dashes. Many publishers require that an en dash rather than a hyphen be used to indicate inclusive page numbers or page ranges. In order to indicate an en dash, as in "dogs, 35–40," the following codes would be used:

ANSI/NISO Code: `&ndash;`
dogs, 35`&ndash;`40

Chicago Code: `<n>`
dogs, 35`<n>`50

In both examples the en dash code is set tight. That is, there are no spaces in front of or behind the code.

Typeface changes. Many indexes contain *See* and *See also* cross-references. Frequently *See* and *See also* are set in italic type. To indicate italics—as in "books. *See* publishing"—ANSI/NISO uses the following codes:

```
ANSI/NISO Code: <it> to start; </it> to end
books. <it>See</it> publishing

Chicago Code: <i> to start; </i> to end
books. <i>See</i> publishing
```

Special characters. As appendixes D and E indicate, there are codes for special characters. Many European characters are included in appendix D. Both the ANSI/NISO and University of Chicago code sets contain many more codes than are illustrated in these two appendixes. Indexers who need to code characters that do not appear here either can refer to the appropriate publication of ANSI/NISO or, for the University of Chicago Press, can devise a unique code and advise the publisher what they have used. Following is an example of two methods used to code for the non-ASCII characters in the word Pâté—the circumflex and the acute accent:

```
ANSI/NISO Codes: â = &acirc; and é = &eacute;
  P&acirc;t&eacute;

Chicago Codes: â = <cir>a and é = <ac>e
P<cir>at<ac>e
```

It is not hard to imagine how difficult it would be to proofread a heavily coded electronic manuscript. Luckily, such files are imported directly into the target system's software and printed so that it can be quickly seen whether or not the coding is correct. Indexers who use dedicated indexing software can have the software automatically insert generic codes into the index text file. Coding a text file manually would be very time consuming and errors easily introduced. Some indexing software vendors provide the ability to insert standardized sets of generic codes as well as the ability to build user-defined code tables.

Layout of the Index

Rather than an exhaustive discussion of typography and layout considerations regarding indexes, this section is a discussion of general page design principles for attractive index presentation. Additionally, since many publishers work with page design software in house to produce camera-ready copy, formatting suggestions for desktop publishing software will be presented.

Most of the discussion that follows will focus on the layout of an indented style index. As was pointed out earlier, an indented index is the most usable format. A run-in index format should be used only as a last resort when the number of pages available for the index is at a premium.

Index Title and Introductory Note

The index should be titled. If there is only one index, then the simple title *Index* appears at the top of the first index page. Under the *Index* title is a good place to include the index author's name if the indexer is credited:

Index
Written by Tom Smith

If there are multiple indexes, each should be clearly titled—for example, Subject Index, Name Index, Author-Title Index, Index to Cases.

An introductory note is needed to explain any special conventions used in the index. The note appears at the beginning of the index, between the index title and the beginning of the index entries.

Type Size and Columns

Indexes are usually set in two or more columns per page in a type size that is smaller than the type used in the body of the book. The type size for the index is often two points smaller with the leading reduced proportionately.

At first it may seem that printing the index in the same type size as the book at one column per page would help the reader—the larger type size would be easier to read. But if the body text of the book is 10-point type with 12 points of leading, an index formatted in this size can be quite lengthy. If the index were printed at one column per page, readers would have many more pages to thumb through in order to locate index entries. The index would be quite cumbersome.

The index page design goal is to fit as many entries on a page as possible while ensuring that the entries are easy to scan. The page designer should remember that indexes are not read like the body text of a book. Instead, index users jump into the index at some point and scan the pages for the alphabetic section that contains the index entry sought. Ideally readers will be able to ascertain easily where they are in the index at any point on a page.

Text Alignment and Hyphenation

As noted earlier in this chapter, the alignment of the right margin of the index text is usually ragged right, or unjustified. When words in index entries are hyphenated, more characters will fit on an index column line. Many desktop publishing programs offer automatic hyphenation. If this feature is activated, the production editor will need to review the hyphenation carefully so as to avoid unsightly and confusing breaks within index lines. See the discussion about bad breaks below for more information.

Indention and Turnover Lines

In an indented index a style must be established that clearly indicates the distinction between different levels within entries. Indention within an index visually establishes the hierarchy of the index entries. When the hierarchy is clearly presented, the usability of the index is greatly enhanced. The indention levels, although related to index usability, also impart information. For example, a reader scanning an index entry that contains indented sub-subentries knows that the specificity of entries changes as the indention level increases.

Publishers often use a combination of em spaces to indicate indention levels. Generally, the main heading is set flush left with no indention, subentries are indented 1 em, sub-subentries are indented 2 ems, and so on.

Many desktop publishing programs allow for the use of points as a linear measurement. Such programs also offer other linear measures such as inches or centimeters. Regardless of which unit is used, a consistent indention measurement must be set up for each level present in the index. Each indention level is indicated by an even, incremental increase in indent length. If inches is used as the linear measure, main headings are set flush left, subentries could have an indent of .20 inches, sub-subentries could have an indent of .40

inches, and so on, with each subsequent level .20 inches greater than the preceding level.

Index text files that will be imported into desktop publishing software are often formatted by the indexer with main headings flush left, subentries indented 1 tab, sub-subentries indented 2 tabs, and so on. The actual linear measure of the indent is set up within the desktop publishing program by defining a particular length for the tab character. In the example described above, the tab would be set equal to .20 inches. Or if points are used as the measure and the index is set in 8-point type, the tab will be set equal to 8 points.

Closely connected to the formatting of indention levels is the formatting of turnover lines. If each line in an index always fits within the column width, turnover lines would not be a problem, since there would not be any. It is extremely rare, though, to find an index with no turnover lines. A turnover line must be indented in a way that will easily distinguish it from a subentry or sub-subentry indentation. The example below illustrates the problem that arises when a turnover line is indented with the same measurement as a subentry indent.

> journals
>> abbreviations of titles, 34–38, 54, 90, 115
>> copyediting of, 23
>> printing cost reduction using offshore printing
>> facilities, 120–25
>> storage of back issues
>>> in sealed containers, 67
>>> warehouse facilities for, 234
>> worldwide distribution of, 335

The third subentry above ("printing cost reduction . . .") is a long line that will not fit across the column width; it turns over and continues on the next line. Since the turnover line indent is not set correctly, the last portion of the entry, "facilities," appears to be another subentry that is not in alphabetic order. As the example shows, it is necessary to set up a specific way of handling turnover line indention.

Many publishers handle turnover line indention by indenting both main-heading and subentry turnover lines by the same amount of space; often this amount is slightly more than the indent for a subentry. This method works quite well for two-level indexes—that is, indexes that do not have sub-subentry levels—and is the method used to format the index in *The Chicago Manual of Style*.

Another method of handling turnover line indention is to add a discrete measure to the indention of the particular level of the index that is affected. Many typesetters use an en space as the turnover line indention increment. An en space is equal to half of an em space. If the em space is equal to 8 points, then the en space will be equal to 4 points. In this case the turnover line indent for a main heading will be 4 points (1 en space), the turnover indent for a subentry will be 12 points (1 1/2 ems), and a sub-subentry turnover line will be indented 20 points (2 1/2 ems). The turnover line indent is arrived at by adding 1 en to the em space indention for each level.

We can use the same method when working with inches as a linear measure. If the indention levels are in increments of .20 inches, then the turnover line indentions will be an increment of .10 inches (half of .20 inches). The entry below, using inches as a measure, illustrates the various indentions for levels within the entry and turnover lines within levels.

```
0" for main heading
 .10" for main heading turnover line
  .20" for subentry indent
  .20" for subentry indent
  .20" for subentry indent
   .30" for subentry turnover line
  .20" for subentry indent
  .20" for subentry indent
    .40" for sub-subentry indent
    .40" for sub-subentry indent
     .50" for sub-subentry turnover line
    .40" for sub-subentry indent
  .20" for subentry indent
  .20" for subentry indent
```

What's important in the above is that the turnover line indents are different from the indents that indicate subentry levels. The turnover line indention length is a static number that is added to the indention of the level of the line that turns over.

If the "journal" entry example were formatted with a correct turnover line indent, it would look like this:

```
journals
    abbreviations of titles, 34–38, 54, 90, 115
    copyediting of, 23
    printing cost reduction using offshore printing
       facilities, 120–25
    storage of back issues
       in sealed containers, 67
       warehouse facilities for, 234
    worldwide distribution of, 335
```

Notice that the term "facilities" is indented differently from either the subentry indent or the sub-subentry indent.

Bad Breaks

Bad breaks are unsightly and confusing line breaks from column to column and from page to page in the index. Bad breaks compromise the usability of the index. Bad breaks do not become apparent in the index until the type and layout of the index pages are set. Reformatting the index in order to remove bad breaks is usually the responsibility of the production editor. Dealing with bad breaks should not begin until it is certain that the text of the index is stable. Adjusting for a bad break on one page of the index often has a domino effect on the pages that follow. In other words, adding a line to the second index column on the fourth page of the index can move all the remaining index lines back another line, thus creating new bad breaks later in the index.

One of the most common types of bad breaks is the splitting of an entry's subentries from one column or page to another. The result is a new column that begins with a subentry:

```
journals                             storage of back issues
    abbreviations of titles, 34–38, 54,     in sealed containers, 67
       90, 115                              warehouse facilities for, 234
    copyediting of, 23                      worldwide distribution of, 335
    printing cost reduction using off-
       shore printing facilities, 120–25
```

Users looking at the entry on the right have no way of knowing that the entry "storage of back issues" is a subentry of the main heading "journals." A simple way of dealing with this problem is to repeat, at the top of the continuation page or column, the main heading with the word *continued,* in parentheses, inserted as demonstrated below:

journals	journals (*continued*)
abbreviations of titles, 34–38, 54,	storage of back issues
90, 115	in sealed containers, 67
copyediting of, 23	warehouse facilities for, 234
printing cost reduction using off-	worldwide distribution of, 335
shore printing facilities, 120–25	

Notice that the correct indention of the various levels is maintained in the example above. The word *continued,* often in italic type, follows the level at which the break occurred. If the break occurred within the sub-subentries for "storage of back issues," the carried-over part of the entry would look like this:

journals	journals
abbreviations of titles, 34–38, 54,	storage of back issues (*continued*)
90, 115	warehouse facilities for, 234
copyediting of, 23	worldwide distribution of, 335
printing cost reduction using off-	
shore printing facilities, 120–125	
storage of back issues	
in sealed containers, 67	

Again, notice how the correct indention levels are maintained so that readers can easily see the entry's hierarchy. In order to save space and avoid turnover lines, many production editors abbreviate the word *continued* as *cont'd.*

Ideally, any break within an index entry will be noted with the use of the carried-over part of the entry followed by *continued,* including breaks that occur between columns on the same page. The use of *continued* lines is particularly helpful to readers of indexes of large-format books with three or more columns of index text per page. When *continued* lines are provided in such indexes, readers can look at the top of each index column and easily know where they are in the index. Examples of such attention to detail by production editors can be found in the indexes that have been awarded the ASI–H. W. Wilson indexing award. A list of winners of the ASI–H. W. Wilson Company Award for Indexing is provided in appendix F. The award-winning books are examples of not only excellence in indexing but also excellence in index page design and layout.

Although dedicated indexing software can automatically insert *continued* lines in an index, such software is rarely used to typeset index pages. In order for *continued* lines to be placed within the index, the production editor must insert them in handwriting in proof, line by line. Obviously this can be a very time-consuming endeavor. Many publishers choose to use *continued* lines only when an entry breaks at the end of the last column on a right-hand page and carries over to the left column on a left-hand page.

Some editors suggest that intercolumn breaks on the same page of an index do not need to be adjusted with the use of *continued* lines because readers can easily scan the bottom of the previous column to locate the entry that is modified. But editors almost unanimously agree that a break that occurs between a right-hand page and a left-hand page must be compensated for by the insertion of a *continued* line.

Other types of bad breaks include the top of an index column beginning with reference locators that are carried over from another entry:

> 67, 82–89, 135
> dogs, 55
> donkeys, 89

In addition to being unsightly, this arrangement leaves the reader fumbling for direction and, hence, is unacceptable.

Another type of blemish to avoid is a single line at the beginning of an alphabetic section standing alone, "widowed" at the end of a column, or a single line of an alphabetic section standing by itself, "orphaned" at the top of a column. Readers could easily miss these entries.

Bad breaks such as the three described above can often be eliminated by reducing the leading within a column so that one or two more index lines can fit within the column. If the leading is increased, one or two more index lines can be forced to the next column. Another remedy for these types of bad breaks is to move a line of the index from one column to the next. This method works quite well when the index columns are not vertically justified on the page.

Sometimes an entry can be shortened by judiciously tightening up the language. But such editing must be done in such a way as not to change the meaning of the entry.

Page Design Tips

When working with a lengthy, dense index that is set in small type (anything less than 9 points), page designers might consider using a dictionary-style "guide word" across the top of each page. As in dictionaries, the running head on the even-numbered pages would contain the main heading that begins the page; the running head on the odd-numbered pages would contain the main heading that ends the page.

Indexes that make heavy use of special notation within the entries will contain a note that explains the notation. If several items require explanation—for example, abbreviated, compound reference locators that refer to different volumes in the collection—the designer may consider adding a running footer to each index page that translates the abbreviations. This would save readers time; they would not need to turn over and over again to the headnote at the beginning of the index.

"Header letters" are sometimes used to distinguish the individual alphabetic sections within a lengthy index. In an index that is set in 8-point type, a large (14-point) capital *A* could appear before the A section, a capital *B* before the B section, and so on. Such visual guides can greatly help readers navigate through the index pages. If there is not enough space for header letters, an attempt can be made to provide at least a blank line or two between the alphabetic sections.

9

EDITING THE INDEX

> When the indexer comes to the last page of a great book
> he rejoices to have finished his work; but he will find by
> experience, when he calculates the arrangement of his
> materials, that he has scarcely done more than half of
> what is before him.
>
> Wheatley, *How to Make an Index*

In 1979 G. Norman Knight found Wheatley's comment a fitting introduction to his chapter on editing indexes. It is just as meaningful now as it was in 1902 when Wheatley's book, *How to Make an Index*, was published.

This chapter will discuss three editing roles: editing by the indexer, editing by the book author, and editing by the copyeditor. Unfortunately, many indexes do not receive treatment from all three parties. Quite often professionally prepared indexes are not reviewed by authors. Authors who prepare their own indexes frequently turn over to their copyeditors material that is in need of extensive editing that is best done by the person who indexed the book.

It is extremely important for all parties to budget time for review and editing of the index. Professional indexers should build editing time into their work schedule. If an index is to be reviewed by an author, a minimum of three to four days should be added to the schedule so that the author has time to receive the index, review it, and work with the indexer to integrate any changes. After the author and indexer have completed their collaboration, the index is turned over to the copyeditor at the publishing house. The copyeditor may be expected to deliver the index to the production department within a day or two after its receipt. Of course, the time estimates above are very tentative. Long and complex indexes will obviously require more editing time.

Authors must understand how little time is available for index review. Because of time considerations, many publishers do not encourage the author to review the index at all. One editor describes the situation in this way:

> We give the author very little time for review. The index is sent by Federal Express to her in manuscript—only if she asks for it. She has to phone in her changes, but she is not encouraged to have any. Otherwise, the author receives page proofs to look at [via Federal Express again, any response must be made by phone]. This last chance is all we give the author. Of course, by this point it is mostly a pro forma OK we are looking for.

EDITING BY THE INDEXER

Like any piece of writing, an index will require editing by its author. When an indexer reaches the last page of text and enters the last entry, what lies before her is a first draft of the index. The editorial work that follows involves several types of editing skills: substantive editing, copyediting, and proofreading. While the publisher will undoubtedly perform copyediting and proofreading tasks, the indexer should provide an index manuscript that is in need of few, if any, copyediting or proofreading changes.

Because an index is internally complex, substantive editing tasks should be left to the indexer alone. Decisions regarding the rewriting or reorganization of material in an index are best made by the indexer. Careless reorganization of an index can easily result in a breakdown of the conceptual interrelationships within the index.

Editing is an integral component of the indexing process. As an indexer works with the text, editing decisions are made along with entry selection decisions. Frequently the structure of the index does not emerge until after a few chapters of a book have been indexed. Early in the indexing process the indexer may return to the first 25 percent of the index entries and completely restructure them.

The index is molded and remolded throughout the first "sweep" through the text. This is one reason that an editor's or author's interim review of an index is often not of great benefit. The draft of the index that is sent off for review on day ten may bear little resemblance to the index on day fifteen. An index contracts and expands as it develops. Term selection that made sense on page 125 may not make as much sense by the time the indexer reaches page 230. She may go back to the entries on page 125 and rephrase them in light of the new information on page 230.

As the indexer adds new entries, old entries are constantly being manipulated. A biological metaphor for this process would not be far off the mark. New cells grow and old cells divide; synergy is at work that results in a functioning organism in which renegade or mutant aberrations have been identified and eliminated. Index writing integrates substantive editing into the initial creative writing process.

The important role that dedicated indexing software plays in the editing process cannot be ignored. Indexers who are able to work with the emerging index in sorted order at all times are able to get a sense of the overall structure of the index quickly. Global search and replace operations greatly aid in the restructuring of entries. Indexers who work with this type of software claim that many editing tasks are completed during the index-writing stage; there is far less editing to do at the final stages of the indexing process.

Perhaps this intense integration of editing into the index-writing process occurs because of the short amount of time allowed for indexing. Whatever the cause, experienced indexers know when the proper structure for an index has emerged. They can feel it. Once the structure is in place, the cadence of work changes. Term selection seems to move faster. The indexer knows where to place new entries within the index network.

Experienced indexers also know when the structure is not working. But the sense that an index structure is not working is often a good sign. It is what precedes finding the proper structure. Indexers must pay attention to their "inner voice." Indexers have even been known to discover the key while dreaming at night. In the morning they return to their index, rework it, and "feel" the index fall into place.

One of my colleagues, when asked the question, "What is it that really goes on in indexing?" answered, "Magic!" While magic may or may not play a role, the intense synergy between creativity and editing that grips the indexer is an integral part of the indexing process. It is this aspect of indexing that is difficult to describe and impossible to teach.

By the time the indexer has reached the last page of text, a definite index structure will be in place. It is now time for the indexer to change modes; the final editing process requires a very different perspective than did the writing process.

Substantive Editing Tasks

The most difficult and time-consuming aspect of editing for the indexer will be the review of the structure of the index. The indexer, while intimately involved with the index, must be able to develop an "editorial distance" from the work and view it with the eyes of the readers.

Main headings. Main headings need to be evaluated one by one, keeping in mind that they are the primary access points in the index. Do they make sense? Are they clear and concise? Are they worded in the way that readers are likely to look them up?

As the indexer proceeds through the index, inevitably inconsistencies and new relationships between concepts will emerge. Inconsistencies should be eliminated; new relationships must be molded into the structure of the index. The need for consistency in an index is paramount. For example,

        baseball, 35–49
        football
            history of, 80–82
            professional teams, 92–95
            rules of, 82–91
            San Francisco 49ers, 94

The entries above reveal an inconsistent treatment of a similar topic. Assuming that the discussion of baseball covers the same type of topics as the football discussion, either the baseball entry should be divided into subentries or the football entries should be condensed into one main heading "football, 80–95." If space allows, the baseball entry could be reworked as

        baseball
            history of, 35–36
            professional teams, 42–49
            rules of, 37–42

The football entry contains one more inconsistency. Why are the San Francisco 49ers the only team mentioned as a subentry? What about the Chicago Bears or the Washington Redskins? If in fact all the football teams are discussed on pages 92–95, there is no need to list individual teams under the heading "football." Instead, the subentry "San Francisco 49ers" should be eliminated and changed to a main entry. The indexer should also check the teams described on pages 92–95 to be sure they all appear as main headings within the index.

Similar kinds of topics in an index should be treated in a consistent manner. Readers depend upon this consistency when using the index.

Long strings of undifferentiated reference locators at the main heading level should be broken down into subentries. Exactly what constitutes a "long" string of page numbers is often defined in a publisher's style guide or, unfortunately, by the space allowed for the index. A common rule of thumb is that more than five reference locators should be differentiated by the addition of subentries:

dogs, 23, 29, 35–39, 98–103, 123–127, 158–164, 213–220

The number of locators provided in the entry above places an excessive burden on the reader. The entry is in need of further analysis by the indexer. The indexer will likely return to the text and provide subentries:

dogs, 23, 29
    breeding of, 35–39
    as companions, 158–164
    military use of, 213–220
    obedience training, 98–103
    search and rescue operations with, 123–127

Subentries. Subentries, like main headings, must be evaluated for their clarity and conciseness. Do they make sense? Are they worded in a way that readers will be likely to look up? Are they necessary? At the subentry level, typical candidates for editing are the single subentry under a main entry and the group of subentries that all have the same page number. The entry

> chicken recipes, 45–49
> Chicken Divan, 53

can be condensed to "chicken recipes, 45–49, 53" without a loss of information.

In the next example the subentries should be eliminated and then examined as possible main entries:

> file management, 35–36
>   copying files, 36
>   deleting files, 36
>   moving files, 36

If these subentries do not already appear as main entries, the indexer may decide to convert them to main entries:

> copying files, 36
> . . .
> deleting files, 36
> . . .
> file management, 35–36
> . . .
> moving files, 36

This type of rearrangement leaves intact the information provided by the original main heading, "file management," and at the same time provides multiple access points for specific information about the topic.

Cross-references and double-postings. Each cross-reference in an index must be verified. The indexer must be sure that the referenced term does in fact exist in the index. If a cross-reference reads "Judiciary, federal. *See* Federal courts," the indexer must be sure that there is a complete entry for "Federal courts." Remember that a complete entry will contain at least reference locators and often subentries as well. All circular cross-references must be eliminated:

> Judiciary, federal. *See* Federal courts
> . . .
> Federal courts. *See* Judiciary, federal

Cross-references must also be direct. We do not want to send the readers on a convoluted path to the proper term. If the indexer has decided to post information at "Federal courts," then all cross-references from synonyms should directly lead to "Federal courts." The following cross-references are in need of editing:

> Courts. *See* Judiciary, federal
> . . .
> Federal courts, 35–42
>   appointment of judges, 67
>   jurisdiction of, 78
>   political influence in, 83
> . . .
> Judiciary, federal. *See* Federal courts

The entry "Courts. *See* Judiciary, federal" should be changed to "Courts. *See* Federal courts."

Cross-references that send the readers elsewhere in the index only to pick up one or two references can often be changed to double-postings:

> autos. *See* cars
> . . .
> cars, 67–72

Rather than force readers to spend time going to another portion of the index, the indexer could add the page numbers at the "autos" entry and eliminate the cross-reference. Such double-posting is often best done during the final editing stage. Indexers should be cautious of double-posting information while writing the index. The danger is that the two double-posted entries may not contain the same information in the long run.

A crucial part of the final editing process is checking to see that all double-posted entries are mirror images of each other:

> autos, 67–72
>   compacts, 74
>   sedans, 128
> . . .
> cars, 67–72
>   compacts, 74
>   sedans, 128
>   station wagons, 88–89

In the example above, the double-posted information under "autos" is incomplete. Readers turning to the "autos" entry will not find the information about "station wagons." Readers should be able to go to an entry and feel confident that all related information about the topic has been gathered together at the entry. Readers should not have to second-guess the indexer and try to think of synonymous terms.

While it is often beneficial to provide multiple access points for information, the danger in excessive double-posting is that information will be scattered in the index. Scattered information forces readers to look in many places in order to gather all information about a topic. It is the indexer's job to pull related information together. The following series of entries is an example of scattered information:

> oak trees, 82–88
> . . .
> pine trees, 89–93
> . . .
> trees, 78–80

Ideally, the indexer will add subentries to the "trees" entry and the page numbers for the general "trees" references to the two other entries:

> oak trees, 78–80, 82–88
> . . .
> pine trees, 78–80, 89–93
> . . .
> trees, 78–80
>   oak trees, 82–88
>   pine trees, 89–93

Lastly, the indexer will review the treatment of synonyms in the index. As noted above, posting information at two or more synonymous terms may lead to scattered information. Such problems must be resolved during the final editing stage. But often during final editing the indexer will add cross-references for synonymous terms. The addition of such cross-references will add to the usability of the index and provide for a more coherent structure.

After the indexer is satisfied that the structure of the index is robust, still more editing tasks remain. The indexer must now wear the hats of a copyeditor and proofreader.

Copyediting and Proofreading Tasks

Many of the tasks that follow are performed by the indexer throughout the indexing process. However, all index manuscripts will benefit from a final review of the following items.

Alphabetizing

All main headings and subentries must be sorted in the alphabetic order desired by the publisher. Even if the indexer uses dedicated indexing software, a review of alphabetic order is still needed. Check the publisher's style guide at this stage just to make sure that desired alphabetic order has been followed.

Spelling

All words in the index should be spelled correctly. Any proper terms, such as personal names, must be proofread against the text. Indexers who use computerized spelling checkers must still manually review the spelling of terms in the index because, as we all know, computerized spelling checkers do not catch all spelling errors. The other problem with computerized spelling checkers is that many of the specialized, as well as proper, terms in an index will not appear in the online dictionary; the spelling checker will tag these terms as misspellings.

Accuracy of Reference Locators

All reference locators must be correct. Undoubtedly during the editing process, the indexer looked up many entries in the text. But there certainly will not be time at this point to check the accuracy of each and every entry. The indexer can at least make sure that reference locators are sensible. A locator such as "7883" may be in need of a hyphen or an en dash: "78–83." More troublesome is the incomplete locator, say, "125–." In this case the indexer must return to the text and supply the missing portion of the locator. Finally, all reference locators should appear in ascending numeric order, generally with Roman numerals preceding all Arabic numbers.

Parallel Construction

Main headings and subentries will follow a consistent grammatical format, whenever possible and whenever parallel construction does not distort the meaning of the entries or make them unwieldy. In the example below, the subentry "move" can be changed to "moving of" so that parallel construction is maintained within the entry:

> files
> copying of
> deleting of
> move

Punctuation

All entries must be checked for the correct use of punctuation in accordance with the publisher's style guide. A comma followed by a space separates multiple reference locators. Multiple cross-referenced terms are separated by a semicolon followed by a space. Neither the reference locators nor the multiple cross-referenced terms are run together without punctuation followed by a space character.

Main headings that are followed immediately by a comma and one subentry may benefit from rewording:

> books, teenagers and, 90

In the example above, "teenagers and" turns out to be the only subentry for the main heading "books." The entry would read better as "books and teenagers, 90."

Capitalization

The index must be reviewed for correct capitalization. If a publisher asks that every main heading be capitalized, this must be checked. If only proper names and nouns are to be capitalized, this too must be checked.

Format of the Index

If an index is presented in an indented format, indention levels must be consistent and correct. Any lines that turn over must follow the correct indention for turnover lines. Indexers producing a run-in index format should have been given explicit instructions by the publisher regarding margin settings for the index manuscript. The indexer must ensure that the margin instructions have been followed.

Cross-reference Format and Placement

The indexer must check that correct style and placement of cross-references have been followed throughout the index. For example, if *See also* cross-references are to appear as the last subentry, then there should be no *See also* cross-references running off from main headings that are followed by subentries.

Special Typography

The indexer must be sure that the correct typography has been used throughout the index. Titles of works are usually printed in italics and underlined in the index manuscript. Any other special elements used in the index must be thoroughly reviewed. If italic page numbers indicate pages containing illustrations, the indexer must check the page numbers for italic. At this point it would help to check the index citations against a list of illustrations from the publisher.

Query Resolution

Any unanswered questions that have emerged during the indexing process must be resolved. For instance, if the indexer has noted inconsistent spellings of an individual's name, the editor or author must be queried unless the indexer is certain of the correct spelling. If the indexer is certain that a name or term has been misspelled, it is kind to provide the editor with this information so that the misspelling can be corrected in the text.

There are types of queries that should not be left until the end of indexing. If the indexer notices any error that may affect the placement of text on pages of the book—such as a misplaced illustration—the editor should be contacted immediately.

Introductory Note

If the index includes any use of special symbols, abbreviations, unconventional sorting methods, or typography, the indexer will write a note that explains the use of such devices. Additionally, if portions of the text are deliberately not indexed, this information is included in the note. The introductory note is placed at the beginning of the index, preceding all entries. It should be worded as succinctly as possible. If it looks too lengthy, users of the index will resist reading it.

Submission Format

An index is usually submitted in two formats: as manuscript copy and as a text file on disk. Any last minute changes that are written on the manuscript copy must also be integrated into the electronic file. While the manuscript submission format is usually straightforward, the electronic submission format can be complex. As was pointed out in the previous chapter, many indexes submitted on disk are heavily coded. Some are difficult to read due to the codes. At a minimum, the indexer will check the text file for proper coding. If the coding has been inserted automatically by the computer, then it is necessary to check only a handful of typical entries. For example, one could locate a term that should be coded for italics and make sure that the beginning and ending codes are correct. Codes that indicate levels in the index should be checked. If end-of-line codes are required, a spot-check of a few of these will reveal whether the correct codes have been inserted. The indexer should be sure to scroll through the index to make sure that the entire index, from A to Z, is included in the file.

Indexers who insert the codes manually have a huge proofreading task awaiting them. As those of us who use them know, computers are very literal. A misplaced generic code can cause havoc once the file containing it has been accessed by the client's publishing system. Files that contain manually inserted codes must be checked line by line for accuracy.

Indexer's Editing Checklist

Main headings: clear, concise, sensible

Subentries: clear, concise, sensible

Cross-references: verified

Cross-references: correct format and placement

Double-postings: complete "mirror images" of one other

Alphabetizing

Spelling

Accuracy of reference locators

Parallel construction

Punctuation
Capitalization
Format of the index
Special typography
Query resolution
Introductory note
Submission format

Editing by the Author

Authors who prepare their own indexes should also perform the editing tasks described in the previous section. Authors who review an index prepared by someone else will do best to focus on the conceptual content of the index. Of course, if the author notices any misspellings or typographical errors, these errors should be pointed out to the indexer.

Authors need not concern themselves with stylistic matters. Rather, they should review the index for completeness and access to information. Before actually looking at the index, some authors find it helpful to reflect on the content of their books and to compose a list of their major topics. With this list in hand, authors can check their indexes by looking up the terms in the index.

Some authors prefer to sit down with the index and read it. They will look up in the text any entries whose meaning is unclear. Authors can also randomly flip through their set of final page proofs and attempt to locate index entries for selected pages.

The author may find it very helpful to have in hand a listing of index entries in page-number order as well as a manuscript copy of the formatted index. The page-number-order listing can be used when the author cannot locate index entries for a particular item on a particular page. The page-number-order listing will provide a list of entries for the page in question; the author will doubtless locate the entry in this listing. It is possible that the indexer has phrased the topic differently than the author would have. At this point the author may suggest a cross-reference that will guide most readers to the entry. Or the author may wish to have the entry changed.

Authors must try to avoid substantial restructuring of the index. If entries are not phrased in the same manner that the author might phrase them, then cross-references can be inserted in the index. Undoubtedly the author will be reminded by both the copyeditor and the indexer that there is very little time available for review and reworking of the index. Authors are often expected to return comments about the index within a day or two of its receipt.

It is best if the indexer makes the author aware of any restrictions that the publisher has placed on the index. Many problems that arise during the author review stage are due to the author's lack of understanding of the constraints under which the indexer worked. The most common restriction is space—forcing the index into a limited number of pages. If the indexer has followed particular space-saving procedures, the author needs to know what they are. If written works are posted only as titles and not by authors' names, for example, this convention should be explained to the author.

The author who has abdicated involvement with the index up to this point is not in a good position to insist on major changes that would affect the length of the index or the production schedule for the book. On finding the index unsatisfactory, the author should contact the editor immediately and be prepared to clearly and calmly indicate the structural problems of the index.

A properly prepared index will very likely impress the author. It is easy for the author to be "swept away" by the depth and intricacy of the index and fail to review it in a detailed manner. Many authors look at a well-prepared index and say, "I didn't realize that I discussed all of that!" Authors must try to approach the index from the perspective of their intended audience. They should look up concepts and topics in the index as a reader might do.

If particular topics seem to be missing, authors should contact the indexer. Chances are good that the material is covered somewhere in the index. The indexer and the author can then discuss a better way of providing access to the information.

Ideally, the author will have an opportunity to review the index before it is sent to the publisher and the indexer will be allowed to integrate the author's suggestions into the index before the index is submitted to the publisher. But the publishing world rarely operates within an ideal time frame. It is more likely that the author will receive the index from the publisher after the indexer has submitted it. All too often the indexer is "out of the loop" at this point; the index is in the hands of the editor, and few authors have the right of consultation. However, any substantial changes in the index should be discussed with the indexer, who is in the best position to revise the index. Frequently the indexer is not consulted about such changes and the integrity of the index is compromised.

It may come as a surprise to many authors that no one outside the publishing house will review the final page proofs of the index. Although many indexers offer to review the final pages of the index, rarely are they given the opportunity. All indexers have stories to tell about gross formatting errors in at least one of their indexes. This type of error could have been easily avoided had the indexer been able to review the page proofs. If authors want to see the final pages of the index, they must make this desire known to their editor early in the production cycle so that time can be allocated for this final review. Authors may also wish to include the right of final review of the index in their book contract.

EDITING BY THE EDITOR

Ideally, by the time the editor receives the index, little editing will be required if the indexer has done a good job. If the indexer and the author have worked together on the index, the editor need only proofread the index and review it for conformance to desired specifications. After that, the editor need only copyfit the index and send it to the production department for typesetting and final layout.

But most editors will not receive indexes that have been both professionally prepared and thoroughly reviewed by the book author. All too often at this critical point in the production cycle, an editor receives an index that is in need of heavy editing.

The advice found in *The Chicago Manual of Style* is worth repeating. "Copyediting a well-prepared index can be a minor pleasure, an ill-prepared one, a major nightmare. You cannot, as editor, remake a really bad index yourself. . . . you cannot turn a sow's ear of an index into a silk purse" (13th ed. 18.126; see also 14th ed. 17.132).

Copyediting Tips

The copyeditor's first task is to assess the overall quality of the index. Ill-prepared indexes fall into one of two categories: salvageable and unsalvageable. Since time is of the essence at this point, editors must be able to judge indexes quickly. Following are a few tips that may help the editor assess overall quality:

Length. A very short index is immediately suspect. If an index is excessively short, it is most likely unsalvageable. The ideal solution would be to have the material reindexed. An index that is excessively long poses different problems. Such an index is probably in need of thorough and time-consuming restructuring. Information in the index is probably scattered, with little or no pulling together of related information. While this type of index may be salvageable, salvaging it will require the attention of someone very familiar with the text and with indexing. The time required to edit an index of this type must be balanced against the time required to reindex the material from scratch.

Undifferentiated reference locators. Another telltale sign of an ill-prepared index is the appearance of entries followed by long strings of reference locators. While an editor may be able to live with eight or ten locators following an entry, having twenty or more locators is unacceptable. At first glance it may appear that breaking down these strings of locators into subentries will fix the problem. But the fact that long strings of undifferentiated locators exist at all is symptomatic of a lack of analysis in the index that will very likely affect other aspects of the index.

Cross-references. An index that lacks cross-references is suspect. However, if the index passes muster in other respects, the editor can add appropriate cross-references without unduly compromising the production schedule.

Term selection. The editor must review the conceptual content of the index, just as we recommended that authors do. When the editor is familiar with the text, checking for coverage of major topics will not be difficult. If major topics are missing, the quality of the index is suspect. If, upon looking up several entries in the index, the editor still does not understand the meaning of the entries, the quality of the index is in serious doubt. When the scope and depth of an index do not reflect the scope and depth of the text, the material most likely needs to be reindexed.

A word of caution is called for here. Frequently the editor who receives the index is not the book editor and is, instead, a production editor or project manager familiar only with the table of contents, the style sheets, and the type specs for the book. Review of term selection in an index should not be attempted by editors who are not intimately knowledgeable about the content of the book. If the book editing has been contracted to a freelance editor, the index should be sent to the freelance editor for review.

Accuracy. A copyeditor's rule of thumb for checking accuracy in an index is to randomly look up 10 percent of the entries in the referenced pages. If only one or two inaccurate entries are discovered, then the editor should check another 10 percent of the entries. If no inaccuracies are found in the second group, one can hope that the inaccuracies of the first group are anomalous. But if more inaccuracies are discovered, the entire index must be checked. This can be a tedious and error-prone task. The main problem is how to resolve the inaccuracies. If an entry cites page 78 as its reference when in fact the page should be 178, it could be very difficult for the editor to locate the correct reference. The editor who attempts to resolve such inaccuracies will only have time to check for inverted digits (such as 87 instead of 78) and dropped digits (such as 178 instead of 78), but not to leaf through the text, hunting for other kinds of errors. If the reference cannot be corrected quickly, it should be deleted. If an index is full of inaccurate reference locators, it is not usable.

Ill-prepared Indexes: Available Options

An editor has three options for dealing with bad, unsalvageable indexes: (1) publish the index as is; (2) leave the index out of the book; or (3) delay production and have the index redone, preferably by a professional indexer.

Unfortunately, in this age of "bottom-line publishing" we see the first option frequently exercised. Assuming that the index fits in the space reserved, publishing it "as is" in the short term is the most cost-effective approach. It is easy to sympathize with editors who are tired of dealing with troublesome authors and have little energy left to demand that the index be rewritten. It is also understandable that delaying the production schedule in order to rework an index can be costly. By the time the index is in the hands of the publisher very likely not much remains in the book's budget to accommodate preparation of a new index.

However, the publication of ill-prepared indexes can have long-term, undesirable effects. First and foremost, such an index reflects badly on the author and the publisher; it indicates a lack of quality and professionalism. In some books the index has a direct effect on sales. For example, instructors reviewing books for classroom use rely heavily on the index. When an instructor is faced with six possible textbook choices, the index is often the initial filter in the review process. If the instructor cannot find pertinent topics in the index, very likely the book will be put aside and the next index scanned. Acquisition librarians have strong feelings about good indexes in books. When it is necessary to decide between various books for purchase, the acquisition librarian will be more likely to purchase the book with the better index.

The second option available to the editor, not publishing an index at all, is the least desirable of the options. Access to information is severely compromised if an index is lacking. But if a given index would be an embarrassment to print, it might be better to be criticized for not providing an index rather than ridiculed by reviewers for publishing a bad index. Another problem with bad indexes is that they can be very misleading. Potential buyers of a book may look at an index, not find a topic, and assume that the topic is not covered in the text, concluding that the book is of little or no value to them. It may not occur to the potential buyer that the index is bad; indeed, many people will assume that the index accurately reflects the content of the book.

The third option, delaying production and having the index redone, may be the most desirable option, but it is probably the least feasible. It is the rare production schedule that has an extra two or three weeks available for last-minute reindexing. And locating an indexer at the eleventh hour can be very difficult.

What is especially frustrating about the submission of bad indexes is that the situation is avoidable. Many publishers are acutely aware of the need to employ or contract with skilled editors, skilled proofreaders, skilled production personnel, and skilled printers and binders. It would be unthinkable for a publisher to turn over a book-length manuscript to an individual for copyediting when that individual has demonstrated no experience in copyediting. And yet, often little thought is given to the professional qualifications of the writer of an index.

As soon as an author has submitted a manuscript, the editor should begin thinking about who will index the book. If the editor knows that the index will be written by an inexperienced indexer, every effort must be made to include time in the production cycle for extensive revision or rewriting of the index. Just as someone who has never before copyedited would not be expected to provide satisfactory services the first time around, so too would it be rare for someone who has never before indexed to provide a satisfactory index.

Good Indexes: What to Do with Them

The editor who receives a good index that has benefited from thorough review by the indexer/author must still examine the index. An index, like any other piece of writing, will benefit from another stage of copyediting and proofreading. If the index has been submitted electronically, it should be printed as soon as possible to ensure that no "computer problems" are lurking in the background.

The following checklist is for editors who find the structure of the index in good order and must perform only basic copyediting and proofreading tasks.

COPYEDITOR'S CHECKLIST

Check alphabetizing of main entries and subentries
Check order of subentries if the order is not alphabetic
Check spelling of all words in the index
Check punctuation
Verify cross-references
Check accuracy of reference locators
Check typography
Check that formatting is correct, especially of cross-references

Some of the editing tasks listed above can be done at the manuscript stage. Other tasks, though, are best left until the index page proofs are in hand. In particular, matters relating to typography will need to be checked on the final typeset pages. Those editors who must mark up an index manuscript for typesetting should follow the same general procedures used for the markup of any manuscript copy.

REDUCING THE LENGTH OF AN INDEX

For the purpose of the discussion that follows, we will assume that all layout and formatting options that squeeze more index entries onto a page have been fully exploited and still an index needs to be reduced in size. Eliminating entries from a well-prepared index is a thankless task. Eliminating entries from such an index reduces to some extent the access to information in the index; it should be attempted only by someone intimately familiar with both the index and the text. Ideally, the indexer will be asked to reduce the size of the index. The indexer knows the index thoroughly and will be in a better position to shorten it without severely compromising its internal structure.

The number of index lines that need to be deleted should be ascertained. If only a 1 percent reduction in size is needed, removing the necessary amount of entries will not be difficult. However, a 10 percent reduction in size can prove to be quite complicated.

In an indented style index, the first candidate for elimination would be sub-subentries. All sub-subentries can be eliminated and their reference locators pulled up to the subentry they modify.

If the index is a two-level index (main headings and subentries), the editor can scan the index looking for subentries that are followed by only one page number. These subentries can be eliminated and their reference locators pulled up to the main heading that they modify.

Another method that can be used to save space is to examine all the index lines that turn over in an indented index. It may be possible to rephrase the entry so that it fits on one line. In a run-in index, the same method can be used: shorten as many entries as possible without distorting the meaning of the entry. Always make sure that rephrased entries are alphabetized correctly.

If the index needs to be additionally shortened, the next items to consider deleting are the *See also* cross-references to obvious synonyms. It is strongly recommended, however, that an attempt be made to retain all cross-references since they are integral navigation aids.

If it is house style to distinguish between continuous and noncontinuous discussion of a topic on consecutive pages, editors are cautioned to resist the temptation to consolidate page numbers like "Faulkner, William, 65, 66, 67"—and change them to "65–67." Remember that the comma indicates separate discussion about a topic on the referenced pages whereas the en dash indicates a continuous discussion.

After the index has been reduced in size, it must be copyedited again. First, any entries that have been rephrased need to be checked for correct alphabetization. Second, all cross-references must be checked again. Entries that were referenced in cross-references in the original index may have been eliminated. The editor must make sure that terms referred to in cross-references still exist.

Revising an Index for a Revised Edition

When a revised edition of a book is published, the editor must decide whether to revise the original index or to write a new one. Three factors that will determine which is the better option are (1) the quality of the index to the original edition, (2) the extent of changes in the text, and (3) whether the original index exists in electronic format. The discussion that follows assumes that the person revising the index either is the author of the index or has obtained revision rights through copyright assignment or some other contractual agreement.

If the original index is not of good quality, there is no point in revising it. The revision process is not likely to improve the quality of a bad index.

Changes in the text can be editorial additions or deletions and pagination changes. If editorial changes are isolated and not extensive, chances are good that the original index can be revised. But if editorial changes are sporadic and occur throughout the book, probably revising the index will not save time. One critical factor is the effect of editorial changes on the original pagination of the book. If new material is added in chapter 3 of a book and the pagination after the addition is increased in regular page increments, the index entries that are attached to the remaining pages can also be increased by adding the difference to the original reference locators. But if the editorial changes result in the movement of text by paragraphs rather than full pages, repagination of existing index entries can be very time consuming.

Even when an indexer is able to work with an older index in page-number order, tracking new pagination on a paragraph-by-paragraph basis is very tedious. If the "creeping paragraphs" are restricted to a discrete portion of text, say, twenty pages in chapter 4, it may be cost effective to revise the index entries for the affected pages and then repaginate the remaining entries automatically.

However, in order to make a reasonable decision about the revision or rewriting of indexes, the editor must keep track of the changes in the text. Ideally, an editor who decides to revise an index will provide the indexer with the changed pages and a copy of the old pages. For example, the indexer may receive 50 new pages of a 300-page book. The pages may be from chapter 5. The indexer's assignment is to revise the entries for those 50 pages. The entries from chapter 6 onward will be repaginated by adding an increment of 13 to each page number.

An unsatisfactory and expensive arrangement would be to give the indexer old pages and new pages and ask the indexer to figure out where the changes have occurred. It is much better if during the revision process the editor has tracked every textual change that might affect index entries and every pagination change that will affect index entries. Armed with this information, the editor will be in a good position to ascertain if revising an index is feasible.

If the editorial changes to a book are substantial, the index should be completely rewritten. Changes affecting more than 30 percent of the text are considered substantial. Because the index is an intricate network of interrelationships, substantial changes in the text will greatly impact the inherent structure of the index. An index structure that worked well for the original text may need extensive revision if it is to fit the new text. A properly prepared index is not a structure that lends itself well to insertion or deletion of its modular parts.

If the original index does not exist in electronic format, any thought of revision of the index is best approached with great hesitation. Revision of an index should not be attempted unless it is possible to work with the index entries in page-number order. The absence of a page-number-order listing of index entries greatly increases the opportunity for error. Anyone revising an index must be certain that all entries on the changed pages have been found on the text pages. The only way to ensure 100 percent accuracy is to work with a page-number-order listing.

Since the mid-1980s, professional indexers have had access to dedicated indexing software that allows them to retain archive copies of index files that can be used at a later date for revision purposes. Many publishers receive indexes in electronic format. However, the electronically submitted indexes are generally formatted versions of the index. Many publishers fail to ask for (or require) simultaneous submission of the archive index files that could be used in the future.

If an index archive file, or data file, is not available, some formatted index files can still be successfully converted to a data file format. There are conversion services and programs that can prepare a formatted index file for import into a dedicated indexing program.

But it is often the case that no electronic version of the index exists. Sometimes publishers find it to be cost effective to have the original index pages optically scanned. The files created by the OCR (optical character recognition) process are then edited, converted into index data file format, and imported into dedicated indexing programs for revision. The cost effectiveness of this procedure must be weighed against the cost of reindexing from scratch.

It would appear that the use of embedded indexing software would greatly alleviate the problems associated with the revision of indexes. Indeed, the ability to quickly generate revised indexes from original text files is the primary raison d'être for embedded indexing software. However, the use of embedded indexing software is not without its problems. In the next chapter the advantages and disadvantages of embedded indexing software will be discussed.

Planning Ahead for Revisions

Many publishers know from the beginning that a book will go through revisions in the future. Planning for later editions can help make the indexing revision process manageable. The primary index component to consider is the format of the reference locator.

Using section or paragraph numbers as reference locators in the index, as in legal indexing, may be helpful. The primary benefit of using a section or paragraph number as the reference locator is that it is not tied to the actual pagination of the book. Paragraphs can be inserted, deleted, and edited; they can shift from page to page without affecting the index entries that follow.

Publishers of computer documentation revise their material frequently. Quite often computer documentation is paginated using a chapter–page-number sequence. The pagination for each chapter begins anew with page 1. With this pagination method, an unlimited number of editorial changes can be made to one chapter without affecting the index entry pagination for other chapters.

In some material, changes to the text are so frequent that a unique reference locator format must be designed. But all too often, little or no thought is given to the index reference locator format during the book design process. Updating and maintaining a thorough and accurate index under such circumstances can be a maddening and difficult task. Early consultation with an indexer can be very beneficial. For example, I was asked by a book design consultant to work out a pagination format for a set of policy and procedures manuals for a large bank. There were approximately fifteen hundred pages of text. The publications manager for the bank said that various portions of the text were revised on a biweekly basis. The publications department needed to be able to insert new pages at virtually any point within the set of manuals. The department also wanted to be able to produce a monthly cumulative index for all the manuals. A reference locator format was eventually designed that could accommodate the almost continuous revision of material. With the use of dedicated indexing software, the revisions were handled quickly and new cumulative indexes generated as desired.

Finally, electronic versions of indexes should be retained for future use. Both the formatted version of the index and an archive data file version of the index should be stored by the publisher. In the future, when a revised index is needed, the index data files can be put into a dedicated indexing program that generates index entry listings in page-number order and later can be used to repaginate entries in even increments. Remember that the index data files will not con-

tain any editing changes made to the index after it was submitted
to the publisher. So it is also a good idea to retain a copy of the
edited index manuscript. Should the index data files be used in
the future, the original editing changes can be incorporated into
the new index.

10

TOOLS FOR INDEXING

THE PRECEDING CHAPTERS have presented different aspects of index structure and design. This chapter will discuss various methods used by indexers to produce indexes. Regardless of which tool the indexer uses, the index must meet the specifications of the publisher that assigned the work. The adage "the right tool for the job" is as appropriate here as it is in carpentry. Just as the carpenter can choose between a hand drill and a power drill, so, too, the indexer can choose between manual and electronic tools. The first portion of this chapter will present manual methods for index production. The automatic indexing tools will be discussed next, followed by a discussion of computer-aided software tools. Lastly, ideas about the future of indexing and indexing tools will be presented.

Each indexer has her or his own way of working. There is great truth in what Delight Ansley said about methods of producing indexes: "The best way to make an index is the way that the indexer finds most convenient. If the result is a good index, nobody will care whether it was made with a notebook, a computer, or knots in a piece of string" (quoted in Knight 1979: 39).

For many indexers the first step in index production, regardless of which tools are used, is the marking of page proofs (see the discussion in chap. 3, "Getting Started," on term selection and the marking of page proofs). What concerns us in this chapter is what to do with the terms once they have been selected as entries by the indexer. This chapter will focus on the tools used to manipulate the entries and to produce the document we refer to as an index.

MANUAL METHODS

In this age of the computer, many scoff at the notion of using manual methods to produce an index. While professional indexers may find the idea of writing index entries by hand on 3″ × 5″ cards ludicrous, the manual method of indexing still has its place. Authors without computers who wish to write their own indexes are unlikely to invest several thousand dollars in hardware and software so that they can use a computer for one book index. Aside from the capital investment required to take advantage of computer-aided indexing tools, there is also a significant time factor to consider. Learning to use dedicated indexing software requires an investment of time. In the long run, occasional indexers may be able to produce indexes more quickly using manual methods.

Long before the appearance of the computer, indexes were produced manually, and various manual methods have emerged over the years. Here, only two methods—the use of index cards and the typing of entries into a text file on a computer—will be presented. G. Norman Knight describes several other manual methods in his chapter "The Mechanics" (1979: 33–39).

The 3″ × 5″ Index Card Method

We have all used index cards for one thing or another. These cards can also be used to produce an index. The procedure involves writing entries on the cards, alphabetizing the cards, editing the cards, and typing an index manuscript from the cards.

In the past, many style guides have suggested that indexers type the entries on cards (see *Chicago* 1982: 525). While typewritten entries will be easier to read and less likely to be misread than handwritten entries, most indexers who use cards do not type entries onto them. Rather, they write entries by hand. Those who wish to type entries on the cards can use continuous forms in the typewriter or printer. These forms can be ripped apart later to 3″ × 5″ index card size.

Each card usually has only one index entry. In this context, an index entry refers to a main heading, subentry, and reference locator; or a main heading and cross-reference. If sub-subentries are used, then the card will contain the main heading, subentry, sub-subentry, and reference locator. The following formatted index entry would be broken down into three index card records:

dogs
  feeding of, 56

  walking of, 89
  See also American Kennel Club

The alphabetized cards would look as they do in figure 10.1 (read up from the bottom).

Many indexers place more than one index entry on each card. However, beginning indexers should work with one entry per card until, with more experience, they learn how to judge what entries will be likely to fall next to one another.

When the cards are first written, they are not immediately alphabetized. Instead, the cards are placed face down in a stack so that before the entries become scattered throughout the alphabetic sections of the index, the indexer can verify the reference locator for each card. Prior to alphabetizing, the cards will be in page-number (or other locator) order. Such a stack of cards in entry order might look as they do in figure 10.2.

After the page numbers have been checked for accuracy the next step is to alphabetize the cards and place them in a container with alphabetic dividers. There are special filing boxes built to hold 3" × 5" index cards; these boxes can be several feet long. Shoe boxes can also be used to hold the cards. In any case, a box of some size will be

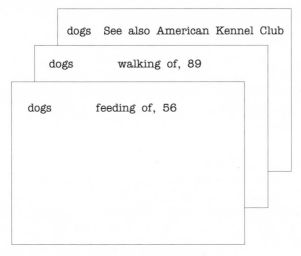

FIG. 10.1. ALPHABETIZED INDEX CARDS.

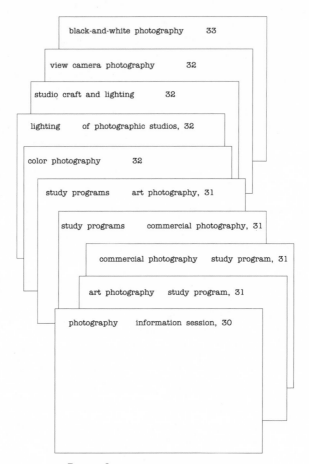

FIG. 10.2. INDEX CARDS IN ENTRY ORDER.

needed for a book-length index, which may require several thousand index cards.

Once a batch of perhaps several hundred cards has been alphabetized and filed, the indexer will perform editing tasks when filing new cards. Entries on previously filed cards will be looked up to ensure consistency in terminology.

Once the first sweep through the page proofs has been completed and cards have been written and filed for all entries, the next step is to edit the cards. At this point, a large work space is helpful. The index cards can be spread out on a large table so that various entries can be compared. Many of the editing tasks described in chapter 9 are performed at this time, as are reorganization and rearrangement of the entries. Corrections to entries are written on the cards. If necessary, the edited card is realphabetized. The goal at this stage is to prepare the cards for typing.

The last stage of the process is typing the index manuscript. At this point all term selection decisions and editing tasks have been completed. Indexers who must deliver the index on disk may choose to turn the cards over to a word processor operator. If the cards are neat and legible, the word processor operator should be able to produce both an index manuscript and an index text file on disk. If the index cards will be turned over to someone else for typing, a strong argument can be made for typing the entries instead of writing them by hand.

The Text File Method

Using a computer as a manual indexing method may seem a contradiction. But when the indexer must perform such mundane tasks as alphabetizing, we are still in the realm of manual methods of indexing. Indexers who have access to a computer may wish to use their computer to create an index by typing entries into a file and alphabetizing the entries manually. Please see the next section of this chapter for a discussion of more sophisticated computer-aided indexing methods.

The "text file method" of index production is quite simple. The entries are typed into a text file. Subentries are placed under main headings and indented, usually with a tab character. As the indexer adds entries to the file, the entries are placed in alphabetic order. For example, the subentry "painting, 149" would be inserted as the third line of the following:

    art classes
        monoprinting, 56
        watercolor, 89

One drawback to this method is that the indexer must think of not only term selection but also alphabetizing at one and the same time. The indexer working with index cards can focus on term selection and perform alphabetizing tasks at another time. Another drawback to the text file method is that as the file grows in length, moving from the end of the file to the beginning of the file to insert a new entry in the various sections of the alphabet can be quite tedious. One way to speed up this process is to insert alphabetic header letters in a unique way that allows for quick searching. For example, on the line above the *C* entries, the indexer can place the sequence "C$." When it is necessary to go to the *C*'s to insert an entry, the indexer can search for C$ and quickly be taken to the *C* portion of the index.

Benefits of the text file method include the ready availability of common word processing tools. For instance, the text file can be quickly searched if the indexer wishes to look up another entry. Many word processors include spell checking features. The index can be printed in manuscript form at any time; a printout can be a useful reference for the indexer working with long indexes. The primary benefit of this method is that there is no separate step required for typing the index manuscript. Assuming that the indexer is able to alphabetize quickly, the text file method may save more time than the index card method.

Indexers who use the text file method will naturally be tempted to let the computer alphabetize the index entries. As we shall see in the discussion that follows about embedded indexing software, allowing the computer to sort the entries is not an option. Even if the sorting modules available in word processing software could sort properly, there is the added problem of subentries beginning with a tab character or spaces that indicate an indention level. The character or characters used to indicate indention levels will be sorted along with the text characters that follow if a line-by-line sorting method is used. Such a sorting method will completely jumble the structure of the index.

AUTOMATIC INDEXING

automatic: *adj.* **1.** having the power of self-motion; self-moving or self-acting: *an automatic device.*
(Webster's *Encyclopedic Unabridged Dictionary of the English Language*)

Automatic indexing conjures up images of indexing at the push of a button, the computer taking care of all the drudgery and the thinking involved in creating an index! With respect to the way that indexing has been discussed in this book, the phrase *automatic indexing* is an oxymoron. There is nothing automatic about the index-writing process. There is no automatic indexing tool available that could produce the index in the back of this book. Many of the automatic indexing tools available are not intended to be used with book-length narrative text. Instead, they were designed to process massive amounts of textual data stored as titles of articles and reports. So automatic indexing is not *indexing* as the word is used in this book. In many cases, a more descriptive term for automatic indexing would be *automatic list generation*.

Automated indexing tools vary a great deal in complexity. An entire book could be written about the tools currently available, but here we will briefly survey some of the more common tools, one of which, the concordance generator, is found in many document processing software programs. Suggestions for further reading will be presented at the end of this section.

Automatic indexing tools can be divided into two types: (1) those that produce a listing derived from, but independent of, the document being indexed, and (2) those that are used to retrieve information in the online environment. The discussion here will focus on the first type of automatic indexing.

Intellectual versus Algorithmic Analysis of Text

Automatic tools for indexing are distinguished from computer-assisted indexing tools primarily by their lack of intellectual analysis of text. When computer-assisted tools are used, a human selects the text to include in the index; the computer manipulates the text and produces a listing in the format of an index. When automatic tools are used, the software selects text for the index on the basis of the algorithms that are part of the software's instruction set.

The distinction between the intellectual and algorithmic analysis of text has particular importance in regard to the writing and preparation of indexes as stand-alone documents. While there is interesting and challenging work going on in natural language research, computers are not able to analyze and synthesize text as efficiently as can the human mind. No automated indexing program currently available can compete with the experienced human indexer. No automated indexing program available can produce an index that conforms to the ASI–H. W. Wilson Award criteria for the content of an index. None can fulfill the British indexing standard's criteria for the function of an index. Most significantly, no automated indexing program available can be used to produce a proper book index.

The previous statement might appear to be incorrect since a common feature of most PC-based word processing programs is automatic indexing. And although many of the word processing programs also offer computer-assisted embedded indexing functions, it is the automatic indexing feature that we see advertised. What we have here is a terminology problem. The common feature found in word processing software is not *automatic indexing;* rather, it is *automatic concordance generation.* A concordance is a list of words that appear in a document followed by a reference locator. Unlike an index, no analysis of the text is required to produce such a list. There will be no subentries in such a list, no cross-references, no gathering together of related information.

Concordance generators are the simplest forms of automated tools. A concordance generator scans the text files and compares the character strings with an *exclude list.* The exclude list, also called a stop list, is composed of common articles, prepositions, conjunctions, and other terms that are to be excluded from the final concordance listing. In other words, the concordance generator will not list every occurrence of the word *and* or *the.* Any term not included in the exclude list will appear in the concordance in an alphabetic order which is often a modified ASCII order. A reference locator will be attached to each word in the list.

As an example, I used the section from the British indexing standard entitled "The Function of an Index," which appears in chapter 1 of the present volume, as a sample text file. I then ran the concordance generator that is part of the word processing software I used to write this book (WordStar) against the text excerpted from the British standard. Following is the concordance that I produced in this manner (the reference locators have been removed):

CONCORDANCE LISTING

Analyse	Headings	Produce
Arrange	Helpful	Relationships
Arrangement	Identify	Relevant
Based	Index	Scattered
Being	Indexed	Seeking
Chosen	Indicate	Series
Concepts	Information	Significant
Cross-	Locate	Subheadings
references	Material	Subject
Direct	Means	Subjects
Discriminate	Mention	Synthesize
Document	Nothing	Systematic
Entries	Offers	Terminology
Exclude	Order	Terms
Function	Passing	Treated
Group	Potential	User

As you may recall, the portion of text being "indexed" here consists of nine short paragraphs, 113 words. The list above is composed of 47 words. Approximately 42 percent of the words in the original text appear in the concordance list. The ratio of the number of concordance terms to the number of words in the original text decreases significantly as the size of the original text increases. But the number of undifferentiated reference locators increases dramatically in a concordance for book-length material. The term *cross-reference* has probably been used several hundred times throughout the text of this book. A concordance for this book would list each page on which the term appears. Although we can agree that the concordance generator is exhaustive in that every occurrence of a term will be identified, the usefulness of such a listing is limited when compared to the *cross-reference* entry in the index for this book. The index entry for this term is analyzed, whereas a concordance listing is unanalyzed.

Another type of automated indexing tool that has been around for many, many years is the KWIC generator. KWIC is an acronym for Key Word in Context. Closely related to KWIC generators are

KWOC (Key Word out of Context) and KWAC (Key Word alongside Context) generators. Wellisch refers to this trio as "The Three Stooges" (1991: 199), and I find the allusion to the famous comedy team appropriate.

KWIC and KWOC generators can be viewed as slightly more sophisticated concordance generators. Like a concordance generator, the KWIC and KWOC generators scan the character strings in the text and compare the terms in the text to the terms in an exclude list. If a term does not appear in the exclude list, it is added to the KWIC or KWOC listing. Unlike the concordance generator that lists only a term and its reference locator, KWIC/KWOC lists provide a specified amount of *context* in which the term appears. The context is a certain number of other characters in front of and behind the appearance of the term.

An example of KWIC and KWOC listings will better illustrate their capabilities. Again, the excerpt from the British standard, "The Function of an Index," is used as the sample text. The reference locators have been removed, and an exclude list has been used. The keywords in the KWIC listing (table 10.1) run down the middle of the page. The text to the left and right of the keyword is the context that wraps around the keyword.

The KWOC listing, which appears as table 10.2, places the keyword in the left column. The context appears in the right column. Unlike in the KWIC listing, which shows us the keyword within its context, we must look through the KWOC listing to find the keyword (buried) within its context.

KWIC and KWOC listings are very lengthy and dense. Like a concordance, these listings are exhaustive. A KWIC or KWOC listing cannot provide the same level of access to information that we find in an index written by a human. Even when these tools are used with article title collections, they are of limited value. As Wellisch (1991: 199) points out:

> Despite the pun in its name, a KWIC index is actually neither an index nor is it quick to use (though it is admittedly quick and cheap to produce). It is not a real index because title words alone seldom if ever express the entire subject matter of a document, and sometimes do not express it at all, as in the title of Lenin's famous pam-

phlet, *What Is to Be Done?*, published in 1902, which laid the groundwork for the Russian Revolution in 1917.

These types of information access devices have enjoyed widespread use over the years primarily in bibliographic collections. For a detailed treatment of this topic see chapter 12, "Word Indexes and Concordances," in Borko and Bernier (1978). Also of interest is Lancaster's discussion of precoordinate indexes (1991: chap. 4). Borko and Bernier (1978: 170–71) conclude that

> the permuted (KWIC, KWOC, revolved, rotated, term-pair) index is far from perfect from the searcher's viewpoint, but from the producer's viewpoint it offers a way of providing prompt guides to words in titles without the use of indexers and index editors and with only the help of keypunchers, a computer, and an available program.

Thus far our discussion of automated tools has focused on extremely unsophisticated, simplistic tools. There is far more interesting work being pursued in the information science community on automated indexing methods and information retrieval. Readers unfamiliar with information science or statistical information retrieval models may wish to read Bruce Croft's (1989) article "Automatic Indexing" for a gentle introduction to this subject area. Those who are comfortable with statistical analysis should read Gerard Salton's (1988) *Automatic Text Processing.*

Because the automated methods discussed in the referenced texts above are heavily oriented toward online access to information, they will not be discussed here, where our focus is the writing and preparation of indexes that are independent, structured documents. Most sophisticated automatic tools are not designed to produce indexes that are stand-alone documents. The algorithmic analysis of text, be it natural language processing or the application of statistical models, is certainly interesting. But when such methods are used to truly analyze text, they fall pitifully short when compared to the power of the human mind.

A computer is capable of quickly processing massive amounts of data while humans can process only limited amounts of material at one time. But when access to information is the goal, the intellectual and analytical skills of human beings are far superior to the algorith-

based on its terminology.	|ANALYSE	|concepts treated in the document so as to produce a series of headings
that is scattered by the	|ARRANGE	|entries into a systematic and helpful order.
to produce a series of headings	|ARRANGEMENT	|of the document. Group together information on subjects
information within the material	|BASED	|on its terminology. Analyse concepts treated in the document so as
cross-references. Direct the	|BEING	|indexed. Identify and locate relevant
terms not chosen for the index	|CHOSEN	|for the index headings to the headings that have been chosen, by means of
on its terminology. Analyse	|CHOSEN	|by means of cross-references. Direct the user seeking information under
Indicate relationships between	|CONCEPTS	|treated in the document so as to produce a series of headings based
	|CONCEPTS	
	|CROSS-	
by means of	REFERENCES	|Direct the user seeking information under terms not chosen for
to the headings that have be	|DIRECT	|the user seeking information under terms not chosen for the index headings
passing mention of a subject.	|DISCRIMINATE	|between information on a subject and
Analyse concepts treated in the	|DOCUMENT	|so as to produce a series of headings based on its terminology.
by the arrangement of the	|DOCUMENT	|Group together information on subjects that is scattered
Arrange	|ENTRIES	|into a systematic and helpful order.
headings and subheadings into	|ENTRIES	|Synthesize
to the potential user.	|EXCLUDE	|passing mention of subjects that offers nothing significant
	|FUNCTION	|of an Index
arrangement of the document.	|GROUP	|together information on subjects that is scattered by the
Synthesize	|HEADINGS	|and subheadings into entries.

so as to produce a series of	|HEADINGS	based on its terminology. Analyse concepts treated in the document
information under terms	|HEADINGS	that have been chosen, by means of cross-references. Direct the user seeking
the user seeking informat	|HEADINGS	to the headings that have been chosen, by means of cross-references. Direct
entries into a systematic and	|HELPFUL	order. Arrange
	|IDENTIFY	and locate relevant information within the material being indexed.
Direct the user seeking in	|INDEX	Function of an
within the material being	|INDEX	headings to the headings that have been chosen, by means of cross-references
	|INDEXED	Identify and locate relevant information
	|INDICATE	relationships between concepts.
Discriminate between	|INFORMATION	on a subject and passing mention of a subject.
Group together	|INFORMATION	on subjects that is scattered by the arrangement of the document.
have been chosen, by means of c	|INFORMATION	under terms not chosen for the index headings to the headings that
Identify and locate relevant	|INFORMATION	within the material being indexed
Identify and	|LOCATE	relevant information within the material being indexed.
relevant information within the	|MATERIAL	being indexed. Identify and locate
chosen for the index headings t	|MEANS	of cross-references. Direct the user seeking information under terms not
on a subject and passing	|MENTION	of a subject. Discriminate between information
Exclude passing	|MENTION	of subjects that offers nothing significant to the potential user.
mention of subjects that offers	|NOTHING	significant to the potential user. Exclude passing
mention of subjects that	|OFFERS	nothing significant to the potential user. Exclude passing
into a systematic and helpful	|ORDER	Arrange entries
information on a subject and	|PASSING	mention of a subject. Discriminate between

(continues)

Exclude	PASSING	mention of subjects that offers nothing significant to the potential user.
nothing significant to the	POTENTIAL	user. Exclude passing mention of subjects that offers
in the document so as to	PRODUCE	a series of headings based on its terminology. Analyse concepts treated
Indicate	RELATIONSHIPS	between concepts.
Identify and locate	RELEVANT	information within the material being indexed.
information on subjects that is	SCATTERED	by the arrangement of the document. Group together
that have been chosen, by me	SEEKING	information under terms not chosen for the index headings to the headings
the document so as to produce a	SERIES	of headings based on its terminology. Analyse concepts treated in
of subjects that offers nothing	SIGNIFICANT	to the potential user. Exclude passing mention
Synthesize headings and	SUBHEADINGS	into entries.
between information on a	SUBJECT	and passing mention of a subject. Discriminate
and passing mention of a	SUBJECT	Discriminate between information on a subject
Group together information on	SUBJECTS	that is scattered by the arrangement of the document.
Exclude passing mention of	SUBJECTS	that offers nothing significant to the potential users.
	SYNTHESIZE	headings and subheadings into entries.
Arrange entries into a	SYSTEMATIC	and helpful order.
series of headings based on its	TERMINOLOGY	Analyse concepts treated in the document so as to produce a
by means of cross-references.	TERMS	not chosen for the index headings to the headings that have been chosen,
Group	TOGETHER	information on subjects that is scattered by the arrangement of the document.
Analyse concepts	TREATED	in the document so as to produce a series of headings based on its terminology.
headings that have been chosen,	USER	seeking information under terms not chosen for the index headings to the
significant to the potential	USER	Exclude passing mention of subjects that offers nothing

TABLE 10.2: KWOC LISTING

|ANALYSE	|Analyse concepts treated in the document so as to produce
|ARRANGE	|Arrange entries into a systematic and helpful order.
|ARRANGEMENT	|by the arrangement of the document.
|BASED	|a series of headings based on its terminology.
|BEING	|material being indexed.
|CHOSEN	|chosen for the index headings to the headings that have been
|CHOSEN	|chosen, by means of cross-references.
|CONCEPTS	|Analyse concepts treated in the document so as to produce
|CONCEPTS	|Indicate relationships between concepts.
|CROSS-REFERENCES	|chosen, by means of cross-references.
|DIRECT	|Direct the user seeking information under terms not
|DISCRIMINATE	|Discriminate between information on a subject and passing
|DOCUMENT	|Analyse concepts treated in the document so as to produce
|DOCUMENT	|by the arrangement of the document.
|ENTRIES	|Arrange entries into a systematic and helpful order.
|ENTRIES	|Synthesize headings and subheadings into entries.
|EXCLUDE	|Exclude passing mention of subjects that offers nothing
|FUNCTION	|Function of an Index
|GROUP	|Group together information on subjects that is scattered
|HEADINGS	|Synthesize headings and subheadings into entries.
|HEADINGS	|a series of headings based on its terminology.
|HEADINGS	|chosen for the index headings to the headings that have been
|HEADINGS	|chosen for the index headings to the headings that have been
|HELPFUL	|Arrange entries into a systematic and helpful order.
|IDENTIFY	|Identify and locate relevant information within the
|INDEX	|Function of an Index
|INDEX	|chosen for the index headings to the headings that have been
|INDEXED	|material being indexed.
|INDICATE	|Indicate relationships between concepts.
|INFORMATION	|Discriminate between information on a subject and passing
|INFORMATION	|Group together information on subjects that is scattered
|INFORMATION	|Direct the user seeking information under terms not
|INFORMATION	|Identify and locate relevant information within the
|LOCATE	|Identify and locate relevant information within the
|MATERIAL	|material being indexed.
|MEANS	|chosen, by means of cross-references.
|MENTION	|mention of a subject.
|MENTION	|Exclude passing mention of subjects that offers nothing
|NOTHING	|Exclude passing mention of subjects that offers nothing
|OFFERS	|Exclude passing mention of subjects that offers nothing
|ORDER	|Arrange entries into a systematic and helpful order.
|PASSING	|Discriminate between information on a subject and passing
|PASSING	|Exclude passing mention of subjects that offers nothing
|POTENTIAL	|significant to the potential user.

(continues)

TABLE 10.2: CONTINUED

|PRODUCE	|Analyse concepts treated in the document so as to produce
|RELATIONSHIPS	|Indicate relationships between concepts.
|RELEVANT	|Identify and locate relevant information within the
|SCATTERED	|Group together information on subjects that is scattered
|SEEKING	|Direct the user seeking information under terms not
|SERIES	|a series of headings based on its terminology.
|SIGNIFICANT	|significant to the potential user.
|SUBHEADINGS	|Synthesize headings and subheadings into entries.
|SUBJECT	|Discriminate between information on a subject and passing
|SUBJECT	|mention of subject.
|SUBJECTS	|Group together information on subjects that is scattered
|SUBJECTS	|Exclude passing mention of subjects that offers nothing
|SYNTHESIZE	|Synthesize headings and subheadings into entries.
|SYSTEMATIC	|Arrange entries into a systematic and helpful order.
|TERMINOLOGY	|a series of headings based on its terminology.
|TERMS	|Direct the user seeking information under terms not
|TOGETHER	|Group together information on subjects that is scattered
|TREATED	|Analyse concepts treated in the document so as to produce
|USER	|Direct the user seeking information under terms not
|USER	|significant to the potential user.

mic skills of the computer. It is unfortunate that the sheer mass of material published in both the print and the electronic media precludes the writing of indexes for each and every document.

COMPUTER-AIDED INDEXING

Tools for computer-aided indexing manipulate index entries by alphabetizing and merging the entries, and formatting the entries into a structured index. Entry selection is performed by the indexer. The indexer decides exactly how to phrase all index entries. Ideally, computer-aided indexing tools free the indexer from mundane tasks such as alphabetizing and allow the indexer to focus attention on term selection and the structure of the index.

Computer-aided indexing tools can be divided into two categories: embedded indexing software and dedicated indexing software. Embedded indexing software is generally a feature found in word processing or page design software such as WordPerfect or Ventura Publisher. Embedded indexing software allows the indexer to insert index entries (or tags for entries) directly into the document's text files. Dedicated indexing software is stand-alone software that requires the indexer to type index entries and reference locators into the program. The sole purpose of such software is the production of indexes. Programs such as Macrex and Cindex are examples of dedicated indexing software. Both types of computer-aided indexing tools will be discussed in this section.

Embedded Indexing Software

Embedded indexing software allows the indexer to insert index entries (or tags for the entries) into a document's text file(s). The indexer inserts entries in one of two ways: (1) the entries are typed using special codes or commands that distinguish the entries from the actual text, or (2) terms in the text are marked in a unique way that identifies them as index entries. After entries are embedded, the software will generate an index by scanning the text, extracting the embedded entries, attaching page numbers to the entries, and then sorting and merging the entries to construct an index.

Embedded indexing software is a common feature found in most document processing programs. Many programs—WordPerfect, Microsoft Word, XyWrite, WordStar, FrameMaker, and Ventura Publisher, to name a few—contain an embedded indexing module. Several mass-market document processing programs have contained embedded indexing modules since the mid-1980s. While we have witnessed dramatic improvements during the past decade in the capabilities of document processing software, the indexing modules have remained surprisingly unsophisticated. The discussion that follows is based upon the state of embedded indexing tools in the early 1990s. It is fervently hoped that future software development will render moot the portions of this discussion that are critical of embedded indexing tools.

Although the way that index entries are embedded in text files varies from program to program, some generalizations can still be made about this method of producing an index. In some programs, embedded index entries are treated as "hidden" text. This means that after an entry has been inserted, the index entry is not visible on the computer screen unless a special command is issued to display the entry text. Other programs require the indexer to type the index entry on a separate line preceded by special codes that indicate that the text is an index entry. When index entries are embedded in this way, they are usually visible on the screen at all times. Embedded entries can be edited like other text in the file.

Regardless of how entries are embedded, when the document is printed the index entries do not appear with the rest of the text. Embedded index entries will appear in the index only after the indexer has asked the software to generate an index.

Most embedded indexing software provides two ways to designate entries for the index. One method involves marking text in the document file itself and issuing a command to include the marked text as an entry for the index. The second method is used when the indexer needs to include an index entry that does not appear verbatim in the text. The indexer moves to the exact place in the text where an entry should be embedded. A command is issued to indicate that an entry should be embedded at a particular point in the text. The indexer then types the exact text for the index entry.

Indexers who embed entries in the text files need not worry about assigning reference locators; the software adds the locators to the entries when the index is generated. That index entries can be written independent of the assignment of reference locators provides two primary arguments in favor of this indexing method:

1. Indexing can begin before final page proofs are ready.
2. Future revisions of the text will not require reindexing of the entire text since index entries will be retained in the text that remains unchanged. Since the entries are not tied to locators, additions or deletions of text will not affect the entry locators because the software will assign new locators if the text is repaginated.

On the face of it, these two arguments in favor of embedded indexing are quite convincing. However, very serious problems with embedded indexing tools lurk beneath the surface. In the discussion that follows every effort has been made to distinguish between technical problems with embedded indexing software and practical problems with this method of index writing. Technical problems can be solved by reprogramming. Practical problems require reevaluation of the entire approach to indexing in this manner. The practical problems will be discussed first.

Practical Problems

Time is of the essence at the time an indexer is creating an index from final page proofs of a book, as has been pointed out many times. Once final page proofs have been produced, the book is almost ready to go to the printer for manufacturing. Any indexing method that would give the indexer more time to write the index is alluring. Using embedded indexing tools, index writing can begin before the final page proofs are generated. However, we must ask ourselves, at what point is it practical to begin indexing?

It is sometimes suggested that index entries be embedded by authors as they write their text. But as noted earlier, writing narrative text and writing index text are two very different forms of writing. How many authors are capable of switching from one writing mode to another in midstream? How many would *want* to? If index entries are embedded in concert with the writing, how many index entries will remain through the editing and rewriting stages? How many first drafts of a book go unchanged? How much of the original indexing work will have to be eliminated as the text is edited?

Many authors who do embed index entries do not do so as they are in the process of writing the text. Instead, they return to the text files and embed index entries as a procedure separate and distinct from the writing process. Some wait until the text has gone through several stages of review and editing. Often the indexing does not begin until the document is undergoing a final review. While the author waits for comments from the final reviewers, index entries are embedded in text that is assumed to be fairly stable. Authors who wait until the final review stage to begin indexing have a much clearer picture of the structure of the book. Far less time will be spent reorganizing and rethinking the index if the general structure of the book is known before indexing begins.

Many writers use a computer and word processing software to produce their text. But most writers whose books are published by book publishers are not using the software that will be used to typeset and paginate their books. For example, authors may use Word-Perfect and deliver WordPerfect files to their publisher. What often happens at this point is that the WordPerfect files are converted by the publisher or typesetter to another format for typesetting. The page breaks in the WordPerfect file are not the same as the page breaks in the typeset copy of the file. In order for the correct page numbers to be assigned to embedded index entries in the Word-Perfect file, authors will need to go through the WordPerfect text files and repaginate the files, usually by forcing new page breaks, to duplicate the pagination of the typeset book copy. This will mean waiting until the final page proofs of the book are in hand. After they receive final page proofs, authors can go through their text files, which already contain embedded index entries, and repaginate the files so that the page breaks (and pagination) match those of the final page proofs. At best, this is a tedious, time-consuming, error-prone task to perform on three-quarters of a megabyte of text files—a common size for a book-length manuscript.

Thus far this discussion has assumed that the author will be embedding the index entries in the text files. These days, however, publishers, particularly technical documentation publishers, are more commonly asking professional (contract) indexers to embed index entries in text files. Aside from the great number of technical difficulties with this approach, there is the practical problem of providing the indexer with final versions of the files. Working with files that will undergo extensive changes is pointless; the indexer must use stable text files. The indexer cannot work on one set of text files while the author edits another set of text files. Thus, the advantage of beginning the indexing early in the publishing process is lost.

Another problem with current embedded indexing software is that it is very cumbersome for the indexer to move between various parts of the text. Many indexers refer forward and backward through the pages of a book while indexing to check other discussions of similar material. Most book-length documents are not stored in one file; instead, the text is often divided into separate files, perhaps one chapter per file. To refer to other parts of a book while online, one usually must open separate files to examine text in another chapter. The indexer will often avoid this step and instead leave loose ends that will have to be cleared up later during the editing stage.

Technical writers who index their own work using embedded indexing tools frequently work from a printed copy of their documents before embedding entries in the text files. These writers claim that they save a great deal of time by marking entries on the printed pages, primarily because the printed pages are much easier to read than is the computer screen. They also keep a printed copy of the entire manuscript close by solely for the purpose of referring to other portions of the text while indexing. Another advantage of working with printed text pages is that the writers can indicate exactly where to embed entries on the printed page. When they work with the text file, they know where to insert the index entry. Later when the index entries need to be edited, they can refer to their marked copy of the pages and easily locate the embedded entry.

By far, the most important reason cited above for embedding index entries in text files is to avoid reindexing the text when it is revised in the future. Even in the face of technical problems that increase the time needed for indexing by two- to threefold when compared with the use of dedicated indexing software tools, many publishers of frequently revised documentation claim that embedded indexing is still cost-effective.

In chapter 9 some of the problems inherent in the revision of indexes were presented. Even if we put aside the technical problems found in current versions of embedded indexing software, we are still faced with the practical problems of revising indexes. While it is true that embedded entries will be carried along when text is moved from one part of a document to another, it is also true that embedded entries will be deleted when the text is deleted. When a document is extensively revised, we must ask ourselves how much of the original indexing work will remain? Do the remaining entries still make sense, or has the basic organization of the index been undermined? If a significant portion of the index entries is eliminated, those entries that remain must be reexamined in light of the changed material, whether that material has been added or removed.

An index is an interconnected network of access points to information in the text. Tampering with the network links through deletions and additions of entries can significantly affect the integrity of the entire index structure. When a document undergoes extensive revision, the new index that is generated from the embedded entries must be thoroughly reviewed and edited. This type of review, in and of itself, can be very time consuming. The structure of the entire index must be examined. Every cross-reference must be verified. The new index must be compared to the old index to make sure that important entries have not been left out by mistake. When we add up the time it took to embed the entries in the first version and add the additional time it took to embed new entries in the second version and then add the editing time needed to ensure that the integrity of the index structure has not been compromised, we see that it would often take far less time to reindex the material from scratch.

If the document is moderately revised, the extra time involved in embedding index entries in the first version still cannot truly be cost-effective. A moderate revision can be efficiently handled without embedded entries by working with an index text file produced by a dedicated indexing program in page-number order. The entries affected by the new changes can be isolated in the page-number-order file, they can be edited or deleted, and a new index can be regenerated quickly.

For example, if it takes an indexer twenty-three hours to write an index using dedicated indexing software, we can assume it will take at least twice as long, forty-six hours, for the same index entries to be embedded in the text files. A minor revision of an index often involves only a few hours of editing and revision time when the indexer can work with the original index in page-number order. (A common feature of dedicated indexing software is the ability to quickly produce an index file in page-number order.) It is possible that such revision can be completed in an hour or two. A great many revisions of this type would be required in order to justify the investment of the additional twenty-three hours needed to embed index entries in the original document.

Another problem with revision of text that contains embedded index entries is the physical placement of the embedded entries. Many embedded indexing programs require that the indexer insert an embedded entry tag for each page associated with the entry. If "dogs" are discussed on pages 5 through 8, the indexer would insert embedded entry tags for "dogs" on pages 5, 6, 7, and 8. The indexing program would assign page numbers to the entries and merge them together in the index as "dogs, 5–8." Unfortunately, most embedded indexing programs do not provide a "copy previous entry" command.

Even though the embedded entries are not tied to the pagination of the text, the indexer's decision regarding the placement of embedded entry tags is often based upon the page breaks within the text. Many

programs that contain embedded indexing modules are WYSIWYG
(What You See Is What You Get). This means that the current page
breaks and other text formatting elements are visible on the computer screen. The problem with this approach arises when the text is
revised. At the time of indexing, the indexer cannot possibly know
where future page breaks will occur when the text is revised. Placement of an embedded index entry during the original indexing may
not be adequate when the text is revised. Figure 10.3 should help to
make this problem clear.

In figure 10.3, embedded index entries are indicated by "<entry
#>." When the embedded tags were originally inserted into the text
file, <entry 2> covered a paragraph of discussion that occurred on
page 12. Dark shading indicates the text referenced by <entry 2>.
The original index correctly cited this reference as "<entry 2>, 12."
However, eight months later the text for this chapter is revised. New
text is added at the top of page 12. The addition of new text moves
the paragraph that contains the <entry 2> tag to the bottom of page
12, with part of the original paragraph moving to the top of page 13.
The new index that is generated does not cite the continuation of
discussion on page 13 because the <entry 2> tag appears only on
page 12.

While embedded indexing software that allowed for *begin entry*
tags and *end entry* tags would solve the problem of creeping paragraphs and repagination, new problems could easily emerge. Using
the "dogs, 5–8" entry mentioned above, the indexer could insert a
"begin dogs entry" tag at the appropriate spot on page 5 and an "end
dogs entry" tag at the appropriate spot on page 8. If new text were
added prior to the page 5 tag, new pagination would be picked up
correctly by the indexing program if the text moved significantly.

Original Text   Edited Text
FIG. 10.3. TAGGED BOOK PAGES.

But we must consider what would happen to a paragraph within the discussion of dogs that was moved outside the begin/end tags. Let's say that the paragraphs on the original page 6 are moved to the end of the chapter and are now found on page 28. Unless the indexer remembers to insert new index tags within this text, entries tied to this text will not appear in the index.

It may appear from this discussion that embedded indexing is never warranted. While embedded indexing tools are extremely cumbersome and time-consuming to use, in three situations they may prove useful.

Material that will be published in both a printed and electronic format is a candidate for embedded indexing. Embedded index entries in online text files that can be dynamically tied to an online index greatly improve access to information. The index itself can serve as the structure for hypertext linking of online information. A more detailed discussion of hypertext and the indexing of electronic documents is provided by Liebscher (1993), Marchionini (1993), and Mulvany (1993) in *Indexing Electronic Images and Text* (Bellardo et al.).

As "custom" publishing, also known as "demand" publishing, becomes more widespread, embedded indexing software will be a useful adjunct tool. Custom publishing involves the production of selected portions of a book. Custom published books are now offered by some of the large American textbook publishers. For instance, an accounting textbook may in its entirety be 600 pages with fourteen chapters. In the past, instructors assigned the book for their classes but often did not require the students to read the entire book. A 600-page textbook could easily cost the students $50.00. But if the textbook publisher is involved in custom book production, instructors can specify which portions of the book they wish to use. For example, an instructor might request chapters 1–4, 7, and 12. The publisher would then produce in small quantities a book that contains only the specified chapters. A custom publishing system makes the production of such a book relatively easy. The text does not change, and therefore neither do the page breaks within the chapters. The new text pages are repaginated, beginning with page 1; a new table of contents and index are generated for the repaginated book pages. Because the pages of the book are not actually revised, embedded index entries are practical because only page numbers change.

The two applications of embedded indexing discussed above, online text and custom publishing, are practical if two criteria are met. First, the text itself must be relatively stable, that is, not subject to extensive revision. Second, the technical problems with embedded indexing software must be overcome.

The third situation in which embedded indexing may prove useful is when authors are the ones who will be using it. During the editing and revision of book-length manuscripts it is often necessary to refer to various portions of the text. It can be maddening for writers to search through a whole manuscript visually, looking for a particular discussion of a topic. They know the topic is discussed; they just don't know where! Authors who embed index entries in their manuscript can create a personal index that will be helpful during the editing process. While this index need not conform to their publishers' style guides, it can prove to be a very useful tool for navigating through a lengthy manuscript.

Technical Problems

Technical problems with embedded indexing software are related to software design or hardware limitations. Unlike some of the practical problems discussed above, technical problems can be resolved through reprogramming and the use of more capable hardware. A detailed discussion of the technical limitations of popular, PC-based embedded indexing programs can be found elsewhere (Mulvany 1990; Wittmann 1991). The discussion here will focus on general problems common to most embedded indexing programs. Technical problems can be divided into two categories: (1) problems related to actual index entry manipulation, and (2) problems related to user interface design.

Index entry manipulation. Index entry manipulation includes the sorting of entries, the formatting and placement of cross-references, the handling of reference locators, and the formatting of the index as a whole. As has been pointed out in previous chapters, there are different ways to sort entries in an index. The indexer needs the flexibility to sort index entries in a manner that will provide the best access to information for readers. In addition to choosing between a word-by-word or letter-by-letter alphabetizing sequence, the indexer must be able to control the sorting of numeric entries and special types of entries, such as names beginning with *St.* or *Mc.* Many embedded indexing programs do not even offer a choice between word-by-word and letter-by-letter alphabetizing.

The least sophisticated programs alphabetize the index entries in strict ASCII order. It is easy to spot this type of sorting because capitalized entries will precede all entries beginning with lowercase letters. One notch above the programs that rely on a strict ASCII sort are those that use a slightly modified ASCII sort. This type of program will typically sort letters without regard to whether they are upper- or lowercase. However, the extent of the modifications to a strict ASCII sort is usually limited to letters of the alphabet and letters that appear in the international character set. Often punctuation marks and other symbols are not assigned a new sort order; they retain their ASCII sort values. For example, "Who Is Sylvia?" will sort before apples because the ASCII value of the double quotation mark (034) is lower than the ASCII value of a lowercase *a* (097).

Some embedded indexing software is programmed to ignore such characters as double quotation marks and parentheses. But as a rule, these programs do sort on the space character, which means that letter-by-letter alphabetizing is not possible. Even if word-by-word alphabetizing is desirable, embedded indexing programs usually do not sort numbers in ascending numeric order.

The documentation for most of these programs rarely provides a thorough discussion of the sorting sequence used, but the indexer needs to know how entries will be sorted. Following is a short list of terms that can be used to test the sorting order of an embedded indexing program. These terms are sorted in three ways: (1) in strict ASCII order, (2) in word-by-word order, and (3) in letter-by-letter order. In both the word-by-word and letter-by-letter lists numbers have been sorted in ascending numeric order.

Strict ASCII Sort	Word-by-Word Sort	Letter-by-Letter Sort
"Who Is Sylvia?"	data structure	database
FORMAT statement	database	data structure
Intel 80386	format command	format command
Intel 8088	FORMAT statement	FORMAT statement
data structure	Intel 8088	Intel 8088
database	Intel 80386	Intel 80386
format command	"Who Is Sylvia?"	"Who Is Sylvia?"

Embedded indexing programs that do not allow the indexer any control over the sort order of the entries force the indexer to carefully review and alphabetize the index entries manually. In a book-length index, resorting index entries can take a great deal of time.

Most publishers require that leading prepositions, articles, and conjunctions in subentries not be sorted. Additionally, many publishers ask that names beginning with *St.* or *Mc* be sorted in a special manner. Lastly, many publishers require that numbers be sorted as if they were spelled out. Some embedded indexing programs allow the indexer to force a particular sort order through the use of a "Sort as" field. The program often provides the indexer with a dialog box where the index entries are input along with any "Sort as" instructions. For example, if the indexer wanted the subentry "of host mode" to sort as "host mode," the index entry dialog box might look like figure 10.4.

The "Sort as" field instructs the computer to ignore the *of* when this subentry is sorted. Likewise, the indexer could instruct the computer to sort a numeric entry as though it were spelled out, as in figure 10.5.

In theory, the indexer could force a letter-by-letter sort through the use of a "Sort as" field. Using the entry list above, the "data structure" entry could be entered in the dialog box as shown in figure 10.6.

In practice, however, indexers are unlikely to have the time to force a letter-by-letter sort in this way. Even with the use of efficient indexing tools, the index-writing process takes time and concentration.

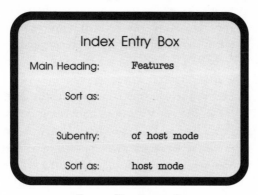

FIG. 10.4. DIALOG BOX 1.

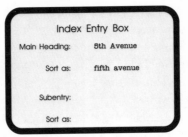

FIG. 10.5. DIALOG BOX 2.

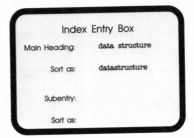

FIG. 10.6. DIALOG BOX 3.

While the addition of a "Sort as" field does allow the indexer to specify a desired sort sequence, the use of this feature requires a great
deal more time because of the additional typing of entries that is
required. Users of embedded indexing software have to spend a great
deal of time overcoming the limitations of the software itself—time
they could be devoting to the index-writing task at hand.

Most embedded indexing programs allow the indexer to insert *See*
and *See also* cross-references. The indexer, however, is usually limited to one pre-defined format for cross-references and a pre-defined
placement for cross-references. Some programs will automatically
place a *See also* cross-reference as a subentry at the end of a subentry
list. If the indexer or the publisher/client wants the cross-reference
placed at the top of the entry, run off from the main heading, the
cross-reference will have to be moved manually after the index has
been generated. Some programs will not merge multiple cross-
references into a single entry, so the indexer must add multiple cross-
references all at one time or merge them manually after the index
has been generated. For example, some programs produce

> See also formatting commands
> See also graphics

instead of

> See also formatting commands; graphics

Unlike some dedicated indexing programs, embedded indexing software does not always provide for cross-reference verification. The indexer will have to make a manual check that each referenced term in a cross-reference exists elsewhere in the index.

Embedded indexing programs will assign page numbers to embedded index entries. Some programs will automatically concatenate consecutive page numbers to form a page range. For example, "dogs, 3, 4, 5, 6" will appear as "dogs, 3–6" in some indexes. However, the indexer usually does not have the option of making distinctions between a consecutive discussion of a topic on pages 3–6 and a sporadic discussion on pages 3, 4, 5, and 6. The page-number concatenation feature is frequently automatic and cannot be turned off.

A handful of embedded programs provide for page-range compression or elision of numbers. The few programs that do perform compression of page numbers often follow the abbreviation sequence used in *The Chicago Manual of Style* (13th ed. 8.67; 14th ed. 8.69); other compression methods—which may be required by clients—are not allowed.

Those embedded indexing programs that can handle multipart page numbers allow the indexer to specify the character(s) used as the page-number concatenator. In a book that renumbers pages with each chapter, the following format for a page range is possible:

> roses, fertilizer for, 4–5 to 4–10

Most embedded indexing programs will assign only page numbers as reference locators. It is not possible to use a section number or paragraph number as a reference locator.

While many of the programs allow the indexer to specify that a page number be printed in italic or bold type, annotated page numbers are usually not allowed. For example, the indexer could not use the following types of notations:

Beef Wellington, 34–36, 42(illus.)
minimalist writing techniques, 124n

The majority of indexes produced by embedded indexing programs are printed in indented style, although a handful of programs can format a run-in style index. But when compared to the formatting capabilities of dedicated indexing software, embedded indexing software formatting options seem extremely limited. Turnover line indention is frequently incorrect. The bad breaks that appear throughout an index need to be corrected manually by the indexer or production editor.

User interface design. User interface design refers to the way a user works with software and includes what the user sees on the computer screen. In document processing software, user interface design varies greatly. While it is difficult to address the specific aspects of the user interface design of individual embedded indexing programs, some general comments can be made.

Many embedded indexing programs, particularly those written for PCs, are designed to tag index entries in text files. This means that the indexer can mark a word in the text file and the software will automatically include that word in the index. The design of these programs is based upon the spurious notion that index entries appear verbatim in the text files. Unfortunately, many if not most index entries do not appear verbatim in text files. It is extremely unlikely that a main heading and its subentry will appear in natural form in the text file. So, ultimately, the marking of existing terms in the text files as index entries is of little use to the indexer. Instead, it is often necessary for the indexer to type the entry in a form appropriate to the index.

On the whole, embedded indexing programs require the indexer to perform more typing tasks than do dedicated indexing programs. For instance, most embedded indexing programs do not include an automatic inversion function. If an indexer wants to include both "California, counties" and "counties, California" as entries, the indexer must type the two entries individually. On the other hand, many dedicated indexing programs will automatically invert the first entry (thereby creating the second entry) at the touch of a key.

In order to indicate a continuous discussion of a topic, the indexer must often embed the entry on each page on which that topic is discussed. Such a program should include a way to copy an entry automatically rather than requiring that the entry be retyped several times.

The weakest aspect of the user interface design of embedded indexing programs becomes apparent during the index-editing process. When working with the text files, the indexer is writing the index "in the dark"; the indexer cannot see the previous index entries. The primary way to view previous entries, aside from scrolling backwards through the text file looking for embedded entries, is to leave the editing mode and generate the index. The work area context is not right; rather, it is backwards. The indexer is striving to create an index, a separate document, and yet the context of most embedded indexing programs is the document being indexed, not the index itself. This is comparable to a writer watching text disappear every time a sentence ends; it is impossible to see an entire paragraph, much less the entire context of a discussion. So, too, index writers are extremely handicapped when they cannot work dynamically with the structure they are trying to mold.

The inability to view previous index entries easily leads to many editing problems later. For example, it is not uncommon to index a term in two forms, the singular and the plural (e.g., "book market" and "book markets"). This results in two distinct entries in the index which must be reconciled. If the indexer were able to work directly with index entries in alphabetized order, such problems could be eliminated during the entry-writing stage. Ideally, embedded indexing software should provide a window that contains a sorted and simply formatted listing of index entries.

In chapter 9, "Editing the Index," it became clear that even under the best of circumstances editing an index can be a very time consuming task. Editing an index produced by embedded indexing software is extremely tedious and will take longer than editing index cards or an index produced by dedicated indexing software.

Most embedded indexing programs generate the index as a separate text file; users of these programs are understandably tempted to edit the index text file only, without returning to the original text file to correct the embedded entries. If the embedded entries are not corrected, the entire purpose of embedding entries in the first place is defeated.

The practice of editing only the index text file is quite common. Many technical writers tell me that one of the first things they do when they revise a manual written by another writer is to generate an index from the unrevised text files. Frequently, the index generated from the embedded entries turns out to be quite different from the index printed in the manual. Apparently, the original writer made changes in the index text file without returning to the text files to correct the embedded entries.

We might find the following entries in the first draft of an unedited index:

book market, 34, 56, 191
book markets, 20–26, 139

If the indexer wanted to post all the references at the entry "book markets," the entries for "book market" would all have to be changed to the plural form. The text for a book-length document is commonly divided into many separate files. In the example above, the indexer might need to go into three separate files to locate and change the "book market" entries.

Since so much typing is required to get embedded entries into the proper form for the index, there will undoubtedly be spelling errors. Most embedded indexing programs do not allow a spelling checker to run against index entries alone. Correction of spelling errors in index entries can be another tedious task.

Massive restructuring of embedded index entries is rarely attempted because of the time that would be required to locate and change the entries. Since the practice of editing only the index text file is so widespread, what is sorely needed is software that will automatically update the embedded entries to reflect changes made in the index text file. Just as writers can fine-tune documents in their final, formatted state, so, too, indexers should be able to work with a formatted index and have the embedded entries or their tags automatically updated.

Summary

For the most part, the sorting routines employed in embedded indexing software do not conform to standard alphabetizing requirements of American publishers or national and international index standards. The formatting capabilities of embedded indexing software are extremely limited. The time required to enter embedded index entries and then edit embedded entries is much greater than the time required to perform the same tasks using other index-writing tools. The following conclusions of a few years ago about embedded indexing software are still applicable (Mulvany 1990: 113):

> The current capabilities of the indexing modules of text processing software are inadequate. Even the most simple needs of the professional indexer are left woefully unfulfilled. At a point in the publishing process when users should be able to focus on the content and structure of their indexes, they are required to spend far too much time "cleaning up" the index that is generated by these programs. Users of such programs clearly should not be forced to devote so much time to mundane and repetitive tasks that could and should be handled by the software.

Dedicated Indexing Software

Dedicated indexing programs are devoted solely to the preparation of indexes. They are stand-alone programs in that they do not work with the text files of the document being indexed. Instead, they are designed to enable indexers to type in index entries and reference locators while working from final page proofs of the document. Such programs free the indexer from devoting time to clerical tasks such as the sorting and formatting of index entries; the indexer is able to focus on term selection and the overall structure of the index.

At first it may seem that typing in each index entry is a time-consuming task. But dedicated indexing programs offer various features that do reduce the amount of typing—for example, autoinversion of entries, and the ability to copy reference locators and part or all of previous entries.

These programs have also been fine-tuned to sort index entries according to different schemes. The indexer can choose letter-by-letter or word-by-word alphabetizing. Leading prepositions, articles, and conjunctions can be ignored for sorting purposes, if desired. Terms such as *St.* and *Mc* can be automatically sorted as though spelled *Saint* and *Mac.* Entries that contain numbers will be sorted in ascending numerical order. Some dedicated indexing programs will also sort Roman numerals in correct ascending numerical order.

Cross-references can be verified by some of these programs. Various index formats—such as indented or run-in—can be automatically produced. Generic codes can be automatically inserted.

Because dedicated indexing programs are devoted solely to the task of index preparation, a great deal of time is saved when working with these programs. Professional indexers find that the use of such software is the most cost effective way to work. Perhaps one of the strongest features of this software is that the indexer can work with the index in sorted order at all times. Unlike the user of embedded software, who must "work in the dark"—she cannot see the entries that already exist in the index—the user of dedicated software can immediately see the placement of a new entry within the index in sorted order. The structure of the index is constantly emerging and visible. The work area context is the index itself.

Because the indexer can focus on the structure of the index itself, there are far fewer editing tasks at the end of the process. Simple mistakes such as entering a term in singular form instead of plural form can be corrected immediately. Structural changes such as double-posting entries or deleting entries can be accomplished with a few keystrokes.

Even professional indexers who embed index entries in a document's text files often write the index first using dedicated indexing software. After the index is written and edited, the indexer can produce a listing of index entries in page-number order. The page-number-order listing is then referred to when embedding the entries in the document's text files using the word processing or page design software.

It is important to remember that the software needs of professional indexers may vary greatly from the needs of authors who prepare an occasional index. While the professional indexer may need to produce a run-in, word-by-word alphabetized index one week and an indented index, sorted letter-by-letter, the next week, a book author may need to produce an index in a single style only once every few years. Nevertheless, authors would do well to investigate dedicated indexing software. Even the low-end, less expensive programs might enable authors to produce an index more quickly than could many of the other types of index preparation tools.

Dedicated indexing software is specialized software with a relatively small user base. Few resources provide information about it. Reviews of this software are not likely to be found in the mainstream computer press. The most comprehensive source of information is the American Society of Indexers (ASI). Since 1985, ASI has published (and frequently revised) *A Guide to Indexing Software*, written by Linda Fetters. This publication contains reviews of dedicated indexing software. Linda Fetters has reviewed many of these programs for ASI publications as well as for other information and library science publications. Over the years Fetters has developed a list of features that she uses to evaluate and compare different programs. While not all dedicated indexing programs contain all features, this list does provide a cogent overview of the capabilities of this type of software. Following is Linda Fetters's list of features to look for in dedicated indexing software, reprinted with permission:

Basic Features

Record length: The total number of characters available for each entry.

Total entries: Total number of index records that can be contained in a single index file. Most of the programs can get around any limitation by breaking large indexes into smaller alphabetical groups that can later be merged.

Levels of subheadings: The number of subheading levels that can be attached to any main heading.

Editing and Displaying Entries

Copies previous entry: The program has the capability of duplicating all or part of the immediately preceding entry on the screen.

Copies any existing entry: The program can find and duplicate any record previously entered.

Flips entries: Allows the indexer to transpose a main heading with a subheading or vice versa.

Cross-reference verification: Checking of cross-references for missing headings, circular references, and related problems.

Displays specific alphabetic groups: Displays a specified alphabetic group of entries regardless of the case of the first word of the main heading.

Finds text anywhere: The program offers a find or search option to locate text regardless of its location in the index.

Finds and replaces: The program is able to find and replace specified text anywhere in the index.

Groups together similar entries: The indexer can store a group of entries based on results of a search and work with the group as if no other entries existed in the index.

Macros: The ability to store frequently used words or phrases as abbreviations for recall by function keys or other designated keys.

Onscreen editing: The capability of editing entries once they have scrolled off the current work area without having to exit and use a word processor.

Displays final format onscreen: The indexer can view the entire index (or any part) on the screen in the chosen format at any time without first having to print it to a file for viewing with a word processor.

FORMATTING/PRINTING FEATURES

Indented style: Automatically formats and prints the index in the indented (line-by-line) style.

Run-in style: Automatically formats and prints the index in the run-in (paragraph) style.

User-selected format: Allows the user to set some unusual style other than selecting the number of spaces to indent subheadings, page length, margins, and so on. For example, some programs allow users to right justify page references with or without filler text, such as a row of dots preceding the page reference.

Suppresses repeated headings: Suppresses the printing of duplicate main headings or subheadings and combines or concatenates the page references for those duplicate entries.

Combines page references: Combines page references for records with duplicate main headings and subheadings.

Automatic punctuation: The program inserts user-selected punctuation before page references, between page references, before cross-references, between cross-references, and after cross-references.

Creates word-processor files: Prints the formatted index to a text file that can be edited by any word processor.

Two column format: Prints the index in the designated format in two columns on the page.

Style sheets: Allows the user to set up, save, and re-use style sheets (layouts, configuration files, set-up files, format files) to meet the requirements of different publishers or different methods of production. For example, you might have a style sheet for sending an index to a file, for sending the index to the printer, for sending the index to the screen, for including typesetting codes, and so on.

Inserts print codes: The program allows the indexer to insert print codes for word processors or printers which are translated into the desired effect, such as boldface, italics, subscripts, and so on.

Inserts extended ASCII characters: Allows the indexer to include international alphabet characters or symbols from the IBM extended character set.

Inserts typesetting codes: Allows the indexer to choose among preset typesetting codes or to insert specific typesetting codes. The program automatically inserts the codes when sending the index to a disk file.

Conversion to database file: Converts or stores the index entries in the comma/quote delimited field format that can be read by many database management programs. This is useful if the indexer needs a specialized format that the indexing program cannot provide, but which can be created with the report generator of a database management program. It also facilitates the transfer of index files between indexing programs that can read these types of files.

SORTING

Letter-by-letter: Provides letter-by-letter alphabetizing.

Word-by-word: Provides word-by-word alphabetizing.

Page order: The program can sort the index into page number order either within the program itself, or by the use of a separate utility.

Subheadings by page number: Sorts main headings in alphabetic order but sorts subheadings in page number order.

Ignores articles and prepositions: Ignores a specified list of articles or prepositions to be ignored at the beginning of subheadings. Some programs allow the indexer to specify a list of symbols or characters to be ignored, but not a list of words. Others do both.

Hides specified words: Allows the indexer to mark words, symbols, or numbers to be ignored by the sorting routine.

Allows forced sort order: Allows the indexer to insert text enclosed in special characters which forces the program to sort according to the inserted text rather than the word, character, or number at the beginning of the entry. For example, inserting {ninety}90 forces this entry to sort as if the number were spelled out.

Immediate sorting of entries: Sorts entries into the specified order as soon as the entries are stored. This allows the indexer to view the index in alphabetical order at any time without first having to sort the entire index.

Cumulates indexes: Allows the indexer to merge two or more separate indexes into one large index. This capability is limited by the total number of entries that the program allows, but some programs have "work-around" methods for avoiding such limitations.

The Future

Tools for indexing are varied. Indexers will choose the tools best suited to the job at hand. Undoubtedly, we shall see more sophisticated tools become available in the future. Given the widespread use of embedded indexing software, particularly in the technical documentation community, improved tools are long past due. Ideally, we will see the powerful processing power of dedicated indexing software combined with an eloquent user interface for indexing online text. Such a tool will provide the indexer with a flexible workspace context. The indexer will be able to view formatted text on one side of the screen while the emerging index appears on the other side of the screen (see fig. 10.7).

The index entries on the right side of the screen will be dynamically linked to the text that they reference. If the indexer wishes to see the context of any entry, it can be selected and the associated text will be presented. This feature will provide the online indexer with

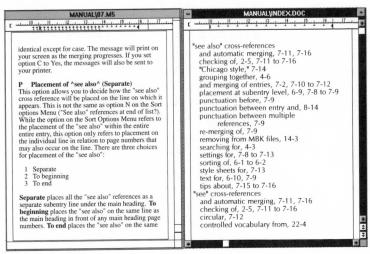

identical except for case. The message will print on your screen as the merging progresses. If you set option C to Yes, the messages will also be sent to your printer.

P   Placement of ^see also^ (Separate)
This option allows you to decide how the "see also" cross reference will be placed on the line on which it appears. This is not the same as option N on the Sort options Menu ("See also" references at end of list?). While the option on the Sort Options Menu refers to the placement of the "see also" within the entire entire entry, this option only refers to placement on the individual line in relation to page numbers that may also occur on the line. There are three choices for placement of the "see also":

    1   Separate
    2   To beginning
    3   To end

Separate places all the "see also" references as a separate subentry line under the main heading. **To beginning** places the "see also" on the same line as the main heading in front of any main heading page numbers. **To end** places the "see also" on the same

"see also" cross-references
    and automatic merging, 7-11, 7-16
    checking of, 2-5, 7-11 to 7-16
    "Chicago style," 7-14
    grouping together, 4-6
    and merging of entries, 7-2, 7-10 to 7-12
    placement at subentry level, 6-9, 7-8 to 7-9
    punctuation before, 7-9
    punctuation between entry and, 8-14
    punctuation between multiple
        references, 7-9
    re-merging of, 7-9
    removing from MBK files, 14-3
    searching for, 4-3
    settings for, 7-8 to 7-13
    sorting of, 6-1 to 6-2
    style sheets for, 7-13
    text for, 6-10, 7-9
    tips about, 7-15 to 7-16
"see" cross-references
    and automatic merging, 7-11, 7-16
    checking of, 2-5, 7-11 to 7-16
    circular, 7-12
    controlled vocabulary from, 22-4

FIG. 10.7. SCREEN DISPLAY.

the same ability to check the context of a discussion as that possessed by the indexer who works with paper pages. Additionally, any changes made in the formatted index will be automatically reflected in the embedded tags for the entries.

Once the basic framework for an effective and efficient embedded indexing system has been created, we can then look forward to tapping the power of the computer environment through the use of linguistic analysis tools. For example, a thesaurus could operate in the background and offer hints for cross-references. If *exit* is entered as an index term, *quit* may be offered as a possible cross-reference, as in "quit. *See* exit."

It is hoped that various post-processing tools will become available. For instance, all *See* cross-references could be evaluated as possible candidates for double-postings. The index structure itself could be analyzed. Entries with too many undifferentiated locators could be pointed out to the indexer. Entries that seem similar could be isolated and reviewed, such as "Eastman Kodak Co." and "Kodak Co." There are a great many possibilities that can be explored once we have a working framework for online indexing.

But whatever tool is used, it is only an adjunct to the intellectual task of indexing. Ideally, our indexing tools will free us from the mundane aspects of index preparation. While we strive to increase the efficiency of our indexing tools, we must remember not to lose sight of the art of indexing.

A tool is just a tool—an implement for facilitating or performing mechanical operations. Instead of shuffling and alphabetizing index cards by hand, we have software that performs this task. However, there is no tool that thinks for us. There is no tool that will decide which terms work as main headings and which terms should be subentries. There is no tool that will automatically control the vocabulary in an index. The indexer must critically read and identify ideas and relationships between ideas.

The indexer's ability to recognize patterns and relationships is a unique human skill that is not capable of becoming automated, at least in the foreseeable future. Computers can build concordances that list every word in a text; they can perform frequency analysis and weighted string pattern matching. But computers cannot identify ideas. Computers cannot construct the intricate network of interrelationships that we call an index. A good index folds the ideas and terminology of a text into patterns that make sense to others. There are many paths that lead to information within the index. This type of access to information has been described as "pre-wiring the thinking so that a person doesn't have to think. You build the links, and if you're good, people aren't even conscious of it. People can find whatever they want without any effort—it's so well organized" (Larson 1989).

Book indexes have been the subject of quantitative studies. But counting the numbers of entries per page or the number of words in subheadings or the frequency of cross-reference use does not get to the heart of the matter. Until we know more about the human ability to identify ideas and provide public access to those ideas, there will be an aspect of indexing that seems like magic.

Neil Larson (1989) said that "indexing is adding value that never existed in the original material." That is the magic of an index. The index goes beyond the words in a text. It provides a gateway to ideas and information that is accessible to others. An index, whether it appears in the back of a book or on a CD-ROM, is a knowledge structure. Access to information is the added value the indexer brings to the material.

Without a doubt, indexing software tools will improve and the demand for indexing will increase. Given the profusion of published material, another certainty is that there will not be enough people skilled in knowledge structure design to meet the information access needs of the marketplace. The book or online text that includes a thoughtfully written and structured index will stand out from the crowd.

The back-of-the-book index is not a relic of seventeenth-century technology; rather, it is an excellent prototype of an efficient information access device. Master the art of book indexing, and you will experience the magic of sharing knowledge.

Appendix A: Index Specifications Worksheet

Title _____

Editor (name & phone #) _____

Author (name & phone #) _____

Number of indexable pages _____

Indexer will receive proofs

    ☐ as one complete set; Date of delivery _____

    ☐ In batches:

        Date of delivery of initial portion _____

        Date of delivery of last portion _____

Date of delivery of the index _____

Table of Contents provided? ☐ Yes   ☐ No

Bibliography provided?   ☐ Yes   ☐ No

NUMBER OF INDEXES

☐ Single index ☐ Multiple indexes   ☐ Author-title

                                    ☐ Authors cited

                                    ☐ Other _____

STYLE GUIDE FOR INDEX

☐ Chicago (13th ed.)   ☐ Chicago (14th ed.)   ☐ House style

FORMAT OF INDEX

☐ Indented (number of levels allowed_____)

☐ Run-in (only 2 levels)

ARRANGEMENT OF ENTRIES

Main heading alphabetizing

    ☐ Word-by-word   ☐ Letter-by-letter

Subentry arrangement

☐ Alphabetic   ☐ Chronologic   ☐ Page-number order

Arrangement of Numbers in Entries

☐ Numeric order ☐ As spelled out ☐ By size

Arrangement of Symbols in Entries

☐ ASCII order ☐ As spelled out ☐ Another order

Cross-reference Format and Placement

Main heading cross-references
    ☐ term. *See* xyz   ☐ term, *see* xyz   ☐ term (*see* xyz)
    ☐ *See also* xyz   ☐ *see also* xyz   ☐ (*see also* xyz)

See also placement
    ☐ At the top of the entry run off from the main heading
    ☐ At the bottom of the entry as the last subentry
    ☐ Indented as the first subentry

Punctuation before *See also* in run-in format _____

Subentry cross-references
    ☐ term. *See* xyz   ☐ term, *see* xyz   ☐ term (*see* xyz)
    ☐ *See also* xyz   ☐ *see also* xyz   ☐ (*see also* xyz)

See also placement ☐ run off from the subentry
    ☐ Other _____

Punctuation

Indented index
    ☐ No special punctuation
    ☐ Colon after main heading/subentry without locators

Run-in index
    Punctuation after main headings without locators _____
    Punctuation after main headings with locators _____
    Punctuation between multiple subentries _____

Between an entry and locators   ☐ Comma followed by a space
    ☐ Two spaces

Between multiple locators   ☐ Comma followed by a space
    ☐ Semicolon followed by a space for change in volume number

Between cross-references   ☐ Semicolon followed by a space
    ☐ Other _____

Main Heading Capitalization

☐ Proper names & nouns only   ☐ First letter only
☐ Entire heading

Reference Locators

Citation unit
- ☐ Page numbers, consecutive
- ☐ Page numbers, modular
- ☐ Paragraph/section numbers
- ☐ Other unit

Format for continuous discussion of a topic
- ☐ Numbers in full with en dash (125–129)
- ☐ Numbers compressed; what style? _____

Modular number concatenator
- ☐ 10-5 to 10-8
- ☐ Other

Format for noncontinuous discussion on consecutive pages
- ☐ Follow style above for continuous discussion (15–17)
- ☐ Separate pages numbers with commas (15, 16, 17)
- ☐ Use *passim* (15–17 passim)
- ☐ Other format required _____

Miscellaneous

Footnotes: Indexable? ☐ No   ☐ Yes
Locator format _____

Display material: Indexable? ☐ No   ☐ Yes
Locator format _____

Length of Index

Is there a length limit? ☐ No   ☐ Yes
If yes, number of index lines allowed _____
number of characters per line _____

Delivery Format of Index

Typed manuscript: ☐ double-spaced   ☐ single-spaced
Disk type: ☐ IBM   ☐ Macintosh
Disk density _____
Text file format
- ☐ ASCII with generic codes
- ☐ Word processing program file _____
☐ Deliver by modem (phone #_____)
Baud rate _____ ; ☐ E71 or ☐ N81; protocol _____

Appendix B: ASCII Table

Decimal Value	Character	Decimal Value	Char-acter	Decimal Value	Char-acter	Decimal Value	Char-acter
0	null	32	space	64	@	96	'
1	^A	33	!	65	A	97	a
2	^B	34	"	66	B	98	b
3	^C (break)	35	#	67	C	99	c
4	^D	36	$	68	D	100	d
5	^E	37	%	69	E	101	e
6	^F	38	&	70	F	102	f
7	^G (bell)	39	'	71	G	103	g
8	^H (bksp)	40	(	72	H	104	h
9	^I (tab)	41	)	73	I	105	i
10	^J (lf)	42	*	74	J	106	j
11	^K (v tab)	43	+	75	K	107	k
12	^L (ff)	44	,	76	L	108	l
13	^M (cr)	45	-	77	M	109	m
14	^N	46	.	78	N	110	n
15	^O	47	/	79	O	111	o
16	^P	48	0	80	P	112	p
17	^Q	49	1	81	Q	113	q
18	^R	50	2	82	R	114	r
19	^S	51	3	83	S	115	s
20	^T	52	4	84	T	116	t
21	^U	53	5	85	U	117	u
22	^V	54	6	86	V	118	v
23	^W	55	7	87	W	119	w
24	^X	56	8	88	X	120	x
25	^Y	57	9	89	Y	121	y
26	^Z (eof)	58	:	90	Z	122	z
27	esc (escape)	59	;	91	[	123	{
28	fs	60	<	92	\	124		
29	gs	61	=	93	]	125	}
30	rs	62	>	94	^	126	~
31	us	63	?	95	_	127	rubout

NOTE: Characters with decimal values from 0 to 31 are control functions, and those with decimal values from 32 to 126 are text characters. The caret (^) that appears before characters 1 through 26 represents the Control (Ctrl) key on the keyboard, so that, for example, ^A is entered by holding down the Control key and then pressing A. ASCII = the American Standard Code for Information Exchange.

Appendix C

SUMMARY OF GENERIC CODES MOST OFTEN NEEDED IN ELECTRONIC INDEX MANUSCRIPTS

Purpose of Coding	ANSI/NISO Code		Chicago Code	
	Start	End	Start	End
Main heading[1,2,3]	`<itm>`		`<p>` or `<x1>`	`</p>` or `</x1>`
Subheading[1,2,4]	`<sit2>`		`<p>` or `<x2>`	`</p>` or `</x2>`
Sub-subheading[1]	`<sit3>`		`<x3>`	`</x3>`
Space between alphabetical groups[5,6]			`<sp>`	
En dash (used between inclusive numbers)[7]	`&ndash;`		`<n>`	
Boldface[8]	`<b>`	`</b>`	`<e1>`	`</e1>`
Italics	`<it>`	`</it>`	`<i>`	`</i>`
Subscript[9,10]	`<u.inf>`		`<sub>`	
Superscript[9,10]	`<u.sup>`		`<sup>`	

NOTE: This summary does not address characters for foreign languages, mathematical symbols, or other general use symbols.

1. ANSI/NISO does not require an end code.

2. The Chicago start code `<p>` must be preceded by three spaces.

3. The Chicago `<p>` and `</p>` codes are used for a one-level index; `<x1>` and `</x1>` (x "one") codes are used for an index with two or more levels prepared in indented style.

4. The Chicago `<p>` and `</p>` codes are used for a two-level index prepared in run-in (paragraph) style; `<x2>` and `</x2>` codes are used for an index prepared in indented style.

5. ANSI/NISO does not define a code for space between alphabetical groups.

6. Chicago does not require an end code. The `<sp>` code is placed flush with the left margin on a line by itself.

7. No end code is required by either ANSI/NISO or Chicago because the en dash is a single printed character.

8. The Chicago codes indicated assume that emphasis code 1 (e "one") has been defined as boldface.

9. The ANSI/NISO codes indicated are user-defined.

10. End codes are not required by either ANSI/NISO or Chicago because the start codes apply only to the character immediately following them.

Appendix D

Summary of Generic Codes for Roman Characters for Latin-based Languages

Character	ANSI/NISO Code	Chicago Code	Description	Decimal Value[1]
á	&aacute;	\<ac\>a	Small a with acute accent	160
â	&acirc;	\<cir\>a	Small a with circumflex accent	131
à	&agrave;	\<gv\>a	Small a with grave accent	133
å	&aring;	\<oc\>a	Small a with ring (overcircle)	134
Å	&Aring;	\<oc\>A	Capital A with ring (overcircle)	143
ä	&auml;	\<um\>a	Small a with umlaut mark	132
Ä	&Auml;	\<um\>A	Capital A with umlaut mark	142
æ	&aelig;	\<U.lcae\>[2]	Small ae ligature	145
Æ	&AElig;	\<U.ucae\>[2]	Capital AE ligature	146
ç	&ccedil;	\<ced\>c	Small c with cedilla	135
Ç	&Ccedil;	\<ced\>C	Capital C with cedilla	128
é	&eacute;	\<ac\>e	Small e with acute accent	130
É	&Eacute;	\<ac\>E	Capital E with acute accent	144
ê	&ecirc;	\<cir\>e	Small e with circumflex accent	136
è	&egrave;	\<gv\>e	Small e with grave accent	138
ë	&euml;	\<um\>e	Small e with umlaut mark	137
í	&iacute;	\<ac\>i	Small i with acute accent	161
î	&icirc;	\<cir\>i	Small i with circumflex accent	140
ì	&igrave;	\<gv\>i	Small i with grave accent	141
ï	&iuml;	\<um\>i	Small i with umlaut mark	139
ñ	&ntilde;	\<tid\>n	Small n with tilde	164
Ñ	&Ntilde;	\<tid\>N	Capital N with tilde	165
ó	&oacute;	\<ac\>o	Small o with acute accent	162
ô	&ocirc;	\<cir\>o	Small o with circumflex accent	147
ò	&ograve;	\<gv\>o	Small o with grave accent	149
ö	&ouml;	\<um\>o	Small o with umlaut mark	148
Ö	&Ouml;	\<um\>O	Capital O with umlaut mark	153
ú	&uacute;	\<ac\>u	Small u with acute accent	163
û	&ucirc;	\<cir\>u	Small u with circumflex accent	150
ù	&ugrave;	\<gv\>u	Small u with grave accent	151
ü	&uuml;	\<um\>u	Small u with umlaut mark	129
Ü	&Uuml;	\<um\>U	Capital U with umlaut mark	154
ÿ	&yuml;	\<um\>y	Small y with umlaut mark	152

1. The decimal value shown is that for the IBM Extended Character Set.
2. Chicago codes of the form \<U. ___ \> are user-defined.

Appendix E

Character	ANSI/NISO Code	Chicago Code	Description	Decimal Value[1]
α	&agr;	\<alpha\>	Small Greek alpha	224
β	&bgr;	\<beta\>	Small Greek beta	225
Γ	&Ggr;	\<GAMMA\>	Capital Greek Gamma	226
δ	&dgr;	\<delta\>	Small Greek delta	235
ε	&egr;	\<epsilon\>	Small Greek epsilon	238
θ	&thgr;	\<theta\>	Small Greek theta	233
μ	&mgr;	\<mu\>	Small Greek mu	230
π	&pgr;	\<pi\>	Small Greek pi	227
σ	&sgr;	\<sigma\>	Small Greek sigma	229
Σ	&Sgr;	\<SIGMA\>	Capital Greek Sigma	228
τ	&tgr;	\<tau\>	Small Greek tau	231
φ	&fgr;	\<phi\>	Small Greek phi	237
Φ	&Fgr;	\<PHI\>	Capital Greek phi	232
Ω	&OHgr;	\<OMEGA\>	Capital Greek Omega	234
¢	&cent;	\<cent\>	Cent sign	155
ƒ	&z.franc;	\<U.franc\>	Franc[2]	159
£	&pound;	\<pound\>	Pound sterling	156
¥	&yen;	\<U.yen\>	Yen[2]	157
¡	&iexcl;	\<U.iexcl\>	Inverted exclamation mark[2]	173
¿	&iquest;	\<U.iquest\>	Inverted question mark[2]	168
≈	&ap;	\<U.approx\>	Approximately equal to[2]	247
°	&deg;	\<deg\>	Degree sign	248
÷	&divide;	\<ds\>	Divide sign	246
≫	&Gt;	\<U.dblgt\>	Much-greater-than sign[2,3]	175
≪	&Lt;	\<U.dbllt\>	Much-less-than sign[2,3]	174
≡	&equiv;	\<U.ident\>	Identical-to sign[2]	240
∞	&infin;	\<U.infin\>	Infinity[2]	236
⌠	&int;	\<U.int\>	Integral operator (top half)[2]	244
⌡	&int;	\<U.int\>	Integral operator (bottom half)[2]	245
∩	&cap;	\<U.cap\>	Intersection[2]	239
≥	&ge;	\<gte\>	Greater-than-or-equals sign	242

Char-acter	ANSI/NISO Code	Chicago Code	Description	Decimal Value[1]
≤	&le;	<lte>	Less-than-or equals sign	243
¬	&not;	<U.not>	Logical not operator[2]	170
±	&plusmn;	<pm>	Plus-or-minus sign	241
√	&z.sqrt;	<U.sqrt>	Square root[2]	251

1. The decimal value shown is that for the IBM Extended Character Set.

2. ANSI/NISO codes of the form &z.____; and Chicago codes of the form <U. ____> are user-defined.

3. The characters for much-less-than and much-greater-than signs (≪ and ≫) can alternatively be used as French guillemets.

Appendix F: Resources for Indexers

PROFESSIONAL ASSOCIATIONS

American Society of Indexers (ASI)
10200 West 44th Ave. Ste. 304
Wheat Ridge, CO 80033
phone: (303) 463-2887
web: http://www.asindexing.org

Australian Society of Indexers (AusSI)
GPO Box 1251L, Melbourne
Victoria 3001, Australia

Indexing and Abstracting Society of Canada (IASC)
P.O. Box 744
Station F
Toronto, Ontario
Canada M4Y 2N6

Society of Indexers (SI)
Blades Enterprise Centre, John Street
Sheffield S2 45U United Kingdom
web: http://www.indexers.org.uk

STANDARDS ORGANIZATIONS

American National Standards Institute (ANSI)
11 W. 42nd Street, 13th Floor
New York, NY 10036

National Information Standards Organization (NISO)
P.O. Box 1056
Bethesda, MD 20827

British Standards Institution
2 Park Street
London W1A 2BS

SGML INFORMATION

Electronic Publishing Special Interest Group (EPSIG)
c/o GCARI
P.O. Box 25707
Alexandria, VA 22313-5707

The *Standard for Electronic Manuscript Preparation and Markup* and four companion guides are available from EPSIG. The guides to the Standard are the *Author's Guide to Electronic Manuscript Preparation and Markup*, *Reference Manual on Electronic Manuscript Preparation and Markup*, *Markup of Mathematical Formulas*, and *Markup of Tabular Material*.

ELECTRONIC CONFERENCES ABOUT INDEXING

Indexing Conference on The WELL in Sausalito, California
The WELL
27 Gate Five Road
Sausalito, CA 94965
(415) 332-4335, voice line

Internet Discussion Group
INDEX-L
To join the group, send the following message (in place of "Jane Doe," use your real first and last name, not your electronic address),

Subscribe INDEX-L Jane Doe

to

listserv@bingvmb.bitnet

TRAINING IN INDEXING

Some colleges and universities offer book indexing courses through their adult education programs. Book indexing courses are often part of a publishing certificate program or are offered through a school of library and information science. The following organizations offer self-paced book indexing courses:

Correspondence Study Program
Graduate School, USDA
South Agriculture Building, Room 1114
14th Street & Independence Avenue, S.W.
Washington, D.C. 20250
(202) 720-7123

Society of Indexers
Mermaid House, 1 Mermaid Court
London SE1 1HR
England

VENDORS OF DEDICATED INDEXING SOFTWARE

All products are for IBM PCs & Compatibles
List taken from *A Guide to Indexing Software*, Fourth Edition, by Linda K.
Fetters (1992), published by the American Society of Indexers.

CINDEX, $485.00
Indexing Research
P.O. Box 18609
River Station
Rochester, NY 14618-0609
(716) 461-5530

IndexAid2, $99.00
Santa Barbara Software Products
1400 Dover Road
Santa Barbara, CA 93103
(805) 963-4886

Indexer's Assistant, $295.00
INQUIRY
195 Sunny Hill Road
Northampton, PA 18067
(215) 837-9615

INDEXX, $99.00
Norman Swartz
1053 Ridley Drive
Burnaby, BC V5A 2N7
Canada
(604) 420-7454

In>Sort for DOS, $79.95
Kensa Software
P.O. Box 4415
Northbrook, IL 60065
(708) 559-0297

MACREX, $495.00
Wise Bytes
P.O. Box 3051
Daly City, CA 94015-3051
(415) 756-0821

NLCindex, $160.00
Newberry Library
60 W. Walton Street
Chicago, IL 60610
(312) 943-9090

wINDEX, $99.95
Watch City Software
24 Harris Street
Waltham, MA 02154
(617) 893-0514

WINNERS OF THE ASI–H. W. WILSON COMPANY AWARD FOR INDEXING

1993	Award not given
1992	Rachel Jo Johnson, indexer
	Matthew Bender, publisher
	The American Law of Real Property (Arthur E. Gaudio, editor)
1991	Nancy Daniels, indexer
	Van Nostrand Reinhold, publisher
	Beyond Public Architecture: Strategies for Design Evaluation

1990   Marcia Carlson, indexer
        Cornell University Press, publisher
        *Nuclear Arguments: Understanding the Strategic Nuclear
        Arms & Arms Control Debates*

1989   Philip James, indexer
        Butterworths, publisher
        Medicine for the Practicing Physician

1988   Jeanne Moody, indexer
        National Wildlife Institute, publisher
        Raptor Management Techniques

1987   Award not given

1986   Marjorie Hyslop, indexer
        American Society for Metals, publisher
        Metals Handbook

1985   Sydney W. Cohen, indexer
        Random House, publisher
        The Experts Speak (Cerf and Navasky)

1984   Trish Yancey, indexer
        Information Handling Services, publisher
        Index and Directory of U.S. Industry Standards

1983   Award not given

1982   Catherine Fix, indexer
        Wm. Saunders Company, publisher
        Diagnosis of Bone and Joint Disorders

1981   Delight Ansley, indexer
        Random House, publisher
        Cosmos (Carl Sagan)

1980   Linda I. Solow, indexer
        MIT Press, publisher
        Beyond Orpheus: Studies in Musical Structures

1979   Hans H. Wellisch, indexer and author
        John Wiley, publisher
        The Conversion of Scripts: Its Nature, History and Utilization

Note: The award is given for an index published during the previous year. Therefore, the 1992 award is for an index published during 1991. Applications for ASI–Wilson Award submissions can be obtained from the American Society of Indexers (P.O. Box 386, Port Aransas, TX 78373).

References

Academic American Encyclopedia. 1990. Danbury, Conn.: Grolier.

American National Standards Institute. 1984. *American National Standard for Library and Information Sciences and Related Publishing Practices—Basic Criteria for Indexes (Z39.4-1984).* New York: American National Standards Institute.

Anderson, M. D. 1987. *Book Indexing.* Cambridge: Cambridge University Press.

Anglo-American Cataloguing Rules. 2d ed. 1988. Chicago: American Library Association; Ottawa: Canadian Library Association; London: Library Association Publishing Ltd.

Bakewell, K. G. B. 1988. *Information Sources and Reference Tools.* Training in Indexing Unit 3. London: Society of Indexers.

Bartholomew Gazetteer of Britain. 1977. Edinburgh: Bartholomew.

Bell, Hazel K. 1989. "Indexing Biographies: Lives Do Bring Their Problems." *The Indexer* 16 (April): 168–72.

———. 1990. "Indexing Biographies: The Main Character." *The Indexer* 17 (April): 43–44.

———. 1992. *Indexing Biographies and Other Stories of Human Lives.* Society of Indexers Occasional Papers on Indexing, No. 1. London: Society of Indexers.

Bellardo, T., Fidel, R., Rasmussen, E., and Smith, P. J., eds. 1993. *Indexing Electronic Images and Text.* Medford, N.J.: Learned Information.

Bishop, Ann P., Liddy, Elizabeth D., and Settel, Barbara. 1991. "Index Quality Study, Part I: Quantitative Description of Back-of-the-Book Indexes." In *Indexing Tradition and Innovation: Proceedings of the 22nd Annual Conference of the American Society of Indexers.* Port Aransas, Tex.: American Society of Indexers.

Booth, Pat F. 1988. *Arrangement and Presentation of Indexes.* Training in Indexing Unit 4. London: Society of Indexers.

Booth, Pat F., and Piggott, Mary. 1988. *Choice and Form of Entries.* Training in Indexing Unit 2. London: Society of Indexers.

Borko, Harold, and Bernier, Charles L. 1978. *Indexing Concepts and Methods.* New York: Academic Press.

British Standard Recommendation for Alphabetical Arrangement and the

Filing Order of Numbers and Symbols (BS 1749:1985). London: British Standards Institution.

British Standard Recommendation for Preparing Indexes to Books, Periodicals and Other Documents (BS 3700:1988). London: British Standards Institution.

Chicago Guide to Preparing Electronic Manuscripts. 1987. Chicago: University of Chicago Press.

The Chicago Manual of Style. 1982. 13th ed. Chicago: University of Chicago Press.

The Chicago Manual of Style. 1993. 14th ed. Chicago: University of Chicago Press.

Cindex. Rochester, N.Y.: Indexing Research.

"Contracted Indexes." 1988. *The Indexer* 16 (October): 100.

Croft, W. Bruce. 1989. "Automatic Indexing." In *Indexing, the State of Our Knowledge and the State of Our Ignorance: Proceedings of the 20th Annual Meeting of the American Society of Indexers,* ed. Bella Hass Weinberg, 85–100. Medford, N.J.: Learned Information.

Diodato, Virgil, and Gandt, Gretchen. 1991. "Back of Book Indexes and the Characteristics of Author and Nonauthor Indexing: Report of an Exploratory Study." *Journal of the American Society for Information Science* 42 (June): 341–50.

Encyclopaedia Britannica. 1990. 15th ed. Chicago: Encyclopaedia Britannica.

Encyclopaedia Judaica. 1972. Jerusalem: Keter Publishing House.

Encyclopaedia of Islam. [1913–36] 1987. Leiden: E. J. Brill.

The Encyclopedia Americana. 1990. Int'l. ed. Danbury, Conn.: Grolier.

Fetters, Linda K. 1992. *A Guide to Indexing Software.* 4th ed. Port Aransas, Tex.: American Society of Indexers.

Gazetteer of the British Isles. 1970. Edinburgh: Bartholomew.

Grech, Christine. 1992. "Computer Documentation Doesn't Pass Muster." *PC Computing* (April): 212–14.

Heywood, Valentine. 1951. *British Titles: The Use and Misuse of the Titles of Peers and Commoners; with Some Historical Notes.* London: Black.

International Organization for Standardization. 1981. *Documentation and Information—Vocabulary—Section 3a: Acquisition, Identification, and Analysis of Documents and Data* (ISO 5127-3a) Geneva: ISO.

———. 199x. *Guidelines for Preparing Indexes to Books, Periodicals, and Other Documents* (ISO 999, in draft) Geneva: ISO.

Knight, G. Norman. 1979. *Indexing, the Art of: A Guide to the Indexing of Books and Periodicals.* London: George Allen & Unwin.

Lancaster, F. W. 1991. *Indexing and Abstracting in Theory and Practice.* Champaign: University of Illinois Graduate School of Library and Information Science.

Larson, Neil. 1989. "Hypertext: Fact, Fiction, and Opportunity." Paper presented at 21st Annual Meeting of American Society of Indexers, 19–20 May, in San Francisco, California.

Levin, Bernard. 1987. "Authors and Indexes," *The Indexer* 15 (October): 238.

Liddy, Elizabeth D., Bishop, Ann P., and Settel, Barbara. 1991. "Index Quality Study, Part II: Publishers' Survey and Qualitative Assessment." In *Indexing Tradition and Innovation: Proceedings of the 22nd Annual Conference of the American Society of Indexers.* Port Aransas, Tex.: American Society of Indexers.

Liebscher, Peter. 1993. "Hypertext and Indexing." In *Indexing Electronic Images and Text,* ed. T. Bellardo, R. Fidel, E. Rasmussen, and P. J. Smith. Medford, N.J.: Learned Information.

Locke, Christopher. 1991. "The Dark Side of DIP." *BYTE* (April): 193–204.

Macrex Indexing Program. Daly City, Calif.: Wise Bytes; Tyne and Wear, UK: Macrex Indexing Services.

Maddocks, Hugh C. 1988. *Generic Markup of Electronic Index Manuscripts.* Port Aransas, Tex.: American Society of Indexers.

———. 1991. *Deep-Sky Name Index 2000.0.* Reston, Va.: Foxon-Maddocks Associates.

Marchionini, Gary. 1993. "Designing Hypertexts: Start with an Index." In *Indexing Electronic Images and Text,* ed. T. Bellardo, R. Fidel, E. Rasmussen, and P. J. Smith. Medford, N.J.: Learned Information.

The McGraw-Hill Style Manual. 1983. Marie Longyear, ed. New York, N.Y.: McGraw-Hill Book Co.

Milstead, Jessica. 1984. *Subject Access Systems.* Orlando, Fla.: Academic Press.

Mitchell, AnnMarie Dorwart. 1992. "Myths about Indexing." In *Frontiers: Proceedings of the 33rd Annual Conference of the American Translators Association, November 4–8, 1992, San Diego, California,* ed. Edith F. Losa, 377–86. Medford, N.J.: Learned Information.

Moys, Elizabeth M. 1992. "Legal Vocabulary and the Indexer." *The Indexer* 18 (October): 75–78.

Mulvany, Nancy C. 1990. "Software Tools for Indexing: What We Need." *The Indexer* 17 (October): 108–13.

———. 1991. "Copyright for Indexes, Revisited." *ASI Newsletter* 107 (November/December): 11–13.

———. 1993. "Online Help Systems: A Multimedia Indexing Opportunity." In *Indexing Electronic Images and Text,* ed. T. Bellardo, R. Fidel, E. Rasmussen, and P. J. Smith. Medford, N.J.: Learned Information.

Mulvany, Nancy C., ed. 1993. *Indexing, Providing Access to Information: Looking Back, Looking Ahead, Proceedings of the 25th Annual Meeting of the American Society of Indexers.* Port Aransas, Tex.: American Society of Indexers.

Names of Persons: National Usages for Entries in Catalogues. 1977. 3d ed.

London: International Federation of Library Associations and Institutions.

National Information Standards Organization. 1988. *Standard for Electronic Manuscript Preparation and Markup* (ANSI/NISO Z39.59-1988). Bethesda, Md.: National Information Standards Organization.

———. 1993. *Proposed American National Standard Guidelines for the Construction, Format, and Management of Monolingual Thesauri.* Draft 3. Bethesda, Md.: National Information Standards Organization (ANSI/NISO Z39.19-1993).

———. 1993. *Proposed American National Standard Guidelines for Indexes in Information Retrieval.* Draft 3. (ANSI/NISO Z39.4-199x).

New Catholic Encyclopedia. 1967–79. New York: McGraw-Hill.

The Oxford Classical Dictionary. 1970. Oxford: Clarendon Press.

Oxford English Dictionary. 1971. Compact ed. Oxford: Oxford University Press.

Pocket Pal: A Graphics Arts Production Handbook. 1983. New York: International Paper Co.

Ridehalgh, Nan. 1985. "The Design of Indexes." *The Indexer* 14 (April): 165–74.

Salton, Gerard. 1988. *Automatic Text Processing: The Transformation, Analysis, and Retrieval of Information by Computer.* Reading, Mass.: Addison-Wesley.

Simpkins, Jean. 1990. "How the Publishers Want It to Look." *The Indexer* 17 (April): 41–42.

Spiker, Sina. 1955. *Indexing Your Book: A Practical Guide for Authors.* Madison: University of Wisconsin Press.

Thomas, Dorothy. 1989. "Book Indexing Principles and Standards." In *Indexing: The State of Our Knowledge and the State of Our Ignorance, Proceedings of the 20th Annual Meeting of the American Society of Indexers,* ed. Bella Hass Weinberg, 15–25. Medford, N.J.: Learned Information.

Vickers, John A. 1987. "Index, How Not To." *The Indexer* 15 (April): 163–66.

Webster's New Biographical Dictionary. 1988. Springfield, Mass.: Merriam-Webster.

Webster's New Geographical Dictionary. 1988. Springfield, Mass.: Merriam-Webster.

Weinberg, Bella Hass. 1988. "Why Indexing Fails the Researcher." *The Indexer* 16 (April): 3–6.

Weinberg, Bella Hass, ed. 1989. *Indexing: The State of Our Knowledge and the State of Our Ignorance: Proceedings of the 20th Annual Meeting of the American Society of Indexers.* Medford, N.J.: Learned Information.

Wellisch, Hans. 1991. *Indexing from A to Z.* New York: H. W. Wilson.

―――. 1992. "The Art of Indexing and Some Fallacies of Its Automation." *LOGOS* 3/2: 69–76.

―――. 1993. "Function Words in Subheadings." *Key Words: The Newsletter of the American Society of Indexers* (January/February): 8–10.

Wheatley, Henry B. 1902. *How to Make an Index*. London: E. Stock.

Wheeler, Martha Throne. [1957] 1968. "Indexing: Principles, Rules and Examples." *University of the State of New York Bulletin*. 1445 (January).

Wilson Award Criteria. Available from the American Society of Indexers, P.O. Box 386, Port Aransas, TX 78373.

Wittmann, Cecelia. 1991. "Limitations of Indexing Modules in Word-processing Software." *The Indexer* 17 (October): 235–38.

Words into Type. 1974. 3d ed. Englewood Cliffs, N.J.: Prentice-Hall.

Index

Written by Carolyn McGovern

abbreviations
  alphabetizing, 130
  of company names, 177, 180–81
  cross-references to and from, 102, 128–29
  double-posting, 130
  explaining, 12, 70
  spelling out, 128–29
  for states in U.S., 175–76
access points
  converting subentries to main headings, 219
  main heading as primary, 77, 217
  multiple, with double-posting, 75, 76, 221
accuracy of entries, assessing, 230
acronyms
  alphabetizing, 130
  cross-references to and from, 102, 128–29
  double-posting, 130
  explaining, 12
  spelling out, 128–29
acute accent, generic codes for, 205
adjective-noun compounds, 82–83
adjectives
  hyphenated, sorting of, 115
  as main headings, 71
  structure of, in entries, 82–83
adverbs
  as main headings, 71
  structure of, in entries, 82–83

Afrikaans names, 165
algorithmic analysis of text, 245–46, 249, 254
  See also automatic indexing
alphabet
  non-Roman, transliteration systems used, 168
  order of letters, 113, 115
alphabetization
  of abbreviations and acronyms, 130
  of alphanumeric pagination, 93–94
  basic rules, 120–21
  choosing method for, 55, 110, 111, 126–27, 181–82
  computer-assisted methods, 263–66, 271–72
  editing and proofing of, 222, 225, 232
  house styles of, 55, 56–58, 59–62
  leading function words, 83, 84, 85, 122
  level-by-level, 115
  manual, 241, 243–44, 265
  need for standardization, 114
  nonalphabetic characters, 131–43
  rules adapted from British standards, 115–19
  See also filing order; sorting
alphabetization, letter-by-letter, 111–14
  arguments for, 112–13, 127
  British standard on, 118–19

This index is alphabetized letter-by-letter. Leading function words in subentries are not alphabetized. The page-number compression style follows that in *The Chicago Manual of Style*, 14th ed., section 8.69. The index was prepared with the Macrex Indexing Program. Using the formula on page 64 of this book, this is a 7 percent index. There are 2,026 entries, averaging 7 entries per page.

alphabetization, letter-by-letter *(continued)*
  Chicago style compared to American standard, 119–20
  compared to strict ASCII sort and word-by-word, 264
  house styles, 55, 56–57, 58, 59, 60–62, 113
  nonletter characters, 117
  space character, 114, 117
  standardization of, 115–20
  for technical indexes, 126–27
  variations in, 112
alphabetization, word-by-word
  arguments for, 112, 126, 127
  British standard on, 118–19
  compared to strict ASCII and letter-by-letter, 264
  computer-assisted, 276
  explained, 109–11
  house styles, 57–58, 59, 60, 62
  hyphenated words in, 114–15
  for nonletter characters, 114, 117
  standardization of, 114–15, 117, 118–19
alphanumeric pagination, alphabetization of, 93–94
alphanumeric terms, arrangement of, 134
American Library Association (ALA), 152
American names (U.S.), 165
American National Standards Institute (ANSI), 3, 289
  See also ANSI entries
American Society of Indexers (ASI), 289
  indexing software guide, 273
  judging indexes, criteria for, 11–12
  locating indexers, 26, 151
  publications of, 202, 273
  recommended indexing contract, 29
American Standard Code for Information Interchange. *See ASCII entries*
American standards for indexes. *See* ANSI/NISO Z39.4-199x; ANSI Z39.4-1984
ampersand (&), filing order of, 114, 115, 136

Anderson, M. D., 67
Anglo-American Cataloging Rules (ALA), 152
  compound names, 157, 158
  names with particles, 165–67, 168–73
  Roman names, 164
  titles of nobility, 161, 162
ANSI/NISO Z39.4-199x (draft 3), 14, 15
  arrangement of numerals, 132, 133
  basic index specifications, 60
  compared to Chicago on letter-by-letter, 119–20
  filing order of characters, 113–14
  index specifications, 60
ANSI/NISO Z39.19, thesaurus design guidelines, 147
ANSI/NISO Z39.59-1988, generic codes, 203–5, 285, 286, 287–88
ANSI Z39.4-1984, 14
  index defined, 3
  locator defined, 85
  punctuation in letter-by-letter sort, 113
  revision of, 15
  sequence of alphanumeric terms, 134
Ansley, Delight, 239
antonyms, cross-references to, 102
apostrophes, sorting of, 112, 115, 120, 136
appendixes
  in computer documentation, 44–45
  icons, list of, 142
  indexing of, 20–21, 44–45
  page-number format in, 93
Apple Computer Inc., index specifications, 60
Arabic names, 169
Arabic numerals
  interfiling with Roman, 115, 120, 135
  See also numerals
archive files of index, 236, 237–38
arrangement of entries, 6, 8
  defined, 109
  recognizability of, 12
  See also alphabetization; filing order; sorting

articles
  alphabetizing, in surnames, 165
  alphabetizing, within entry, 123
  ignoring, in sort, 121–22, 265, 271,
    276
  leading, in subentries, 83, 84
  place names beginning with, 175–76
ASCII characters
  insertion in text file, 201–2, 275
  table of, 139, 284
ASCII sort order
  modified, 246, 264
  strict, illustration of, 264
ASCII text file
  defined, 202
  with generic coding, 202–5
ASI. *See* American Society of Indexers
  (ASI)
ASI–H. W. Wilson Company Award
  for Indexing
  criteria for, 11–12, 246
  page design and layout of winning in-
    dexes, 211–12
  recipients of, 292–93
"ASI Recommended Indexing
  Agreement," 29
assigning indexes, 30–31
  cumulative, 145–46
  providing front and back matter to
    indexer, 42–44, 153–54
  space limitations, 63, 64
Association of American Publishers
  (AAP), 203
astronomy, symbols in, 141
audience. *See* readers
AusSI. *See* Australian Society of Indexers (AusSI)
Australian names, 165
Australian Society of Indexers (AusSI)
  address of, 289
  as source of indexers, 26
author
  collaboration with indexer, 31–34,
    214, 227–28
  contractual responsibility for index,
    16–17
  degree of involvement with index,
    27–28
  locating an indexer, 26–27

author *(continued)*
  names and terms preferred by, 18–
    21, 32–33, 129, 144
  reconciling language of, with read-
    ers' needs, 38, 101
  review of index by, 27–28, 32, 33–34,
    215–16, 226–28
author as indexer
  embedding entries, 257–58, 263
  manual method, 240
  size of task, 17–18
  software needs of, 272–73
  strengths and weaknesses of, 21–24
authored works, indexes as, 4
authors, multiple, indexing work of,
  101–2, 143–45
automatic indexing, 244–54, 279
  defined, 245
  word processing modules, 246–47
Automatic Text Processing (Salton),
  48–49, 249

back matter
  components of, 43
  indexability of, 43–45
  usefulness of, to indexer, 153–54
bad breaks
  defined, 210
  and hyphenation, 207
  three types, 210–13
Bakewell, K. G. B., 152, 176
Bartholomew Gazetteer of Britain (Mason), 176
begin/end codes
  end-of-line, 200, 201, 204
  for special typography, 201, 204–5
begin/end entry tags, 261–62
Bellardo, T., 2, 101, 262
Bell, Hazel, 125
Bernier, Charles L., 249
bibliographic reference in notes, indexability of, 46–47
bibliographies, use of KWIC and
  KWOC in, 249
bibliography
  indexability of, 43
  presence of, and indexing of notes,
    46–47
  as resource for indexer, 153–54

bids for indexes, 27, 29–30
binding of book, 36, 37, 41
biographies, subentry order in, 123–25
Bishop, Ann P., 54, 65
boldface
  begin/end codes for, 201
  for main headings, 196
  marking, in manuscript, 197
  reference locators in, 148, 195, 267
book, parts of a, 42–45
book contracts, provisions for index,
  16–18, 23, 228
Book Indexing (Anderson), 67
book pages, ratio of index pages to,
  64–67
book production schedule
  author review of index, 28, 227–28
  editing of index in, 214–15
  embedding indexing before final
    page proofs, 256, 257, 258
  front matter in, 42–43
  index in, 35, 36–37, 39
  indexing contract and, 28
  planning for index revision, 232
  redoing index, 230–31
book revision. *See* revision of books
book sales, impact of index on, 231
books without indexes, 230, 231
book titles, 83, 122, 194
Booth, Pat F., 150, 160, 161–62
Borko, Harold, 249
botanical name index, 150
British names, 165
British standard on arrangement of
  numbers and symbols (BS
  1749:1985), 135
British standard on indexes (BS
  3700:1976), definition of index, 4
British standard on indexes (BS
  3700:1988)
  arrangement of numerals, 131–32
  criteria of, and automatic indexing,
    246
  definition of index, 3–4
  filing order of characters, 115–16
  function of an index, 5–6
  index specifications, 60
  information about, 14

British standard on indexes (BS
  3700:1988) *(continued)*
  names with *Mac, Mc,* and *M',* 159
  names with *Saint (St.),* 158–59
  nonletter characters, sorting of, 111
  purpose of index, 5–8, 49, 74
  recommended alphabetizing rules
    adapted from, 115–19
British Standards Institution, 3–4, 14,
  290
*British Titles: The Use and Misuse of
  the Titles of Peers and Commoners*
  (Heywood), 161
Burmese names, 170
business names
  cross-references to, 177
  See also corporate names

Cambodian names, 173
Canadian names, 165
capitalization
  distinguishing homographs with, 82
  of main entries, 59, 60–62
capital letters, sorting of, 130, 264
caps
  large and small, for names in index,
    195–96
  small, begin/end codes for, 201
card method, 240–44
cases, legal. *See* legal cases
caste names, Indian, 171
cataloging
  resources on names used in, 153
  term assignment in, 49
chemistry
  Greek-letter symbols, 136–37
  numerals in names, 135
Chicago generic codes, 203, 204, 205,
  285–88
*Chicago Guide to Preparing Electronic
  Manuscripts,* 203
Chicago Manual of Style, 15
  alphabetizing rules, 118, 119–20
  authors as indexers, 21
  editing indexes, 228
  homographs, arrangement of, 123
  Hungarian names, 166
  index card method, 240

Chicago Manual of Style (continued)
  index of, turnover indent in, 209
  index specifications, 54, 56–57,
    60–61
  letter-by-letter sort, variations in,
    112, 115, 116
  names with *Mac, Mc,* and *M'*, 159
  names with *Saint (St.)*, 158
  numerals, arrangement of, 131, 132
  organization names, 128
  page ranges, expression of, 87, 267
  ratio of index to book pages, 64
Chinese names
  order of, 170
  Wade-Giles and pinyin translitera-
    tion systems, 168
chronological order
  confusion with page-number order,
    127
  subentries in, 55, 123–25
CINDEX, 291
circumflex, generic codes for, 205
classification
  dangers of, 71–73
  usefulness of, 73–75
clerical titles, 161, 172
codes
  beginning and end of lines, 200
  editing and proofing of, 225
  for publisher's computer system,
    200–201
  typographic, 196, 200, 201
  See also generic codes
colons, sorting of, 136
columns
  identifiers for text in, 98
  index format in, 275
  index page layout in, 206
  vertical, justification of, 212
commands
  index of, 149–50
  shown in Courier font, 195
commas, sorting of, 111, 116, 136
company names. *See* corporate
  names
compound names, 156–57, 167–68
compression of locators. *See under*
  page numbers; reference locators

computer-assisted indexing tools, 245,
  254–77
  See also indexing software, dedi-
    cated; indexing software, embedded
computer manuals
  appendixes in, 44–45
  command index in, 149–50
  commands as main headings, 106–7
  commands in Courier font, 195
  reference locator format in, 92, 237
  symbols used in, ASCII codes for,
    138–41
  uses of, 141–42
  value of index in, 2–3
  See also technical documentation
concatenators, page-range, 86, 92–93,
  204, 267
concordance
  compared to index, 4
  defined, 246
  generation of, 245, 246–47, 248
conference papers. *See* multiauthored
  works
Congressional Quarterly Inc., 178
conjunctions
  alphabetizing, within entry, 123
  leading, in book title, 122
conjunctions in subentries, leading
  controversy on use of, 83–85
  ignoring, in sort, 121–22, 265, 271
context as defined by KWIC and
  KWOC generators, 248
continued lines, 210–12
contracted words, sorting rules on,
  120
contracts for indexing, 28–29
  See also book contracts
control character (^), sort order for,
  140
cookbooks, ratio of index to book
  pages, 65–66
copyediting. *See* editing of index
copying entries, with indexing software, 260, 269, 271, 273
copyright
  for indexes, 4, 28, 29
  revision rights, 234
Copyright Act of 1976, 29

corporate names
    changes in, 179–81
    See also organizations, names of
cost of index
    to author, 17–18
    in relation to layout and typography,
        39, 40
courses, indexing, 290–91
Croft, Bruce, 249
cross-references
    for abbreviations and acronyms,
        128–29
    blind, 108
    to changed names, 155, 179–80
    circular, 108, 219
    completeness of main heading
        pointed to, 107
    double-posting as alternative to, 77,
        104, 220
    evaluating, 12, 229
    format of, 188–91, 192–94, 224, 225,
        232, 266–67
    function of, 68–69, 101
    general, to a class, 194
    to geographic names and terms,
        174–75
    to homophones, 160
    illustrated, 13
    from main heading, 188–91
    to married names, 156
    in multiauthored works, 143–44
    multiple, 107–8, 223, 266–67
    to organization names, 176–77
    to personal name variations, 154–55
    placement of, 188, 189–90, 191–92,
        193–94, 224, 225, 266
    publishers' styles, 56–59, 60–62
    reference locators in, 108
    from subentries, 188–89, 191
    for synonymous terms, 221–22
    with titles of nobility, 162
    types of, 101–8
    verifying, 219–20, 225, 232, 234,
        267, 272, 274
    *See also specific types of cross-
        references*
cumulative indexes, 145–49, 277
    determining need for, 146, 148–49
    reference locator format in, 147–48

custom publishing, 262–63
Czech names, 158

dashes
    sorting of, 110, 111, 115, 117
    See also hyphens
database file, index conversion to, 276
database indexing, classification in, 72
data file of index, use of, in revision,
    236, 237–38
deadlines
    in book production cycle, 36–37
    and delivery of index, 17
    and delivery of page proofs, 28
decimal points, sorting of, 133
dedicated indexing software. *See* in-
    dexing software, dedicated
Deep-Sky Name Index (Maddocks),
    141
delivery formats for indexes. *See* sub-
    mission formats
demand publishing, 262–63
density of indexing, measures of,
    64–67
density of index text
    and reference locator format, 147–48
    and usability, 50–51, 183, 206–7
density of text on book page
    impact on indexing time and cost, 40
    need for column identifiers, 98
depth of indexing
    of appendixes, 45
    constraints of time and space, 50
    defined, 48–50
    ratio of index to book pages, 63,
        64–67
descriptors
    for geographic names, 175–76
    for personal names, 164
    for pseudonyms, 155
    with single forename, 164
design. *See* page design of index
desktop publishing software
    automatic hyphenation in, 207
    embedded indexing in, 254
    indention measurement in, 207–8
    text file submissions in, 199, 200
    use by publishers, 205–6
De Tienne, Andre, 89–90

diacritical marks, sorting of, 121
diagonal slashes. *See* slashes, diagonal
dialog box, in embedded programs, 265–66
Diodata, Virgil, 65
display material, 47–48
display pages, 43
document-image processing (DIP), 2
document processing software. *See* desktop publishing software; word processing software
dog names, 163
double-posting, 75–77
    of abbreviations and acronyms, 128, 130
    in editing stage, 77, 144, 220–21
    excessive, 221
    mirror images in, 76–77, 220–21, 225
    of organization names, 177–78
    origin of term, 76
    in preference to cross-references, 177–78
    of symbols, 140
DTP. *See* desktop publishing software
Dutch names, 165–66, 167

editing of index, 214–38
editing of index, by author, 226–28
    final review, 32, 34, 214, 215
    usefulness of personal embedded index, 263
editing of index, by editor, 214, 228–33
    cumulative, 146
    layout in pages, 212–13
    in manuscript, 197–98
editing of index, by indexer, 50, 214, 215–26
    building into schedule, 214
    double-posting decisions, 77, 104–5, 144
    embedded entries, 258, 259–60, 269–70
    in index-writing process, 33, 215–17
    manual, 242–43
    onscreen, 274
    revision of embedded entries, 259–60

editing of index, by indexer *(continued)*
    substantive, 215–16, 217–22
    tasks involved in, 222–26
editing of text
    effect on embedded index entries, 257
    multiauthored works, 143
editor
    adjustment for bad breaks, 210, 212–13
    assigning and editing cumulative indexes, 145–46
    assigning indexing projects, 30–31, 63, 64
    communicating with indexer, 31, 39–40, 41, 224
    editing of index by, 146, 197–98, 212–14, 228–33
    estimating length of submitted index, 197–98
    evaluating indexes, 228–30, 232
    front and back matter for indexer's use, 42–44, 153–54
    planning for indexing, 146, 196, 232
    queries to, 157, 224, 226
    reducing length of index, 63
    reference locator format, 97
    revised editions and indexes, 234–38
    specifications for index, 54, 63
    style sheet of, 31
    team indexing, planning for, 147
    term selection, review of, 230
    tracking text changes in revision, 235
electronic conferences on indexing, 290
electronic format
    generic codes in, 202–5
    index submission in, 198–202, 232
    revision of index in, 235–36
    work published in print and, with embedded indexing, 262, 263
electronic manuscript preparation
    and book production cycle, 36
    standards on, 203
electronic media. *See* online documents
Electronic Publishing Special Interest Group (EPSIG), 203, 290

elision of page numbers. *See* page numbers, compression of
em
  defined, 86, 185
  em space, 207, 209
embedded indexing
  benefits of, to producer, 256
  methods of working with, 246, 255–59, 272
  uses for, 259, 262–63
  See also indexing software, embedded
en
  defined, 86
  en dash, 86, 204
  en space, 209
Encyclopaedia Britannica, 153
Encyclopaedia Judaica, 153
Encyclopedia Americana, 153
endnotes
  annotated page references for, 96–97
  indexability of, 43, 44, 46–47
  indexed item absent from text page, 96–97
  multiple references to, 97–98
end-of-line codes, 200, 201, 204
entries
  accuracy of, assessing, 230
  consistency of form of, 81
  format of, house styles on, 55, 56, 57, 58, 60–62
  length of, 64, 107
  levels of, generic codes for, 202, 204
  manipulation of, in embedded indexing, 263–68
  number of, per page, 64–67
entry
  basic hierarchy of, 7
  charging by the, 29, 30
  defined, 14, 240–41
  elements of, 69, 70–108
  illustrated, 13
  multiple terms in, 82
EPSIG, 203, 290
European names, particles in, 165–68
evaluating indexes
  ASI criteria for, 11–12
  by editor, 228–30
exclamation points, sorting of, 136

exclude list, 246, 248
exhaustivity of indexing, 48–50
Extended Binary Coded Decimal Interchange Code (EBCDIC), 139

f. and *ff.*, 90–91
Fetters, Linda, 273–77
Fidel, R., 101
filing boxes, 241–42
filing order
  in ANSI Z39.4-1984, 113–14
  in BS 3700:1988, 115–16
  See also alphabetization; sorting
flat fee, 29, 30
flipping of entries, 273
  See also inversion
flush-and-hang style, 184–85
folio, defined, 91
font for index manuscript, 197–98
footnotes
  forms of references to, 95
  indexing of, 10, 43, 46–47
  multiple references to, 97–98
foreign characters. *See* international characters
foreword, 42
format
  aspects of, summarized, 183
  See also indented style; run-in style; submission formats
formatting
  onscreen display of, 97–98, 274
  software features for, 272, 274–76
freelance indexers, directories of, 26–27
French names, 158, 166
front matter
  indexability of, 42
  usefulness to indexer, 42–43
function of an index, 5–6
function words
  in exclude lists, 246
  leading, in subentries, 83–85
  See also articles; conjunctions; prepositions

galleys
  indexing from, 36
  uses of, 35
Gandt, Gretchen, 65

generic codes
   for electronic index manuscripts,
      202–5, 285
   for Greek characters, 287
   insertion of, 199, 272
   proofing, 225
   for punctuation for Latin-based lan-
      guages, 287
   for Roman characters for Latin-based
      languages, 286
   for symbols, 287–88
   user-defined, 205
*Generic Markup of Electronic Index
Manuscripts* (Maddocks), 202, 203–5,
   285–88
geographic features, 173–75
geographic names, 173–76
   author-compiled list of, 18–19, 20,
      31
   cross-references to, 102
   distinguishing, from geographic fea-
      tures, 173
   inversion of, 173–74
   reference sources for, 176
German names, 166, 167
given names, Indian (Asia), 170–71
glossary, usefulness to indexer, 43–44
grammatical relationship of main heading and subentries, 83–84
graphical user interface (GUI), order of
   icons for, 141–43
Grech, Christine, 3
Greek-letter symbols, sorting of, 136–
   37, 287
grouping of related information, as purpose of index, 6, 7, 12, 74
Guide to Indexing Software (Fetters),
   273–77
guide words, 213

hard return, 200, 201, 204
HarperSan Francisco, index specifications, 61
Harvard University Press, index specifications, 61
header letters, 213, 244
headnote. *See* introductory note
Heywood, Valentine, 161
hierarchical style. *See* indented style

homographs
   distinguishing, 81–82
   sequence of, 123
homophones, cross-references to, 160
Hoover Institution Press, index specifications, 61
hour, charging by the, 29
how-to books, ratio of index to book
   pages, 65–66
How to Make an Index (Wheatley),
   214
Hungarian names, 158, 166–67
hypermedia system, defined, 1
hypertext
   defined, 1
   index text as, 69
   links, index as structure for, 262
hyphenated names, 156, 157
hyphenated words, sorting of, 114–15
hyphenation, in formatted index, 207
hyphens
   sorting of, 110, 111, 112, 115,
      117–18
   as symbols, 136, 138, 139

IASC. *See* Indexing and Abstracting Society of Canada (IASC)
IBM Corporation, index specifications,
   62
IBM mainframe, sorting of symbols,
   139
icons, indexing of, 141–43
identifiers. *See* descriptors
illustrations
   annotated page numbers for, 94–95
   italic references to, 195, 196
   whether to index, 47–48
images, indexing of, 142
indented style, 183, 184–86
   checking and editing, 223–24
   cross-references in, 190, 191–93
   in dedicated indexing programs, 274
   in embedded indexing programs, 268
   heading levels indicated in, 202, 204,
      207
   house styles for, 57–58, 60–62
   layout of, 206–13
   shortening index in, 233
   and space considerations, 64

indention
　　coding for, 200–201, 204
　　of cross-references in indented style,
　　　192–93
　　of heading levels, 204, 207–8, 223–
　　　24, 244
　　in indented style, 200
　　maintaining in *continued* lines, 211
　　in run-in style, 186, 187, 200–201
　　of subentries, 185, 208–9
　　of turnover lines, 186, 187, 208–10,
　　　268
index
　　characteristics of, 4–5
　　cost of, 17–18, 39, 40
　　definitions of, 1, 3–5
　　the ideal, 11–12
　　purpose of, 5–6, 49
　　standards for, 3–4, 14–15
　　value of, 1–3, 231
indexable material, determining, 20–
　　21, 41–48
IndexAid2, 291
index card method, 240–44
indexer
　　attributes of, 24, 38, 39, 45–46
　　locating professional, 26–27
　　strengths and weaknesses of, 24–26,
　　　151, 232
　　See also editing of index, by indexer
Indexer's Assistant, 291
Indexers Available, AusSI, 26
Indexers Available, SI, 27
indexing
　　as art, 39
　　history of, 3–4
　　nature of work, 35, 37–39
　　as profession, 1
　　See also methods of indexing
Indexing, The Art of (Knight), 4, 15,
　　73, 156, 168, 214, 239, 240
*Indexing and Abstracting in Theory
　　and Practice* (Lancaster), 51
Indexing and Abstracting Society of
　　Canada (IASC)
　　address of, 289
　　as source of indexers, 26
Indexing Electronic Images and Text
　　(Bellardo et al.), 101

Indexing from A to Z (Wellisch), 4, 48,
　　49, 72, 173–74
indexing software, dedicated, 254, 255,
　　271–77
　　ASCII text files in, 202
　　automatic inversion in, 268
　　contribution to index-writing pro-
　　　cess, 216, 271, 272
　　evaluating features of, 273–77
　　formatting capabilities, 187
　　generic coding insertion, 205
　　layout capability, 184
　　needs of authors and indexers com-
　　　pared, 272–73
　　revision of indexes, 236, 237, 260
　　text file production, 199–200
　　utility programs, 200
　　vendors of, listed, 291–92
　　viewing of alphabetization schemes,
　　　126
indexing software, embedded, 236, 254,
　　255–71
　　entry manipulation with, 263–66,
　　　266–67
　　improved tools for, 277–78
　　practical indexing problems with,
　　　256–63
　　revision of indexes, 236, 259–60
　　technical problems with, 256,
　　　263–71
　　user interface design, 268–70
　　work area context of, 269
　　working time comparison, 258, 259,
　　　269, 270
Indexit, 291
INDEX-L electronic conference, 89–90,
　　290
"Index Specifications Worksheet," 55,
　　281–83
index-writing process
　　editing as part of, 215–17
　　embedded methods, practical prob-
　　　lems with, 256–63
　　human contribution to, 45–46, 245–
　　　46, 248, 249, 254, 278–80
　　interim review interrupting, 33
　　mastery of, 23
　　overindexing, 50
　　page proof markup, 52–53

index-writing process *(continued)*
  repetitive tasks interrupting, 271
  working in sorted order, 216, 272, 277
  writing of entries, 12, 50–51
INDEXX, 292
Indian names (Asia), 170–71
Indonesian names, 171
Information Sources and Reference Tools (Bakewell), 152
In>Sort for DOS, 292
intellectual analysis of text, 245–46, 247, 249, 254
international characters
  and ASCII codes, 201–2
  generic codes for, 286
  sorting order of, 131
International Organization for Standardization (ISO), 203
  See also ISO entries
Internet discussion group, 290
introduction, book, 42
introductory note
  alphabetization scheme, 121, 140, 164
  examples, 70
  inversions, 178–79
  location of, 206, 225
  reference locator format, 91, 96–97, 98, 213
  referring to other indexes, 150
  special typography, 195
  uses of particular terms, 12, 51, 90
  when needed, 69–70, 224–25
inversion
  automatic, 268, 271
  compound names, 156–58
  direct, double-posting as, 76
  geographic names and features, 173–74, 175
  letter-by-letter sort, 112
  names of Christian saints, 159
  need for and examples of, 79–80
  organization names, 177–79
  personal names, 152–53
ISO 646, ASCII character set, 201–2
ISO 999, standard on indexes, 14
ISO 8879, standard for electronic manuscript preparation, 203

Italian names, 158, 167
italics
  begin/end codes, 201, 204–5
  book titles, 195
  in cross-references, 106, 194, 195
  marking in manuscript, 197
  reference locators in, 94, 148, 195, 267

Japanese names, order of, 171–72
Javan names, 171

kennel names, 163–64
keyword
  alphabetizing by, 121–22
  inversion of organization names, 178–79
  in KWIC and KWOC listings, 248
  placement and structure of, in index entry, 50, 79–80, 126
kings, names of, 164
Knight, G. Norman, 15, 214
  classification, 73
  definition of index, 4
  methods, 239, 240
  names, 156, 168
KWAC (Key Word alongside Context), 248
KWIC (Key Word in Context), 247–52, 248
KWOC (Key Word out of Context), 248, 249, 253–54

Lancaster, F. W., 51, 249
Laotian names, 173
Larson, Neil, 279
layout of book pages, elements affecting index, 39–40
layout of index, 184, 185, 205–13
  and density of indexing, 66, 67
  importing of text file into publisher's system, 200–201
  relation to usability, 183, 185–86
  space considerations, 50–51, 63, 67
leader dots, 188
leading, defined, 40
legal cases
  double-posted citations, 76
  table of, 149

legal indexes
    alphabetization scheme for, 126
    boldface main headings, 196
    layout of, 187
    reference locators in, 99, 100
    vocabulary for, 25
length of index
    cross-references adding to, 128
    estimating, 63–67
    factors affecting space allocation,
        39–41
    function words adding to, 84
    length of book, 64–67
    quality of index, 229
    rates of pay, 30
    reducing, 63, 233–34
    variables affecting, 64
letter-by-letter alphabetization. See al-
    phabetization, letter-by-letter
Levin, Bernard, 27
Liddy, Elizabeth D., 54, 65
Liebscher, Peter, 262
line-by-line style. See indented style
line numbers, as reference locators, 100
Literary Market Place (LMP), 26
locators. See reference locators
Locke, Christopher, 2
logical relationship of main heading
    and subentries, 83, 84
lowercase letters, sorting of, 130, 264

Mac, Mc, and M', names beginning
    with, 159–60, 265, 271–72
MACREX, 292, 301
macros in indexing software, 274
Maddocks, Hugh, 141, 202, 203–5,
    285–88
maiden names, cross-references to, 103
main headings
    arrangement of, 121
    boldface, 196
    consistency in treatment of topics,
        217–18
    cross-references from, 190–91
    defined, 13
    double-posting at subentries and, 76
    evaluation of, in substantive editing,
        217–18, 225

main headings (continued)
    form and structure of, 50, 70–77,
        79–85
    function of, 70, 75
    layout of, 187, 207, 208
    parallel construction of, 81, 223, 225
    relation to subentries, 77–78, 83–84,
        223
    singular versus plural, 80–81
    specificity of, 72, 73
    succinctness and clarity of wording,
        50–51
    turnover indentions, 209
Malay names, 172
manuals. See computer manuals; tech-
    nical documentation
manuscript for the index
    edited, retaining copy of, for revi-
        sion, 238
    in progress as reference, 244
    submission format, 183, 197–98
    typing of, 243
Marchionini, Gary, 262
married names, 155–56, 157–58, 166
Mason, O., 176
mass market trade books, index length
    and density of indexing in, 66
mathematical symbols, generic codes
    for, 287–88
McGraw-Hill College Division, index
    specifications, 62
McGraw-Hill Style Manual
    page numbers for noncontinuous dis-
        cussion, 88, 92
    ratio of index to book pages, 64
    word-by-word sort variations,
        114–15
medical indexes
    alphabetization scheme for, 126
    Greek-letter symbols, 136–37
    ratio of index to textbook pages, 66
    terminology for, 25
methods of indexing
    electronic, 239, 254–77
    manual, 239–44
military titles, 160–61
Milstead, Jessica, 2
Mitchell, AnnMarie, 151

modem transmission, 198, 199
modifiers. *See* descriptors
monetary symbols, generic codes for,
  287–88
Moys, Elizabeth, 25
multiauthored works, indexing of, 101–
  2, 143–45
multipart phrases, alphabetizing, 82,
  126
multiple indexes
  determining need for, 149–50
  introductory note on, 69, 70
  revision of, 150
  titles of, 206
multivolume works, indexing, 145–49
Mulvany, Nancy, 29, 262, 263, 271

name indexes, 150, 152
names
  author's list of, 18–19, 31
  chemical, numerals in, 135
  deciding where to post, 152
  dog, alphabetizing, 163–64
  large number of, alphabetization
    scheme for, 126
  See also geographic names; names,
    personal; organizations, names of
names, personal, 152–73
  beginning with *St.* and *Mc*, 158–60,
    265, 271–72
  changes in, 103, 155–56
  cross-references to, 102–3
  descriptors with single forename,
    164
  European, with prefixes, 165–68
  homophones, alphabetizing, 160
  inversion of, 79, 111, 112
  non-European, 168–73
  obscure, 164
  with particles, 164–68, 169
  reference sources on, 152, 153, 159
  research on, by indexer, 152, 153–54,
    155–56, 157, 180
  titles in, 160–62, 171
  variations in, 18–19
  *See also names of specific national
    groups*
n. and *nn.*, 95–98

National Information Standards Organization (NISO), 14, 289
  See also ANSI/NISO entries
New Catholic Encyclopedia, 153, 159
NISO. *See* National Information Standards Organization (NISO)
NLCindex, 292
nobility, titles of, 161–62, 172
nonalphanumeric characters. *See*
  symbols
nonletter characters
  sort order of, 113–14, 115–16
  See also numerals; symbols
nouns, main headings as, 71, 79
numerals
  alphabetizing, as if spelled out, 131–
    33, 265
  arranging, by size, 133–34
  arranging, in ascending order, 120,
    131, 133, 134, 222, 264, 272
  chemical names with, 135
  entries beginning with, sorting of,
    120, 131
  filing order of (ANSI Z39.4-1984),
    113
  filing order of (BS 1749:1985), 135
  filing order of (BS 3700:1988), 115
  interfiling of Arabic and Roman,
    115, 120, 135
  sorting methods, 131–35
  See also Roman numerals

OCR software, as aid to index revision,
  236
online documents
  indexing of, in future, 277–78
  reference locators in, 100–101
  retrieval and processing of, 245, 249
Oregon State University Press, index
  specifications, 62
organizations, names of, 176–82
  abbreviating, 128, 129–30
  alphabetizing, 181–82
  cross-references to, 102
orphans, as type of bad break, 212
outline, index distinguished from,
  78–79
outline style. *See* indented style

Oxford Classical Dictionary, 153
Oxford English Dictionary (OED), 4

page, charging by the, 29–30
page breaks
    of manuscript and typeset pages,
        257–58
    of revised text with embedded in-
        dexing, 260–62
    See also bad breaks
page design of index, 196, 205–13
    See also layout of index
page design software. *See* desktop pub-
    lishing software
page-number order
    in biography indexes, 125
    confusion with chronological order,
        124–25, 127
    house styles on, 58, 61, 62
    index cards in, in manual method,
        241, 242
    index entries in, for author review,
        226
    revision of index, 260
    working with index entries in, 235,
        236, 237, 272, 276
page numbers
    annotated, 94–98, 267–68
    automatic assignment of, 267
    checking accuracy of, 51
    column or quadrant identifiers, 98
    compression of, 56–57, 58, 59, 60–
        61, 87–88, 267
    concatenation of, 86, 91–93, 204, 267
    continuous distinguished from non-
        continuous discussions, 91–92, 234
    cumulative indexes, 148
    format of, in publishers' styles, 55–
        56, 57, 58, 59, 60–62
    forms of, as locators, 86–98
    full expression of, 57–58, 60–62,
        86–87
    italic, for illustrations, 94
    multipart, forms of, 92–94, 267
    noncontinuous discussion, 88–92
    Roman numeral, 42
    See also reference locators
page proofs
    defined, 35

page proofs *(continued)*
    delivery to indexer, 37
    final, 258, 271
    marking, 51–53, 239
    retaining after submission, 198
page proofs of index text, bad breaks
    in, 210
page-range concatenators, 86, 92–93,
    204, 267
page references. *See* page numbers; ref-
    erence locators
pages in book, ratio of index pages to,
    64–67
pagination, alphanumeric, 93–94
pagination changes, 31, 36
    adjusting for bad breaks in index
        pages, 210
    book revision, 234, 235–36
    custom publishing, 262–63
    embedded entries, 256
    text file, 258
paragraph numbers as reference loca-
    tors, 99, 237, 267
parallel construction, 81, 223, 225
parentheses
    cross-reference format with, 189,
        193–94
    footnote numbers in, 95
    sorting of, 112, 116, 117
particles, personal names with, 164–68,
    169
passim, uses of, 88–90
pay, rates of, 28, 29–30
PC Computing reader survey, 2–3
periodical indexing, classification in,
    72
periods, sorting of, 117
Piggott, Mary, 160, 161–62
place names
    in Indian names, 170–71
    See also geographic names
plural, use of, in entries, 80–81
popes, names of, 164
Portuguese names, 167
preface, value to indexer, 42
prefixes
    European personal names with,
        165–68
    Greek, sorting of, 136–37

prepositions
  alphabetizing, within entry, 123
  book titles beginning with, 122
  geographic names beginning with,
    175
  leading, in subentries, 59, 83–85,
    121–22, 265, 271, 276
  names with, 165, 166
press sheets, defined, 40–41
printing of book
  process of, 40–41
  schedule of, 36–37
proceedings. *See* multiauthored
  works
production editor. *See* editor
production schedule. *See* book production schedule
professional associations, 289
proofreading of index, 198, 222–24,
  225–26
pseudonyms, 154–55
publishers' style guides
  alphabetization rules, 55, 56–58, 59–
    62, 114, 118, 121
  British, 59
  changes to, 54–55, 59
  f. and *ff.*, 91
  generic codes, 203
  homographs, arrangement of, 123
  interpreting, 54–56
  letter-by-letter sort, variations on,
    112, 113
  manuscript submission format,
    197–98
  page numbers, consecutive, 92
  passim, 88–89
  samples, 56–62
  sorting of symbols, 137
  table summarizing, 60–62
  See also specifications, client
publishing practices, indexer's familiarity with, 24–25, 39–40
punctuation
  automatic, user-selected, 275
  proofing and editing, 223, 226,
    232
  run-in style, 186
punctuation marks, sorting of, 113,
  115–16, 136, 264

quadrant identifiers, 98
qualifiers
  to distinguish homographs, 123
  See also descriptors
quotation marks, sorting of, 120, 136

ragged right, 184, 207
Rasmussen, E., 101
rates for indexing, 28, 29–30
readers
  anticipating needs of, 25, 38, 39, 49,
    75, 192, 226, 227
  approaches to indexes by, 5, 10–11,
    69
  categories of, 8–11
  language of, 9–10, 24, 75, 77, 101
  usability of style and layout, 50–51,
    183, 185–87, 195, 196, 206–7, 211
reading of text to be indexed, 37–38, 52
reducing length of index, 63, 233–34
reference books
  needs of users, 9
  paragraph numbers as reference loca-
    tors, 99
  ratio of index to book pages, 66
reference locators
  bad breaks in, 212
  column or quadrant identifiers, 98
  compression of, 56–57, 58, 59, 60–62
  cumulative index, 147–48
  defined, 13, 14, 85
  definitions in boldface, 195
  in electronic media, 85–86
  in embedded software, 255, 256, 267
  evaluating, 12
  forbidden in cross-references, 108
  format looking to revision, 236–37
  forms of, 85–101
  full expression of, 57–58, 60–62
  house styles of, 55–56, 57, 58, 59
  illustrations and display material in-
    dicated by, 48, 94–95, 195
  introductory note on, 69–70, 96–97
  line numbers as, 100
  other than page numbers, 99–101
  paragraph numbers as, 99, 237
  punctuation of, 98, 223
  right-justified, 188
  section numbers as, 99, 237, 267

reference locators *(continued)*
  type changes in, 98
  undifferentiated, 12, 77–78, 86, 218,
    229, 247
  verifying, 222, 225, 230, 232, 241
  See also page numbers
Register of Indexers, ASI, 26
Register of Indexers Available, IASC,
  26–27
relevancy, identifying and judging, 5,
  6, 45, 49
religious names, 155
repagination. *See* pagination changes
resources for indexers, 14–15, 289–93
  authors as, 31–32
  geographic names, 176
  personal names, 152, 153, 159
retrieval of information
  exhaustivity of index, 49
  online, with automatic indexing,
    245, 248, 249
  refining search through subentries,
    77, 78
  term selection for, 50–51
review of index
  by author, 32, 33, 34, 214, 215
  by editor, 228–30, 232
  by indexer, 228
revision of books
  with embedded entries, 256
  planning for, 236
  technical manuals, 270
revision of indexes, 234–38
  with embedded index entries, 259–62
  of multiple indexes, 150
Ridehalgh, Nan, 188
right-justified body text, 184
right-justified indexes, 188
Romanian names, 167
Roman names (ancient Rome), 164
Roman numerals
  in front matter, 42
  interfiling with Arabic, 115, 120, 135
  sorting of, 272
  See also numerals
run-in style, 183, 184–85, 186–87
  cross-references from main heading,
    191
  cross-references from subentry, 190

run-in style *(continued)*
  deciding on, 64, 186–87, 206
  house styles, 56–57, 58, 60–62
running footer, translating abbreviations in, 213
running heads, as guide words, 213
runover lines. *See* turnover lines

saints, Christian, names of, 159
Saint (St.), names with, 158–60, 265,
  271–72
Salton, Gerard, 249
  specificity and exhaustivity, 48–49
  term specificity, 49, 71
Scandinavian names, with prefixes, 167
scholarly texts, ratio of index to book
  pages, 66
scope limitations, introductory note on,
  70
search and replace options, 216, 274
section numbers as reference locators,
  99, 237, 267
See also references
  deleting, to reduce size of index, 233
  excess of, 105–6
  formats of, 193–94
  functions of, 105
  general, to class of unnamed terms,
    106–7
  italics in, 194
  placement of, 191–92, 193–94, 224
See also under references, functions of,
  105
See references
  double-posting as alternative to, 77
  format and placement of, 189–91
  functions of, 7, 8, 101–5
  italics in, 194
  sorting of, 116–17
See under references, uses of, 103
semicolons
  ignoring, in sort, 136
  multiple cross-references with,
    107–8
serial commas, in letter-by-letter sort,
  112, 115
setout style. *See* indented style
Settel, Barbara, 54, 65
SI. *See* Society of Indexers (SI)

signatures, defined, 41
signs. *See* symbols
Simpkins, Jean, 59
singular, use of, in entries, 80–81
size of index. *See* length of index
slang, cross-references to, 102
slashes, diagonal
  sorting of, 110, 111, 112, 115, 117–18
  as symbols, 136, 138, 139
small caps
  begin/end codes for, 201
  large and, for names, 195–96
Smith, P. J., 101
Society of Authors, Great Britain, 16–17
Society of Indexers (SI), 14, 289
  as source of indexers, 27, 151
  training manual of, 160, 161–62
sorting
  of alphanumeric page numbers, 94
  in ANSI Z39.4-1984, 113–14
  in BS 3700:1988, 115–16
  with dedicated indexing software, 271–72, 276–77
  determining method of, 110, 111
  with embedded indexing software, 263–66
  of icons, 142–43
  of international characters, 131
  international standards on, 110–11
  in letter-by-letter alphabetizing, 111–14
  of nonletter characters, 110, 111, 112
  of numerals, 131–35
  of symbols, 113–14, 116, 121, 136–41, 264
  of uppercase and lowercase letters, 130
  in word-by-word alphabetizing, 109–11
  See also alphabetization
space
  allocation for index, 39–41, 65, 67
  constraints on index, 49–50, 63, 76, 227
  ways of saving, 78–79, 84, 103, 104, 186–87, 192, 195
  See also length of index

space character
  filing order of (ANSI Z39.4-1984), 113
  filing order of (BS 3700:1988), 115
  sorting, 110, 111, 117, 136
  sorting, by embedded indexing software, 264
Spanish names, 158, 167–68
specifications, client
  in author-indexer interview, 27
  changing, 54–55
  elements of, 31, 55–56, 63
  house styles compared, 60–62
  interpreting, 54–67
  See also publishers' style guides
specificity of terms, 48–49, 71
spelling
  checking of, 222, 225, 232
  variations in, 12, 127
spelling checker software, 222, 270
Standard for Electronic Manuscript Preparation and Markup, 203, 290
Standard Generalized Markup Language (SGML), 203, 290
standards on indexes. *See* ANSI; ANSI/NISO; British standard; ISO
standards organizations, 14–15, 289–90
Stanford University Press, index specifications, 62, 91
stop list, 246, 248
structure of index
  effect of adding and deleting embedded entries, 259–60
  internal and external, 68–69
  readers' understanding of, 11
style guides. *See* publishers' style guides
style of index. *See* indented style; run-in style
style sheets, client-specific, 275
subentries
  action-oriented, 78
  bad breaks in, 210–11
  chronological order for, 123–25
  classification schemes in, 73
  converting, to main headings, 219
  cross-references as, 189
  defined, 13
  descriptive, 95

subentries *(continued)*
  double-posting at main headings
    and, 76
  evaluating, in editing process, 218–
    19, 225, 233
  form and structure of, 77–79, 79–85
  functions of, 77–78, 86, 218
  indented style, 183, 184–86
  indention of, 200, 207–9
  levels of, 59, 185–86, 273
  nonalphabetic arrangement of, 121–
    26, 232
  order of, house styles of, 55, 56–58,
    59, 60–62
  overanalyzed, 78–79
  parallel construction of, 223, 225
  relation to main heading, 77–78,
    83–84
  run-in style, 183, 184–85, 186–87
  singular versus plural, 80–81
  turnover lines, indent for, 208–10
submission formats, 39, 183, 196–205,
    225, 226
  disk, 183, 198
  electronic, 198–202, 232
  manuscript, 183, 197–98
  modem, 198, 199
suffixes in personal names, 162–64
symbols
  ASCII codes, 201–2, 284
  generic codes for, 284, 287–88
  as literals, 138–41
  as punctuation, 136
  as representations, 136–38
  sorting of, 113–14, 116, 121, 136–43,
    264
synonyms
  accounting for, in index, 12
  author-compiled list of, 19–20
  cross-references to, 102, 104
synthesis, as purpose of index, 6, 7–8,
    37–38

tab character, for indention, 200, 208
table of contents, 5, 43
tagging entries, with embedded soft-
    ware, 254, 255–56, 260–62, 268
team indexing, 146–47

technical documentation
  density of indexing in, 65
  embedded indexing for, 258–59
  icons in, ordering of, 141–43
  ratio of index to book pages, 66
  revision of, 270
  symbols beginning entries, sort or-
    der of, 140
  See also computer manuals
technical indexes
  alphabetization scheme for, 126–27
  sort order of symbols, 136–41
terminology
  following text, 6–7, 8–9, 49, 75, 77,
    101
  indexing, 13–14
  legal and medical, 25
  multiauthored works, 143–44
  multivolume works, 145–46
  readers' learning from text, 129
term selection
  assessing quality of, 229–30
  author suggestions on, 26
  computerized, 245, 246
  distractions from, 243–44
  in embedded indexing, 268
  focus on, assisted by computer, 254,
    271
  main heading, 70–75
  and page-number order of suben-
    tries, 126
  specificity and exhaustivity, 48–49
  structuring and placement, 50–51
textbooks, custom publishing of, 262
text file method, 240, 243–44
text files, and embedded indexing, 258,
    262, 263
text files, index
  ASCII, 202–5
  disk, 199–202, 225, 243
Thai names, 172
thesaurus, in future indexing program,
    278
thesaurus design, 146–47
Thomas, Dorothy, 13
time constraints on index, 49–50, 63
Time-Life Books, 145–46
title of index, 206

titles
    clerical, 161, 172
    military, 160–61
    of nobility, 161–62, 172
    with personal names, 160–62, 171
titles of books
    beginning with function word, 83,
        122
    cross-references to, 194
    to, as page-range concatenator, 92–93
trademarks
    business names, 179
    symbols, 138
training in indexing, 290–91
translations, indexes for, 151
transliteration, 168
turnover lines
    and cross-reference placement, 192
    defined, 186
    indention of, 187, 201, 208–10, 224,
        268
    reducing number of, 233
typeface, changes in, generic codes for,
    201, 204–5
typesetting
    electronic submission to, 198, 199,
        200
    generic coding for, 203, 276
type size, of index text, 40, 206
typing
    in embedded indexing, 268, 270,
        271
    of index manuscript, 197–98, 243
typography
    checking, in editing, 224, 226, 232
    elements that affect index, 39–40
    index, 63, 66, 184, 185, 194–96

U, in Burmese names, 170
Ullius, Diane, 145–46
United States Board on Geographic
    Names, 176
unit modifiers, sorting of, 115
University of Chicago Press
    generic codes of, 203, 204, 205,
        285–88
    text file format for index, 199
    See also Chicago Manual of Style

uppercase letters, sorting of, 130, 264
USDA Graduate School, 291
user interface design
    defined, 268
    of embedded indexing software,
        268–70
    graphical interfaces and indexing,
        141–43
users. See readers
U.S. standards. See ANSI entries

Vickers, John A., 21
Vietnamese names, 172–73
vocabulary control
    cross-references for, 101, 191
    multiauthored works, 143–44
    multivolume works, 146–47
volume numbers, in reference locators,
    147–48

Washington Information Directory
    (WID), 178–79
Webster's New Biographical Diction-
    ary, 153, 165
Webster's New Geographical Diction-
    ary, 176
Webster's Standard American Style
    Manual, 64, 88
Weinberg, Bella Hass, 72
WELL, 290
Wellisch, Hans
    authors as indexers, 21–22
    classification in topic index headings,
        72
    endnote references, 96–97
    exhaustivity and specificity, 48, 49
    function words in subheadings, 85,
        122
    history of indexes, 3, 4
    inversion of place names, 173–74
    KWIC, 248–49
Wheatley, Henry B., 214
Who's Who, 153, 161
widows, 212
Wilson Award. See ASI–H. W. Wilson
    Company Award for Indexing
wINDEX, 292
Wittmann, Cecelia, 263

word-by-word alphabetization. *See* alphabetization, word-by-word
word processing software
   ASCII text files for, 202
   author's, and conversion for typeset-
      ting, 257–58
   automatic indexing feature in, 246
   concordance generator in, 246–47
   embedded indexing modules of, 36,
      254, 255–56
   manual indexing with, 243–44

word processing software *(continued)*
   text file submissions in, 199–200,
      275
Words into Type, 86, 87–88
WordStar International, index specifications, 62
work made for hire, index as, 29
wraparound lines. *See* turnover lines
Writers' Guild of Great Britain, 16–17
writing
   indexing as form of, 23
   text and index simultaneously, 257